The Chekhovian Intertext

Dialogue with a Classic

LYUDMILA PARTS

THE OHIO STATE UNIVERSITY PRESS • COLUMBUS

Library of Congress Cataloging-in-Publication Data
Parts, Lyudmila.
The Chekhovian intertext : dialogue with a classic / Lyudmila Parts.—1st ed.
p. cm.
Includes bibliographical references and index.
ISBN 978–0–8142–1083–3 (cloth : alk. paper)—ISBN 978–0–8142–9162–7 (CD-ROM) 1. Chekhov, Anton Pavlovich, 1860–1904—Influence. 2. Chekhov, Anton Pavlovich, 1860–1904—Criticism and interpretation. 3. Russian literature—20th century—History and criticism. 4. Russian literature—21st century—History and criticism. 5. Russia (Federation)—Intellectual life—1991- 6. Russia (Federation)—Civilization—21st century. I. Title.
PG3458.Z8P37 2008
891.72'3—dc22
2007045611

This book is available in the following editions:
Cloth (ISBN 978–0–8142–1083–3)
CD-ROM (ISBN 978–0–8142–9162–7)
Paper (ISBN: 978-0-8142-5675-6)

The author expresses appreciation to the University Seminars at Columbia University for their help in publication. Material in this work was presented to the University Seminar: Slavic History and Culture.

Studies of the Harriman Institute
Columbia University
The Harriman Institute, Columbia University, sponsors the Studies of the Harriman Institute in the belief that their publication contributes to scholarly research and public understanding. In this way the Institute, while not necessarily endorsing their conclusions, is pleased to make available the results of some of the research conducted under its auspices.

Cover design by Jenny Poff
Text design by Juliet Williams
Type set in Adobe Palatino

To the memory of my mother

CONTENTS

ACKNOWLEDGMENTS

While working on this book I received help and support from many people, including Catharine Nepomnyashchy and Cathy Popkin of Columbia University and Ronald Meyer, editor of the Studies of the Harriman Institute.

I am grateful to Laura LaKopp, Nadya Peterson, Valeria Sobol, and Angela Brintlinger for their most helpful comments. And, of course, the biggest credit goes to my family: Vladimir, Yuliya, and Adele Parts.

CHAPTER 1

Cultural Memory, Myth, and Intertextuality

The Intersection

Culture is memory.

—Yuri Lotman, *Conversations about Russian Culture*

Culture is what one remembers after one forgets all the books one has read.

—Charles Newman, *The Post-Modern Aura*

As DEFINITIONS of culture go, Charles Newman's is better than most. It goes straight to the heart of the matter, bringing together texts (books), memory (remembering and forgetting), and the individual consciousness of the reader. Culture, indeed, is a totality of texts. It is an enormous field, since semiotics understands the text as a broad phenomenon limited neither to written documents nor to strictly literary texts. Yuri Lotman's definition of culture as a "non-inherited memory of a collective" posits culture as a system of texts and symbols, whose function is to maintain its own continuity.[1] An encyclopedia definition of culture includes "language, ideas, beliefs, customs, taboos, codes, institutions, tools, techniques, works of art, rituals, ceremonies, and symbols,"[2] all of which serve to accumulate and transmit knowledge through generations. Culture is, therefore, information in all of its various forms, and it is shaped and preserved through memory. Here, I will limit the discussion of culture to its literary form, and of memory to cultural memory.

The division of texts into literary and nonliterary is not self-evident. In Russian literature, for instance, where do we place medieval chronicles and Karamzin's *History of the Russian State,* Dostoevsky's *Diary of a Writer,* and Tolstoy's literary articles? How do we treat journalism and writers' speeches and letters, philosophical treatises, the contemporary essay trend? Perhaps we should simply acknowledge that these examples are misleading because in Russia literature effectively included and/or substituted for journalism, history, philosophy, and sociology. All of the above works have been treated as belonging to the realm of literary texts. But however peculiar the Russian case may seem, it does not go beyond the bounds of contemporary cultural theory. To a certain extent this blurring of borders between literary and nonliterary genres is evident in most cultures, which leaves us with a very vague notion of literary texts as all texts that employ the aesthetic function of language and explicitly work within the space between the signifier and the signified. Russia's difference, then, lies in the paramount, if not unique, importance in Russian culture of the role of literature in constituting cultural memory and national identity.

The term *cultural memory* requires clarification. Sociologists, anthropologists, and historians address memory as individual, group, social, national, collective, public, narrative, cognitive, body, and so on.[3] The terms seem to alternatively overlap and contradict each other. Memory is a container, and it is a process. It is both objective and subjective, rooted in the past and yet outside of historical time. It is a function of the individual brain, and it is controlled by society and ideology. An individual's memory, however private and unique, exists within and is formed by the surrounding culture. Each of us is a part and a product of a group: family, school, profession, religion, ethnicity, race, or nation. Each group in turn combines individual experiences to form cultural narratives and pass them on to new individual members.[4] Collective memory provides a group with material for forming a group identity. Only the material that is most important for that self-image is preserved and is shared by the collective throughout a historical period. At the level of national collective memory, the mechanism of group identity is more complex but essentially the same. Nations need the discourse of the past as a constitutive element for their present collective identities,[5] but not every past will do—only that which upholds the already existing national image. Cultural memory, as a part of collective memory, operates with the totality of culture's texts available to an individual—encompassing national and world literature—but it is not the same as literature, nor is one merely a container for the other.[6] Just as memory in general involves both the storage of information and the process of retrieving it, cultural memory acts as a repository of literature and the active force in its production.[7] However, it still remains to be explained *how* cultural memory performs this function.

Just as the collective memory of a people sorts through past events to privilege those that support the current national identity, cultural memory allots the highest value to texts that confirm and advance this image. Maurice Halbwachs's analysis of the concept of collective memory stresses its reconstructive function. "The past," he writes, "is not preserved but is constructed on the basis of the present."[8] The cultural past, I must add, as well as the historical past in general—economic, military, technological, and ideological—is also constructed according to the needs of a society in each given era. In other words, society chooses the cultural heritage that supports its current self-perception. National literature plays a paramount role in sustaining this vision. Since society's self-perception denies discontinuity, in order to support its validity it needs to establish a lineage with the historical past, and to do so it must "forget" those texts and events that do not support the contemporary perception and promote those that do. New texts all perpetuate to some extent the existing self-image of a culture by drawing on the valued texts as their intertextual sources.

Cultural memory serves the crucial function of selecting and classifying the texts that form a national literature. It preserves and sorts out the multitude of texts into smaller systems governed by a certain hierarchical order. The active role of cultural memory in producing new texts makes it a central force of cultural production: it receives, arranges, and creates texts by providing the literary community with a set of techniques and with extraliterary material. Moreover, memory ensures cultural wholeness by creating self-descriptive discourses, or cultural models. Such discourses may take the form of a *canon* or of a *myth.* While a canon is usually legitimized and fixed by metastructural descriptions, that is, written histories of literature, myth is an elusive but nevertheless powerful presence in cultural memory, ensuring its unity.

Myth has long been a fixture of literary studies in at least two of its forms: as a type of story and as a mode of thought. The first concept, by far the most widely used, refers to

> a traditional tale (transmitted in different ways and with different supports), telling a series of "fundamental" events (concerning the origins of the universe, of a group, of single natural or cultural phenomenon), projected in a fantastic world (mythical events often involve non-human characters and take place in "different" time and space), and with important and specific social functions (myth as sacred narrative), with a strong normative stance to it, where the events are exemplary and paradigmatic for a group.[9]

This type of myth became the focus of myth criticism, a productive approach to literature that views myth as "the matrix out of which literature emerges both historically and psychologically."[10] The second meaning is defined in more or less pejorative terms as "a concept with which many people agree or pretend to agree, although it does not hold true."[11] Viewed less harshly and, most important, without expressing value judgments, this type of myth is best described as a cultural construct employed by every culture to transform the past into a mode of explanation for the present. As with collective memory, what matters in myth is not the reality or truth of events, but how they correspond to a collective's self-perception today. Like memory, myth gives us a vision of the past and defines our expectations of the future. Whether others see a myth as true is not as important as whether a particular group chooses to maintain it.

I therefore address myth as a part and a product of cultural memory; in other words, my interest is not in a particular primordial text or group of texts, but in "a phenomenon of consciousness."[12] Apparently, primordial and modern myths serve similar functions:[13] the former embodied in rudimentary form religious and philosophical conceptions of reality; and the latter has a significantly narrower function alongside now well developed religious and philosophical discourses, but it still defines our perceptions of the world. Modern myth embraces in a compressed form elements of science, art, and law, which together work to create a collective image of the world. It is, thus, a significant part of the "lifeworld, [that] vast and incalculable web of presuppositions [that] members of a speech community must take for granted if they are able to speak to one another at all."[14] If indeed, as Benedict Anderson asserts, nations are "imagined communities,"[15] then they cannot exist without some commonly shared, if imagined, conceptions of themselves. Myth, therefore, is a necessary part of any culture's development; a multitude of cultural myths inform the self-perception of all social, political, and ideological groups.

The vital role of cultural myths is not readily recognized by cultural critics: Roland Barthes, for instance, sees myth in a somewhat limited light, as a strictly ideological tool. For him, myth is a type of speech, a message that is determined by historical conditions; it signifies whatever the contemporary consumer, necessarily conditioned by history, sees as significant. Barthes, however, views myth as a distortion that masquerades as natural fact, while it is instead a social construct. "Ancient or not," Barthes writes, "myth is a type of speech, chosen by history: it cannot possibly evolve from the 'nature' of things."[16] This rigid division between "facts" and society's view of them is questionable: we can never be sure where one ends and the other begins. Our view of history *is* its reconstruction, always subjective, often passionately so, necessarily selective, and governed by national and cultural myths. The only fact we can assert is that whatever the sources of myth, culture employs it as an instrument for creating both artistic and social models of reality. Myth has little to do with the "nature of things," but everything to do with the way things are viewed and remembered.

Myth's relationship to cultural memory mirrors cultural memory's connection to the totality of national culture: both serve as organizing principles. Schematically, the relationship could be presented in ascending order: myth governs cultural memory, and cultural memory, in turn, organizes the vast field of national literature. Myth determines the hierarchical value of texts, promoting those that are most relevant to the existing model of reality. The most relevant texts are brought to the foreground of cultural memory and become the intertextual sources for new texts.

Unlike particular myths—the archetypal stories that have been recorded in some way and are available for interpretation and transformation—myth as a sociocultural construct through which a culture defines itself is not available for reading in any form. In other words, having lost the narrative part, cultural myths become simply "sets of ideas."[17] Myth can be talked and written about, described and disputed, but it does not exist anywhere except in cultural memory. Since every culture produces its own myths, these myths at the same time define a national culture and reflect essential cultural and national differences. The Russian reliance on its literary heritage to form and uphold its national image, the importance of literature in every aspect of public life, makes Russian literature an ideal subject case for the project of discovering the nation in its narration.[18]

> You can not grasp Russia with your mind
> Or cover with a common label . . .
>
> —Fedor Tiutchev

A culture's dependence on its myths differs from nation to nation and within national cultural histories. Yuri Lotman and Boris Uspensky propose a comprehensive classification of cultures based on that criterion. They distinguish between "cultures oriented toward mythological thought and cultures oriented toward non-mythological thought." The two modes are present to different degrees in all cultures: nonmythological thought operates with metalanguages and is thus typical of scientific discourse; mythological consciousness is distinguished by the prominent role of proper names. Lotman and Uspensky posit Russian culture as having a prevailingly mythological orientation. Their examples include the epoch of Peter the Great, when the creation of a new Russia "was conceived of as a general renaming, a complete shift in names,"[19] including the renaming of the state, the capital, and social institutions. The same epoch witnessed the introduction and integration of a number of foreign concepts into collective consciousness, which also were introduced first in the form of names. Mikhail Epstein may not be going too far when, in his search for the Russian roots of the postmodern concept of *simulacra,* he reaches back to the Petrine epoch to conclude that already at that time "we are dealing with the simulative or nominative character of a civilization composed of plausible labels: this is a 'newspaper,' this is an 'academy,' this is a 'constitution,' none of which grew naturally from the natural soil, but were implanted from above."[20] The provocative undertones of his argument obscure the fact that this process has been extremely productive for Russian culture. The implementation of foreign concepts in fact expedited Russian cultural development as the infusion of new concepts demanded their appropriation and interpretation. Russian culture needed to and did develop mechanisms capable of performing these functions, and moved forward in the process.

The orientation toward proper names during some periods of

Russian history, observed by Lotman and Uspensky, testifies to the largely mythological nature of Russian thought, in which "the general meaning of a proper name in its utmost abstraction amounts to myth."[21] The persistent cultural myth of Great Russian Literature—the cultural tradition of seeing literature as a source of national pride—is based on and consists of the names of the writers included in the canon: Pushkin, Gogol, Dostoevsky, Tolstoy, and Chekhov. As canon writers they matter not as authors of actual works that we read, discuss, admire or ignore; as cult figures, these writers are nothing but symbolic entities by and through which culture identifies itself and on which it relies to assure its identity and continuity. This function might be limiting, but it is especially important at times of social and political crisis, as during the twentieth century became evident in the postrevolutionary period and during and after *perestroika*. During the periods of cultural instability, cult names served as pivotal figures who ensured the unity of culture. New texts congregated around them and created a productive field between texts, allowing for interaction among writers of different epochs.

To appreciate the productivity of such interactions, we must dispense with the violence of Harold Bloom's "power struggle" between precursor and follower, which is precisely the shift one must make when speaking of Russian literature. Its continuity is most often achieved through dialogue among its pivotal figures. The always-heard voice of the predecessor provides the new text with a dialogical counterpart in the Bakhtinian sense: two voices with seemingly equal weight clash in the space of a text, and new meaning is born of their interaction. In an intertextually constructed text, "almost no word is without its intense sideward glance at someone else's word."[22] It "speaks" in response to it and could not have existed without it. The status of a follower, of someone who came later and is denied priority (in Bloom's view), has never caused the Russian artist anxiety; rather, it has assured him or her of the rightness of the chosen path. What Bloom calls "the terrible splendor of cultural heritage"[23] is a mythical splendor, a gloriously appealing concept for a culture that has relied on literature to form its cultural identity.

Whether Russian literature is indeed what defines Russian national identity is a question that cannot be answered. What we can assert, however, is that literature is the focus of Russian cultural myths, of the "unique mode of explanation"[24] of how this culture differs from others. It reflects not history and reality (whatever they may be in a given epoch) but the constructed image of it. The fact that Russia's mythical greatness is sufficiently represented by a small number of names is appropriate to myth's semiological structure where one word, one name, can signify an incommensurably rich concept. The names of the classics of Russian literature are such signifiers. Each one stands for a particular concept in cultural memory, and each has a function in the collective memory. As Vladimir Kataev puts it, "the images of the authors of the works of Russian literature are the primary achievement of this literature."[25]

A discussion of the interrelationship among cultural memory, myth, and the creation of new texts brings into focus not so much particular works by the Russian classical authors, their biographies, or even the actual themes and ideas addressed by them, but rather the ways their works, biographies, and themes have been appropriated by critics, readers, writers, and teachers of literature in the time between the moment when a given work first appeared and the present. Every historical person, once he or she has entered the realm of collective memory, is transformed into "a teaching, a notion, or a symbol and takes on a meaning. It becomes an element of the society's system of ideas."[26] A contemporary text enters into dialogue not with the classic authors as such but with their myths, and the reactions and perceptions that their works engendered. The names of Pushkin, Gogol, Dostoevsky, Tolstoy, and Chekhov each acquired an important place in Russian society's system of ideas. While they are united in collective memory as representatives—pivotal figures of Great Russian Literature and its myth—each one represents different aspects of the whole.

To analyze the whole of the Russian nineteenth-century tradition's textual presence in the literature of the twentieth century would require countless studies; it is clear, however, that this presence has largely defined and limited the range of intertextual sources for the twentieth-century writer and reader. Some critics attribute contemporary prose's increasing intertextual reliance on the nineteenth-century tradition to the cultural and ideological crisis in Russian society, to "the kind of situation (condition, diagnosis) in culture when the artist who has lost the gift of imagination, active perception and vital creativity and perceives the world as a text involves himself not with creativity but with construction from components of culture itself."[27] Others see the influence of the Russian classical tradition as generally typical of

Russian culture: "the Golden Age turned out to be, on the historical scale, an explosive flash, a short splendid efflorescence. Nonetheless, it completely entranced and bewitched Russian Literature. Ever since, our literature has moved forward with its face turned backward, always striving to fit itself into forms corresponding to those of the Golden Age."[28] The critic seems to view all nineteenth-century literature as the Golden Age of Russian letters and thus reflects quite accurately the status of the classic writers in Russian cultural memory: such is their entrancing power that every development in literature and in history is measured against the canon, whether it strives to continue it or break with it.

As early as the end of the nineteenth century, the authority of Russia's literary canon spread beyond the boundaries of literature into the area of national consciousness, the area traditionally dominated by religious and political ideas. The logocentric focus of Russian national identity determined the all-permeating presence of literature in every aspect of public life. In specifically literary discourse, the engagement of the main figures of the tradition, the initiation of intertextual dialogue, became one of the most productive creative impulses for each generation of writers, regardless of their political or social stance. The continuous invocation of those pivotal figures crystallized the functions of each of their canonical names. Thus, for instance, in twentieth-century Russian literature, Pushkin represents the part of the myth that pertains to national greatness and artistic perfection and freedom. Gogol invokes notions of the absurd and grotesque, as well as the theme of the "little person." Dostoevsky is summoned when there is a need to set the stage for a philosophical discussion of Good and Evil and other "eternal" questions, and/or to show the dark and scandalous side of life. This is the "*dostoevshchina*" function favored by popular literature. Tolstoy is significantly less appealing to both pre- and post-Soviet literature (despite the great need for the "red" Tolstoys during the Soviet period), perhaps because his function in the myth of Great Russian Literature is that of the great moralizer, and in that role he is hardly available for a dialogue. The image of Tolstoy as the great sage who holds all the answers does not allow for the relevant equality of voices inherent to dialogue. Chekhov's role in contemporary literary production is both most crucial and most complex and will be our main subject. Pushkin's and Chekhov's cases demand special attention and comparison because they have both served as intertextual interlocutors at crucial moments of Russian history of the twentieth century.

Pushkin's role as the national poet of Russia and the ultimate cult figure has been long acknowledged within Russian culture. In the next chapter, I discuss how modernist writers of the beginning of the twentieth century formed their creative universe around Pushkin and how writers of the end of that century attempted to do the same, albeit with different results. However, this discussion will ultimately serve to foreground the case of the writer who is as important to the end of the last century as Pushkin had been to its beginning: Chekhov. The rest of the book is devoted to how Chekhov and his myth supplanted Pushkin as the main cultural figure, the main interlocutor in discussions of Russia's eternal questions. I will discuss the formation of Chekhov myth and its function in contemporary cultural situation. Chekhov is most often the intertextual source when writers turn to the issues of personal responsibility and the pressure of the everyday, of memory and loss, the intelligentsia and the people, or love and duty. The mechanics of the centennial return, the metaphor often applied to Pushkin's relevance for the Silver Age, remain the same for Chekhov at the end of the century, except that this time the presence is even more pronounced. Chekhov's return (or rather his continuous presence) affects contemporary Russian literature to an unprecedented degree.

Like Pushkin, Chekhov is a cult figure of iconic importance, yet unlike Pushkin, Chekhov's name and his texts do not inspire a knee-jerk reaction of awe. Textual engagement with Chekhov does not necessarily mean an engagement with the grand metanarrative of Russian cultural myths, and even when it does, it does not preclude writers from also addressing less ambitious and more immediate concerns. Chekhov's case is thus both exemplary and exceptional in the way it lays bare the concerns and mechanisms of contemporary Russian literature: ensuring survival through intertextual engagement with classics and their myths.

Contemporary Russian literature in general displays a hostility toward metanarratives that in the case of literature manifests itself in antilogocentrism, a natural response to the years of state ideological manipulation of literary discourse. It is seen first of all in the all-encompassing attack on Soviet ideological mythology and is directed at the politicized myth of Great Russian Literature, that is, its Soviet version. Rejecting and disputing Soviet ideology does not automatically entail rejection of the authority of the great Russian writers, however. Instead, the Russian classics are being freed from under the layers of strictly ideological interpretations, as they are reevaluated and reappropriated.

The philosophical discourse of postmodernism has supplied critics with the terminology to connect the political and ideological crisis in Russia with the broad phenomenon of Western thought. Indeed, it seems that Russia has finally "caught up with America," and Russian culture in unison with the West celebrates "the death of myth, the end of ideology and uniformity of thought, the emergence of multiple and diverse patterns of thought, a critical approach to institutions and institutionalized values, a movement from single Culture to multiple cultures, the desecration of the Canon, and the rejection of metanarratives."[29] However, this suddenly emerging, neat correspondence has been troubling for those critics who cannot ignore the differences in the historical development of Russian and Western cultures. They speak of the all-too-real "death of the author" in Russian history, of the absence of such factors central to Western postmodernism as popular culture and the technological progress of late capitalism, not to mention the absence of capitalism itself. Most find a way out of this predicament by looking for the "domestic" roots of postmodernist phenomena. Mikhail Epstein advances the notion of the generally simulative nature of Russian history, where "ideas have always tended to substitute for reality."[30] Mark Lipovetsky, too, stresses the peculiarities of the Russian cultural tradition in which the Word is identical with power, and reality is constructed according to it: "the power of the word and the belief in the truth expressed by the word are a tradition rooted in the Russian medieval period and reinforced by the moral authority of the Russian classics of the nineteenth century."[31]

Lipovetsky describes contemporary Russian literature as following the postmodernist artistic strategy of dialogue with chaos. This view confirms dialogism as the main feature—in fact, the principle—of postmodernism, yet it locks the postmodern artist in a dialogue with a phenomenon so elusive that, by definition, it cannot be described. Lipovetsky's chaos is an unstable system, "a mixture of different voices and images of the cultural past and present" and "a supreme manifestation of freedom from any cultural and ontological limitations."[32] One feels the need for a more concrete picture. In this study, I too speak of dialogue as a principal artistic strategy, yet this dialogue has a specific set of interlocutors and a tangible (if not always intended) effect. The issue of whether dialogue with a classic is a subcategory of the dialogue with chaos or a different kind of artistic strategy depends, I think, on how optimistic one's view of the contemporary literary situation is. I see a number of contemporary artists, regardless of whether the postmodern label can be applied to them, as engaged in a dialogue with Russian classical literature in an effort to make sense of their own cultural situation. Often, engaging the classics is a strategy of "remaining relevant" as Andrew Wachtel puts it: some writers turn to politics or to journalism, others meet the crisis "head-on" and use classics in their struggle to survive as writers.[33] As I will show in analyses of several texts, the very fact of such an engagement ensures that the cultural tradition is preserved and strengthened.

It is clear that Russian culture has entered the age of postmodernism with its own postmodernist baggage; its destructive thrust is concerned less with the regime (whose disintegration coincided with or perhaps started with the publication of forbidden texts) than with the Word itself. It struggles against disintegration, against being discarded together with the totalitarian ideology that exploited the logocentric focus of Russian identity and usurped the authority of the Russian classics. By closing in on itself, by retreating into an intertextual field, contemporary literature attempts to establish continuity with the nineteenth-century tradition on its own terms. Shedding the Soviet official versions of Russian literature—a process that often takes on violently destructive forms, as in works by Vladimir Sorokin, Igor Iarkevich, and Viktor Erofeev—it does not strive to destroy its original and "pure" myth. Rather, we witness an attempt to reinterpret it. Epochs of ideological and political crisis, which threaten society with rupture in historical and cultural continuity, activate the basic defense mechanism of cultural memory, intertextuality.

> Perhaps poetry itself is but
> One magnificent quote.
>
> —Anna Akhmatova

The body of critical literature on intertextuality is enormous. It runs the gamut from Julia Kristeva's original term for the transposition of one system of signs into another that occurs in every new instance of writing, to studies of sources with their concrete classifications of different kinds of quotations, allusions, and other techniques of reference. Kristeva's studies creatively develop Bakhtin's notions of dialogism and Saussurean semiology with its notion of the differential sign. Both Saussure and Bakhtin see the individual act of speech as determined by the system of language, but the two theories are by no means equivalent, for while Saussure views language as a synchronic system that provides the individual with material for communicative acts which are infinite but nevertheless determined by the system, Bakhtin's main interest is in the social determinism of language as well as of every individual utterance. For Bakhtin, language is not an abstract and unchanging construct but a diachronic system in constant evolution; it reflects and is formed by historical and social situations. In both cases the crucial assumption is that no individual communicative act is truly individual and unique; it is always an arrangement of already existing elements of the system. Kristeva's concept of intertextuality applies this notion to larger literary signs—texts that are compilations of elements of preexisting texts: "each word (text) is an intersection of word (texts) where at least one other word (text) can be read. [. . .] [A]ny text is constructed as a mosaic of quotations; any text is the absorption and transformation of another. The notion of *intertextuality* replaces that of intersubjectivity, and the poetic text is read as at least *double.*"[34] She also extends Bakhtin's notion of dialogism beyond the limits of literary texts and into "the basis of our time's intellectual structure."[35]

Kristeva's concept aims at "characterizing the ontological status of texts in general"[36] rather than only those that self-consciously refer to their pre-texts through a set of marked pointers—quotations, allusions, and such. Her dismissal of the intersubjective in literary development is in line with the broad poststructuralist rejection of the subject as a unified, whole, and free entity. Bakhtin sees the subject's voice and consciousness as defined and formed, challenged and strengthened by society and history. One could say that Kristeva misreads Bakhtin were it not for the fact that the concept of misreading has no place in her philosophy. On the one hand, she expands Bakhtin's ideas into all areas, all "texts" of human existence, and yet on the other hand, she denies freedom and subjectivity to participants in a dialogue, treating them instead as objects in the infinite play of social and psychological forces. Writer and reader, character and author are for Kristeva equally un-free participants in a constant flow of signs within various semiotic systems. Writing is thus the subject's effort to test his or her "freedom in relation to the signifier and reality,"[37] but the effort consistently fails to break free of the bounds imposed by those many systems.

The same ideas inform the work of Roland Barthes, who stresses Kristeva's point that intertextuality encompasses *all* texts:

> The intertextual in which every text is held, in itself being the text-between of another text, is not to be confused with some origin of the text: to try to find the "sources," the "influences" of a work, is to fall in with the myth of filiation; the citations which go to make up a text are anonymous, untraceable, and yet *already* read: they are quotations without inverted commas.[38]

This anonymity of parts of the text leads Barthes to announce the Death of the Author, where the author is the origin of the text, temporally fixed and labeled with a unique name, which would undermine the notion of the text as "a tissue of quotations drawn from the innumerable centers of culture."[39]

Kristeva and Barthes place the author as speaking subject outside the literary process both conceptually and temporally. Authors cannot be influenced by other authors, in the Bloomian or any other sense; they cannot engage in an intersubjective exchange, because they do not have any control over the forces that form the large, amorphous, "already read," and always already existing text. This view is sharply discordant with traditional scholarship that focuses on the author-subject in his or her historical situation, but it offers no alternative approach to the study of literary texts. In fact, a concept of intertextuality that excludes intersubjectivity is disadvantageous to literary studies because it disregards any and all specificity: of authors, genres, talents, national culture, and history. These two opposite poles, intertextuality in Kristeva's sense and a formal study of sources and filiations, represent two fundamentally different views on the nature of literature, and yet they are subdivisions of one field of intertextual studies. At its extremes, the author is either maximally removed, metaphorically dead, or locked in and consumed by a filial relationship. I will argue that the concept of cultural memory helps to resolve the long-standing tension between the original concept of intertextuality and its narrower applications as the study of sources, or, in other words, between "all texts" and the texts that self-consciously point to their filial sources.

While in every text "it is the language which speaks, not the author,"[40] in the self-consciously intertextual text of modernism and postmodernism, it is the language of cultural memory which speaks most loudly. While every text operates with elements of language and many present diverse social discourses, it seems unlikely that the cultural sources of texts are indeed "innumerable." In reality, a particular author, as well as a national literature, operates with a limited number of elements, namely, those that make up a vast but definable field of national culture, including world culture as it was transformed and appropriated into one or another national literature. The author's role is defined first by language, then by the historical and social situation, and finally by cultural memory. Thus, in Russian literature of the beginning and the end of the twentieth century, the word (text) is a compilation or, to continue with Barthes' metaphor, "a fabric," and "a tissue," in which one witnesses a narrowing of the choice of the thread, so to speak—the prevalence of quotations, with and without "the inverted commas," from what was written in Russian literature during the previous century.

For some critics engaged in source studies, the term *intertextuality* provided a convenient new name for a very old practice. To some degree, it proved to be of doubtful benefit because it names and explains at the same time. Often it views modernist and postmodernist texts as intertextually constructed, because according to a circular logic, that is the only way they could be constructed. Rarely do the complex cultural, historical, and ideological impulses behind the intertextual references come into play. As useful as the systems and classifications of intertextual signs are in developing a theoretical metalanguage, they can only serve as the first step in an analysis of that complex phenomenon of conscious and subconscious inscribing of previous texts into new ones which is intertextuality. One must take the next step and attempt to uncover the author's aesthetic and philosophical objectives with which he or she enters into dialogue with texts of the past, as well as the less obvious cultural phenomena of which the writer is an agent.

I conceptualize intertextuality as a mechanism for transforming cultural memory into a text. Every instance of intertextuality, whether it is a small quotation or a complex network of allusions, signals the fact that the pre-text or texts are vital parts of culture. The recognition, and the consequent "ramifying growth of meaning," occur only if the reader and the writer carry the same cultural memory. One of the effects of this "semantic explosion that takes place in the collision of texts"[41] is the "rereading" of the pre-text through the new one. The other and often overlooked effect concerns the status of the new text. An intertextually constructed text consciously positions itself on the axis of the cultural tradition; it forces its way into the tradition, intending, among other things, to benefit from proximity to the works already accepted, and often sanctified, by cultural memory. Whatever the individual aim of the writer when he or she employs older texts in constructing his or her own, he or she is relying on the reader's recognition of the referent text. The writer therefore exploits cultural memory and in so doing reconfirms and reinforces it. Even if the text draws on the part of the tradition that it views negatively, as is sometimes the case with parody, it still latently acknowledges that the parodied text is relevant in cultural space.

While all parody is intertextual, not all kinds of intertextual engagement are parodic. Both parody and intertextual dialogue start with the tangible presence of another text, but the similarities end there. Throughout its development and in all its various forms, parody has retained its reliance on the comic.[42] Its attitude is always to some extent "against" the parodied text; Bakhtin, for instance, describes parody as hostile dialogue, one in which the voices are "hostilely opposed."[43] Critics have rightly complicated parody, reconceptualizing it from a kind of literary joke of the everyday meaning into a much more complex literary form. Yury Tynianov views parody as a stage in literary evolution, and Linda Hutcheon as a perfect and principal postmodern form because it "both incorporates and challenges that which it parodies."[44] In all cases, however, parody implies engagement of a very specific kind: even if it does not ridicule, it uses the referent text against itself; in other words, it is explicitly confrontational. Hutcheon's definition of parody either stretches parody to cover too much of literary phenomena or, conversely, limits all postmodern discourse to confrontation of styles, genres, or schools. It seems that this view of parody—as "repetition with critical distance that allows ironic signaling of difference in the very heart of similarity"[45]—limits intertextuality to purely confrontational engagement. Yet, it is clear that intertextual dialogue may encompass a multitude of attitudes. Intertextual dialogue, as a concept and as a literary strategy, creates an independent text that benefits from the association with a well-known text without necessarily confronting it. Moreover, in dialogue, direct quotation is often unnecessary as long as the author signals his or her intention to engage the other text. The new text is always an artifact in its own right. Parody, on the other hand, is a secondary literary form in the sense that it exists solely as reaction to some other text and does not pretend to be an independent literary work.

Bakhtin's definition is most useful here: he sees parody and dialogue (as well as stylization and *skaz*) as phenomena of the same order because they share "one common trait: discourse in them has a twofold direction—it is directed both toward the referential object of speech, as in ordinary discourse, and toward *another's discourse,* toward *someone else's speech.*"[46] Yet, for Bakhtin, dialogue is a much more interesting and productive kind of engagement because it implies and acknowledges the depth and complexity of the other text. In other words, when the referent text is not merely an object of literary manipulation, when a polemic is involved and the equality of texts is implied, then we have a dialogue. In the case of intertextual dialogue with classics, no one expects the dead writers to actively participate in the exchange. Yet that does not preclude a dialogic attitude as long as the contemporary writer sees the older text and its author as interlocutors and not as targets. In dialogue, the referent text is a tool, not a target; the contemporary author makes a statement and addresses the reader with the help of the older one. On the other hand, as Lyudmila Petrushevskaya's and Igor Iarkevich's texts will show, when the author plays up her or his aggressive attitude and makes it into a strategy, when the older text is explicitly the target of an overtly hostile engagement, then dialogue may deteriorate into parody.

Even a cursory glance at the titles of literary works that appeared during the last two decades of the twentieth century reveals a tendency to draw on the nineteenth-century tradition in order to engage it in dialogue.[47] Given the fact that titles are "privileged and hierarchical slots in texts,"[48] intertextually devised titles allow authors to announce their aesthetic and ideological intention quite blatantly. The most persistent emphasis seems to be on the changes in social circumstances by which the status of literature and its potential to exert influence have diminished. A contemporary author finds it increasingly difficult to connect with the reader, to hold his or her attention. The status of literature has changed during the last decades of the twentieth century: it has been undermined by the market economy that places literature on a par with other consumer goods and by the abundance of Western cultural exports and the surge in production of mass pulp literature. Moreover, the reader is skeptical about the whole of Soviet ideological discourse, which overemphasized and travestied the moral message inherent in classical literature. Even though the rejection of the ideological discourse does not necessarily mean the rejection of the texts valorized by it, it does place high literature in a cultural situation where the reader's attention cannot be taken for granted. Thus, consciously or not, the author appeals to the best-known, tried-and-true texts whose high status by association guarantees the new text a position of literary importance. Intertextual titles such as Vladimir Makanin's "Underground or a Hero of Our Time" (*Underground ili geroi nashego vremeni*)[49]; Evgeny Popov's "On the Eve of the Eve" (*Nakanune Nakanune*); Viktor Pelevin's "Ninth Dream of Vera Pavlovna" (*Deviatyi son Very Pavlovny*); and Alexander Lavrin's "The Death of Egor Il'ich" (*Smert' Egora Illicha*), to name just a few, activate cultural memory and capitalize on the authority of the classics embedded in it. The new texts can go in different directions and pursue various goals, from emphasizing (dis)similarities on the level of the plot to parodying the pathos of the older work; in any case, this text's intertextual nature activates and benefits from the mechanism of cultural preservation, memory.

The intertextual dialogue with the classics is not limited to the list above; there is hardly a work (whatever its title) from the 1980s and '90s that does not display this tendency. Makanin's "Underground" laments the loss of "all spiritual mechanisms of resistance that were so scrupulously built by the Russian literature of the last two centuries."[50] Vyacheslav P'etsukh, in *The New Moscow Philosophy* (*Novaya moskovskaya filosofia*), presents a watered-down version of *Crime and Punishment* in order to set the stage for his pale twentieth-century version of Dostoevskian characters engaging in arguments on the "eternal questions." Andrei Bitov, in "The Man in the Landscape" (*Chelovek v peizazhe*), employs the whole of Gogol's associative field to probe questions of art, nature, and culture, while Anatoly Korolev, in "Gogol's Head" (*Golova Gogolia*), holds Gogol responsible for the misfortunes of Russian history.[51] In Lavrin's "The Death of Egor Il'ich," the reader might expect a present-day Tolstoyan character searching for the meaning of his life as it comes to a painful end, but Egor Il'ich is a bookcase, an old, well-crafted bookcase that spent its life holding the riches of Russian literature. Thus the Tolstoyan character merges with the bookcase in Chekhov's *The Cherry Orchard,* to which one of the play's characters famously pays tribute on its centennial. When the loving owner arranges the burial of the bookcase (of Literature?), he imagines himself buried alive inside the case and cannot bring himself to close the grave. In Igor Iarkevich's "Trembling Creature" (*Drozhashchaia tvar'*), the title of which refers the reader to Dostoevsky's Raskolnikov, a literary critic goes around a city killing people with a peculiar weapon—a volume of Tolstoy's *Resurrection* (Tolstoy's most heavy-handedly moralistic novel). Iarkevich, like Sorokin and Erofeev in their stories and essays, attacks the "sacred source," the whole of the myth of Great Russian Literature. Not surprisingly, he constructs his anti-aesthetic position in relation to this myth and from its components. The strength of the tradition, the infallible status of canonical figures, forces writers of all ideological stripes to formulate their positions in relation to the canon.

Canonical writers too, of course, did not create from a void. A key part of the present-day redefinition of Russian culture as a whole, intertextuality as a phenomenon of literary production is as old as textuality itself. In critical thought, it first appeared under the name of imitation. From Plato and Aristotle onward, imitation is a positive term, a form of apprenticeship, a way to learn the craft through the appropriation of earlier masters' achievements.[52] It is, therefore, a universal practice of interpretive reading of the writers' predecessors that results in capturing their techniques, style, and central images. Beyond the apprenticeship stage, such interpretive reading fulfills a double function: to overcome an inhibiting admiration for the older masters while creating one's own style and technique, and simultaneously to make a place for oneself in the tradition, to become one of the threads in the textual fabric of a national culture.

Translation as a form of imitation is a necessary stage of apprenticeship for Russian literature. The common eighteenth-century practice of multiple translations of the same piece by different authors reflects this view of the world cultural tradition as belonging to everyone and no one; if at first there was a need to prove that "the Russian land can give birth to its own Platos and Newtons," by the advent of Romanticism this residual anxiety was well overcome.[53] Russian literature, having produced its own canonical figures, and now undergoing the process of adapting Romantic nationalist ideas, no longer distinguished between works that had a foreign predecessor and those that did not. One important byproduct of this development is that the Russian cultural tradition forever preserved the tendency to strive toward inclusion in the tradition rather than or at least prior to working against it. Having suffered through the anxiety of not belonging, it can never be seriously affected by the anxiety of influence; on the contrary, this Bloomian notion is hardly applicable to Russian literature in the same way as it is inapplicable to American literature, which in Charles Newman's words suffers from the "anxiety of non-influence,"[54] because it has been mostly influenced by literatures in other languages. Rather, we observe Russian writers' tendency to establish continuity and position themselves in the tradition even as they struggle to surpass older figures.

The process of appropriating literary models led to the creation of a national literature. The practice of translation-imitation remained productive well into the nineteenth century. Thus, for instance, the dominant genre of the first third of the nineteenth century, the elegy, can be viewed as a triumphant culmination of "literary transplantation":[55] for almost every elegy by Zhukovsky, Batyushkov, Pushkin, and other poets of the time there exists a foreign source. Locating these sources in no way diminishes the originality and artistic value of this Golden Age genre; rather, it helps to uncover the mechanisms of the literary process. "Elegiac poetics," writes Lidiia Ginzburg,

> are the poetics of recognition. The Russian elegiac style was based on all kinds of transformations of "eternal" poetic symbols and on the imagery system of "light" French poetry and the elegiac lyrics of the eighteenth century, deeply assimilated, reworked in the Russian poetic culture. The narrow circle of readers of the time was very familiar with the French prototypes of Russian elegiac formulas.[56]

Where for the eighteenth-century poet the pool of available models included mostly poets from foreign traditions, the poets of Pushkin's time freely drew on both European and Russian sources.[57] Pushkin's intertextual practices are characteristic of a relatively young literature that creates itself and its tradition, its present and past, at the same time. Pushkin's case, moreover, is exemplary in that he, more than any other nineteenth-century author, both relied on and formed Russian cultural memory. Pushkin's Russian intertextual sources are either his contemporaries or poets of the previous generation or two, much too recent for the distance necessary to create conditions for a struggle for poetic authority. As much as Pushkin (like any poet) was invested in claiming for himself a status of the first and the best, this very process involved his using his contemporaries and predecessors as guarantors and friendly supporters, not opponents. Rather than challenging tradition, Pushkin wrote himself into it by freely using all of its sources, layering his texts, sometimes playfully, sometimes in earnest, with allusions and quotations, thereby creating his own individual and recognizable voice. Oleg Proskurin explores the intertextual layers of Pushkin's texts in order to show how the young poet searched for his own techniques by trying on the techniques of older poets: "Playful reinterpretation of old forms allowed [him] to find in them an unexpectedly rich potential."[58] All of the cultural material available for imitation, from the ancients to his older contemporaries, allowed Pushkin to learn the craft from within, so to speak, to uncover the mechanisms of poetry by appropriating its existing forms. It should be noted that at a time of fixed generic forms, not novelty but rather the perfection of form itself was the aim of the individual author, and this very rigidity allowed Pushkin to overcome generic restraints by tapping into his reader's memory of the genre's conventions. This reliance on cultural memory allows Pushkin, for example, to open the traditionally plotted elegy, "The Young Man's Grave" (*Grob iunoshi*), with three spaced periods, the graphic markers of an ellipsis, as if assuming that "the reader is aware of everything that should have preceded the young man's death, and the main interest is concentrated on that which transpired afterwards."[59] The young Pushkin learned by combining and recombining well-known styles, genres, and even individual texts. At the end of his life, Proskurin asserts, Pushkin employed his own as well as others' texts as intertexts: "directing [the reader] to his own verses, Pushkin at the same time activated their intertextual energy, activated the meanings stored in their previous intertextual connections."[60] The result of this practice is the "multidimensional" and "multileveled" (*mnogomernost' i mnogoplanovost'*) nature of Pushkin's word. The wealth of intertextual relationships in Pushkin and the resulting wealth of meanings is the effect of his use of the poetic tradition in order first to enter it and later to develop it further. Proskurin's analysis of Pushkin's intertextual practices makes use of Kristeva's and Barthes' view of literature as a structure where "writing reads another writing, reads itself and constructs itself through a process of destructive genesis,"[61] but without undue emphasis on the destructive part—without going to the extreme of completely denying the poet the position of a speaking and writing subject choosing his interlocutors. This is precisely the vantage point, the golden middle from which one sees the productive impulse inherent in the theory of intertextuality, if and when it includes intersubjectivity rather than rejecting it.

The narrative of Pushkin's life and work strikes a perfect balance among linguistic, sociohistorical, and cultural factors, all of which together form the most persistent and influential myth in Russian cultural history. David Bethea, in his article, "Where to Begin? Pushkin, Derzhavin and the Poetic Use of Filiation," discusses Pushkin's role in forming his own biographical myth from the limited material provided by his cultural and historical situation. A defining moment of this biography—Pushkin's meeting with the first poet of the eighteenth century, who "blessed" him as he undertook the path of the poet—may have occurred independently of Pushkin's initiative, but he took full advantage of its myth-making potential. In his analysis of literary filiation, Bethea simultaneously undermines and exploits the traditional view of the literary process as centered on the author-subject in a historical context; he operates with the idea of origin and literary filiation even as he questions the origins of a specific myth of Pushkin's biography. The fact that Pushkin consciously used the myth of filiation in creating his poetic biography emphasizes, on the one hand, that the myth is a man-made construction, a useful tool for critics to organize their field of study: Bethea's question, "Where to Begin?," highlights, however playfully, our need for points of origin, for order in our critical universe. Yet, on the other hand, Pushkin's active role in myth creation makes it hard to deny the poet the status of a subject: it is he who provides the raw material for the myth that critics and the reading public eagerly accept and perpetuate.

Bethea's analysis of "Recollection in Tsarskoe Selo" shows how

> the young Pushkin has, on the one hand, *positioned himself* through the inner compositional logic of the poem *as heir apparent to the Petrov-Derzhavin-Zhukovsky tradition* of patriotic singing and imperial celebration. Yet the decidedly public nature of this debut conceals, on the other hand, its own risks, especially for an individual like Pushkin, whose pattern almost invariably will be not to follow

> but to sidestep or, in Bloomian terms, to swerve from a regnant tradition.[62]

Bethea employs Bloomian terms to describe what Pushkin "will do." However, his article is precisely about a Pushkinian tactic that cannot be analyzed in Bloomian terms—claiming a place for himself in the tradition, not breaking with it. The very fact that the two great poets of the eighteenth and nineteenth centuries actually physically meet reminds us how young and "under-populated" Russian literature was then, how much in need of being nurtured, developed, and provided with a narrative of its own creation. "Recollection in Tsarskoe Selo," the poem written by the schoolboy Pushkin, is fused in the reader's cultural memory with the now proverbial line from his "Eugene Onegin," which from a distance of fifteen years puts the final myth-making spin on Pushkin's public reading of his poem in Derzhavin's presence: "The old Derzhavin noticed us and blessed us on his way to the grave." The stress here is on the natural succession, the peaceful passing on of the sacred title of poet. Pushkin is aware of the necessity to position himself on the axis of tradition before proceeding to rework it from within. This awareness puts him into dialogical interaction with both older and contemporary figures and makes him only one of the participants, significant as he is, in a literary intertextual exchange.

It is, of course, common knowledge that Pushkin's works as well as his biography became for later generations of Russian writers and readers a major part of cultural memory and an inexhaustible source of intertextual material. At the same time, virtually every line of Pushkin stored in the collective memory is but one end of a long thread which, interweaved with other threads, forms the tissue of texts of Russian and world literature. Where is the other end? Or, repeating Bethea's question, where to begin? We begin with Pushkin not only because Pushkin is the main figure—in fact, the foundation—of the greatness and the myth of greatness of Russian literature. We begin with Pushkin before proceeding to in-depth discussion of Chekhov because these two classics link the before and after of culture as it passes through the upheavals of two revolutionary periods of the twentieth century. Just as the Silver Age of Russian literature perceived itself as a centennial return to Pushkin's Golden Age, in much the same way the end of the twentieth century saw itself as a centennial return to a Chekhovian time.

The Pushkin myth, its formation and its role in Russian cultural consciousness, had been thoroughly explored. I offer a closer look at contemporary authors' attempts at connection with Pushkin. They provide the necessary background and a starting point for the analysis of the much more recent and much less explored phenomenon of the Chekhov myth and his function in post-Soviet cultural production. Since Chekhov is as central to late-twentieth-century imagination as Pushkin had been to the beginning of that century, what is similar in their cultural significance puts into sharp relief the specifics of their roles during these historical periods. That, in turn, informs us about main thematic, philosophical, and sociopolitical concerns of two crucial periods of Russian history and about the mechanisms of cultural transformation and preservation.

CHAPTER 2

The Pushkin Myth at a Time of Discontent

"Aleksandr Sergeevich, let me introduce myself . . ."

—Vladimir Mayakovsky, *Selected Verse*

THE FORMATION and gradual politicization of the Pushkin myth began in the nineteenth century and was promptly picked up after the Revolution. The blending of the cultural and literary with the national and political in Pushkin's image accounts for the primacy of the Pushkin myth for Russian collective memory, and for the relative harmony between official canon and cultural myth in Pushkin's image. Canon and myth assume greatness and, at the very least, relevance; the difference lies in what they emphasize as the sources of greatness. Canon must concur with popular approbation; and any viable cultural myth must have the potential to cross social, educational, and political boundaries. In other words, the society as a whole, all of its social and political groups, must accept its basic premise. In fact, the wider the range of the myth's manifestations, the stronger are its longevity and its viability.[1]

The official Russian canon has largely reflected the cultural mythology. Thus, in Pushkin's case, the commemorative activities of the unveiling of Pushkin's monument in Moscow in 1880 became the moment when, in Marcus Levitt's words, "modern Russian national identity concentrated around its literature, with Pushkin at its focus."[2] The event was initiated by the intelligentsia, and funds were raised among the public. The official Pushkin Centennial of 1899 (the centennial of the poet's birth), on the other hand, was a grandiose event organized by the government. "The Pushkin Centennial," Levitt points out, "marked a clear attempt to make Russian literature a part of official culture and to consolidate the State's traditional monopoly on nationalism by claiming credit for the vital role of Russian literature in creating a modern Russian national identity."[3] While the intelligentsia resented and refused to participate in the government's exploitation of Pushkin's centennial, they nevertheless responded with a number of publications that at the same time repudiated "the crude image of Pushkin which was being projected during the jubilee" and helped to "propel him once again into the center of Russian literary life, where he has remained throughout the twentieth century."[4] Pushkin's official inclusion in the canon and his status as national hero reflect, therefore, both Pushkin's uniquely high status in the popular national consciousness and the success of the tsarist government's doctrine of "official nationality." Canon and myth reflect the official and the nonofficial systems of values, and in Pushkin's case they are uniquely alike. The difference lies in their palpability rather than in their essence: the canon is documented, whereas myth exists only in cultural memory. This convergence of official and popular approbation has survived the passage of time and political upheavals.

Pushkin's status as a national figure is so absolute that it is unaffected by differences in critical interpretation. Whereas Gogol's position on the ideological scale might depend on whether a critic sees his aesthetics as that of a realist or a "modernist," and whereas different views of Dostoevsky are held by those who see him as a religious philosopher, as an anti-Semite, or an antirevolutionary,[5] the Pushkin myth is immune to changes in political and literary epochs. The culture's need for national heroes ensures him God-like infallibility; since Pushkin's cultural status is not just that of a brilliant versifier and prose writer but also that of the embodied foundation of Russian national pride. His word is more than a poetic word; it is the word of great universal harmony that, by its sheer power, will bring together the European nations, as Dostoevsky claimed in his Pushkin speech. Proclamations of Pushkin's greatness, from Belinsky to Gogol, from Dostoevsky to

Blok, from Stalin onward, may be a cliché now, but such clichés continue to form the fundamental layer of Russian cultural memory. Throughout the twentieth century, Pushkin's absolute and timeless status generated numerous literary responses. The modernists initiated a search for an approachable Pushkin, the man and the poet, a search that was ultimately about their own place in history and literature. The late-twentieth-century writer deals with the Pushkin of myth, a figure that exists independently of time and history. A dialogue with this monumental figure presents the contemporary writer with the unique challenge of dealing simultaneously with literary and national history, official ideology, and cultural myths, but least of all with Pushkin the historical person.

The writer who engages in intertextual dialogue establishes a connection to older texts—and the men and women who authored them—by addressing similarities or contrasts in their respective historical epochs as well as literary and philosophical traditions; out of this juxtaposition of epochs and worldviews the meaning of an intertextually constructed text is born. In the space framed by two texts, the old and the new, history, though compressed and suspended, is deeply felt. Intertextual engagement presupposes a synchronic plane of culture: everything exists simultaneously in cultural memory; classics belong to their time and to now. But how does a writer engage in a dialogue with a figure outside time and history? How does one create a collision of old and new if the referent figure transcends time? Such intimidating absoluteness in Pushkin has induced different responses on the part of the twentieth-century writer: from attempting to connect with the human part of Pushkin's God-like image—Mayakovsky's blunt formula-demand in his 1924 "Anniversary Poem" is "the living Pushkin, not the mummy" (*zhivogo, a ne mumiiu*)—and thus establishing a personal link with Pushkin's life and works, to an outright rejection of his authoritative status and influence.

For the modernist writer, Pushkin was "an absolute and eternal creative principle," "an ideal synthesis of 'life' and 'art' in which the writer-creator-demiurge surmounted the split between his 'human' and 'divine' nature."[6] Yet, the Silver Age poet is aware of Pushkin as a historical person, a man who belongs to a specific historical period even as his art transcends it. Modernists are keenly interested in precisely this juxtaposition of Pushkin the poet and Pushkin the person, certainly two ideal, but nevertheless distinctly separate, images. The tension between the poet and the person, between art-creation and life-creation, informed most of the modernists' discourse on Pushkin.[7] Veresaev's popular biography, *Pushkin in Life;* Blok's and Khodasevich's Pushkin speeches; Bely's and Mandelshtam's reworking of the theme of Petersburg, one of Pushkin's central themes; Akhmatova's elegies and critical studies on Pushkin; Bryusov's and Tsvetaeva's "My Pushkin"; and Mayakovsky's progression from throwing Pushkin off the steamship of modernity to the friendly conversation of the two poets in "Anniversary Poem," all attest to the search for connections between literary generations, between Pushkin's Golden Age and the modernists' Silver Age. The idea of "centennial return"[8] influenced the perception of every event of the first decades of the twentieth century as parallel to those of a hundred years before and made the modernists' connection to Pushkin all the more personal. With time, however, numerous jubilee activities enabled the Soviet government to manipulate Pushkin's image for official purposes in much the same way as the State had orchestrated the official Pushkin Centennial of 1899. The official Pushkin commemorations of the Stalin era claimed Pushkin for the State and put an end to the modernists' search for "my" Pushkin.[9]

Commemoration, the establishing of recurring commemorative practices, is a means of "inventing traditions"[10] and as such presents a paradox: it attempts to initiate a new tradition but has to rely on the collective memory formed by old ones. Official commemorative activity attempts to underplay its manipulation of the collective consciousness, which involves "the coordination of individual and group memory, the results of which may appear consensual when they are in fact the product of a process of intense contest, struggle, and in some instances, annihilation."[11] As a rule, commemorative activity pursues political and ideological ends. This is why commemorative activities of the Russian émigré community, directed as they were against Soviet ideological appropriation of Pushkin, unfolded along the same routes as Soviet official commemorative activities. Émigré communities throughout Europe celebrated Pushkin jubilees by claiming Pushkin as a symbol of Russian culture and history while calling for their preservation. Émigré Pushkin is as much a political entity as the Soviet one.[12] In Soviet Russia, the grandiose Pushkin celebrations of 1937 (with appropriate morbidity marking the centennial of the poet's death at the height of the Stalinist purges), the extensive exploitation of the Pushkin myth at the beginning of World War II, and the postwar jubilee of 1949,[13] all served as a justification for the Soviet regime, as a foundation of Russian nationalism, patriotism, and the Russian messianic mission in the world. Least of all were these celebrations about the poet as an artist and a person. Pushkin, the symbol of artistic perfection and freedom as he was seen by the poets of the Silver Age, was replaced by a political icon, the individual name by the names of streets, cities, and ships. This Pushkin belonged to everyone, always available and present, like his monument in every city, a figure outside time and thus outside the cultural process. In this form of a name turned into a title, of form emptied of its meaning (as Barthes characterizes all myths), the official Pushkin image survived until the end of the Soviet era.[14]

For writers of the late and post-Soviet periods, the time of Pushkin streets and Pushkin museums, the immediate personal connection with Pushkin and his time enjoyed by the Silver Age poets was therefore impossible. Yet they try. The following is an overview of several texts that dramatize just such an attempt at intersubjective dialogue with Pushkin. However different are these authors and their characters' approaches, each text centers on an attempt either to simply talk to Pushkin or to make a symbolic break to him through the layers of ideological gloss: to capture the historical Pushkin on a photograph or, if that fails, quite literally create one's own Pushkin. All of these attempts invariably fail, and instead of "the living Pushkin" the characters are left with various versions of a "mummy": a ghost, a death mask, a blurred photograph, a monument. These texts make a dialogue with Pushkin into a metaphor in their critique of late and post-Soviet cultural reality. The failure is therefore the subject of these stories, not their effect. Such focus is nevertheless revealing: obviously there is a need for a more approachable interlocutor, and yet the very fact that contemporary authors persist in trying to connect with Pushkin testifies to his continuous importance in the cultural process and, even more strongly, to a longing for cultural heroes and for a renewed belief in the power of the Word.

In the Museum

When Vyacheslav P'etsukh attempts just such a personal conversation with Pushkin in the short story "The House on the Moika" (*Dom na*

Moike, 1997), the only "Pushkin" available to him is the poet's ghost wandering around the empty rooms of the museum located in Pushkin's last residence. The narrator embarks on a detailed account of the history of the house from the time it was built during the eighteenth-century reign of Queen Elizabeth I, to 1925, when it became a museum. Shifting attention from Pushkin to the house itself, P'etsukh attempts to reclaim a place for Pushkin in real historical time, among ordinary contemporaries. But as soon as he reaches the moment when the house becomes the Pushkin museum, the narrator realizes the futility of his effort. The account stops here, as if the history of Russia, exhaustively represented by the successive inhabitants of the house, had stopped as well. The museum as a concept has a peculiar relationship to history: while it is ostensibly the place where history is represented, its static nature cuts off temporal connections and undermines the very dynamics of the historical process. The museum in P'etsukh's story has a deadening effect on history; it freezes a moment and in this case a person in time, severing their connections to other moments and other people, past or future. Pushkin's ghost is entombed in the place of his death, his life represented by nothing more than a collection of old mementoes and papers.

In search of connections, P'etsukh's narrator approaches the house on the Moika as if it represented history in very concrete, human forms. He takes up the "before" and the "after" of the moment frozen in the museum—that is, the last six months of Pushkin's life—and lists those who lived there before Pushkin and after him. Whether the house really was occupied by the daughter of the tsarina's lover, Biron, or by the Decembrist Volkonsky and his mother, or by other colorful figures, is of little importance so long as the history of the Russian state passes in front of the reader's eyes in all its colorful improbability. Pushkin's life in the house does not stand out as an extraordinary event, and neither does his death. The fact that Pushkin is allotted just as much narrative space as the other residents of the house marks the narrator's attempt to see him as a real historical person: one of the residents, a family man, a quiet neighbor who did not entertain much. This attempt is unsuccessful: between the Pushkin of the official canon and the Pushkin of the popular consciousness there is no room left for any other Pushkin.

The narration describes residents and historical associations (the famous provocateur Azef regularly had tea there, for example), until it arrives at 1924, by which time the house has been divided into small rooms and crowded with fifteen poor families. Then a commissar enters and announces that the house is to be vacated immediately since Pushkin, "died here at the hand of the monarchy." When the revolutionary workers and soldiers do not react to Pushkin's name with due respect ("What Pushkin?!" they ask), the commissar delivers a short, incoherent, but very effective speech in which Pushkin and ideology are morbidly entangled:

> А такой Пушкин, что если вы не очистите помещение в двадцать четыре часа, то я вам обеспечу равноценную площадь на Соловках! Про Пушкина они не знают, сукины дети, который неустанно боролся против самовластья, который ратовал за пролетарские массы и зорким оком гения предвидел двадцать пятое октября! . . .[15]
>
> *The Pushkin who, which . . . if you do not vacate the premises in twenty-four hours, then I guarantee you equivalent floor space on Solovki! Sons of bitches, they don't know about Pushkin, who fought unrelentingly against the monarchy, who stood up for the proletarian masses and with the alert eye of a genius foresaw the twenty-fifth of October!*

The speech is an outrageous mix of postrevolutionary clichés; nevertheless, the listeners understand the Solovki reference all too well and immediately vacate the house. As a result, "in their unstable minds Pushkin and Solovki became forever intertwined."[16] The discourse of power defeats and drowns out literary discourse. This fusion of a poet's image with a symbol of the State's coercion, Solovki Island prison, is an apt metaphor for the State's commemorative acts: an empty form can be infused with any meaning. Pushkin's name can be used to intimidate or to rally; dropped in different contexts it means whatever the official ideology needs it to mean at the time. Thus, for the museum's future (a future without state funding) the narrator projects a sponsor appropriate for post-Soviet times, a specialist "on the ideological support of private enterprise" (*po ideologicheskomu obespecheniiu chastnogo predprinimatel'stva*).

Because the story presents a politicized and lifeless image of Pushkin, there is hardly a word in it about Pushkin the poet or the person. The omission is especially striking in a story devoted, after all, to

Pushkin's last private residence. The only "human testimony" is the house manager's story about how Pushkin, shallow person that he was, never missed gazing at a single house fire because he liked to see cats rushing about on hot roofs. Two directly opposed forms of Pushkin's image are presented here: the maximally reduced, anecdotal form, used by Daniil Kharms and Abram Tertz to reclaim Pushkin from under the other—the political, in which the ideological supersedes the human and the artistic. Anecdotes about Pushkin, whether literary, such as those by Kharms and Tertz, or anonymous and truly folkloric, provide a counterpart to the official Pushkin, and the reason for their existence lies in their subversive potential.[17] Kharms created bathetic stories about Pushkin with the sole purpose of countering the official iconic image: he "engage[ed] in a polemic with respectful awe."[18] Subversion is the main source of anecdotes' humor and enjoyment. Like parody, its literary counterpart, the anecdote manipulates the subject's status; never does it attempt to understand. In parody and in anecdote, the subject is split, doubled, and polarized at its limits: awe and mockery exist simultaneously. Nowhere between these two extremes does one see the "real" Pushkin or even wonder what that "real" Pushkin means. Pushkin is lost in the ideological battle between myth and antimyth, and that, sadly, amounts to his second death and entombment. Pushkin's melancholy ghost, another empty form, who wanders around the museum at night, is imprisoned there as effectively as he would be on Solovki Island. The poet who for the modernists symbolized the ideal synthesis of life and art is now literally lifeless and silent.

P'etsukh's story starts with an allusion to Pushkin's poem "To the Poet" with its majestic image of a proud if lonely creator, and ends with the last lines of "Winter Evening," with its famous call to drown sorrow in wine: "Let us fill our cups and bury / All our woes in frothing wine."[19] It progresses, thus, from the lofty to the pathetic, going downhill, so to speak, as does the narrator's estimate of one's chances to make any kind of connection with Pushkin the poet or the person. Since Pushkin is both the most significant and the most politicized figure in the Russian classical canon, the distortion of his image exemplifies the fate of the writer in a society that politicizes its poets. P'etsukh's narrator, usually an upbeat and optimistic persona, cannot help being depressed by the fact that present-day political battles keep on killing the dead classics, while the "people's love" is as unreliable as it was in Pushkin's days. The story ends with the narrator wondering what one can say to Pushkin's ghost, beyond perhaps offering him a drink, thus following Pushkin's own words. The ghost remains silent. Dialogue, in fact any connection with Pushkin, even the most mundane one—for example, over a shared drink—is impossible. The pessimism of the story is not relieved even by P'etsukh's wonderful humor. In most of his stories P'etsukh is careful to provide at least a quasi-optimistic conclusion. "The House on Moika" does not have one precisely because Pushkin's case demonstrates the "abuse" of the classics most clearly.

Andrei Bitov has been exploring the problem of Pushkin's place in the contemporary cultural process throughout his writing career. His novel *Pushkin House* (*Pushkinskii Dom* 1971, published in the USSR in 1987), written decades before post-Soviet writers began the process of freeing their cultural past from its ideological restraints, presents an image of Pushkin similar to P'etsukh's: too iconic and weighted down with extraliterary baggage for a dialogue to occur. Instead of a dialogue, Bitov characters produce a monologue, at times even a diatribe.[20] The museum in Bitov's "novel-museum"[21] is a part of the Academy of Science's Institute of Russian Literature, a real place that holds pieces of Russian literary history (as real as the House on the Moika museum) and a symbolic place where memory is catalogued and visualized. The novel, like the museum, is an imaginary space where classics reside in cultural memory with Pushkin as a stand-in for the whole cultural tradition. Everything revolves around Russian literature, from descriptions of the museum's exhibits, to the protagonists' literary treatises, to intertextual chapter titles.

The reproduced image of the Russian classics in Bitov includes disparate material items, from inkwells to dueling pistols, but is best symbolized by Pushkin's postmortem mask—it appears to be a double, a copy, but it cannot be image-productive. As a symbol of death, it is an image that signals the end of creativity. In a pivotal scene, the novel's protagonist, the literary critic Lev Odoevtsev, literally attempts a "destruction of the museum" when he and a friend, both drunk, smash the museum room of the institute. The destruction culminates with the breaking of Pushkin's mask. "Such violence," Mark Lipovetsky points out, "is the only kind of dialogue with a frozen, simulated cultural heritage available to the metafiction of the post-Thaw, post-Socialist Realism culture of postmodernism."[22] Bitov envisions reestablishing ties with the cultural past, severed by Soviet totalitarian culture, and the destruction of the official museum must symbolize the rejection of the Soviet ideological treatment of the classics, with its deadening effect. However, the symbolic breaking of the dead image does not make the dead body of Russian literature come to life again, at least not for Lev Odoevtsev. The Pushkin mask turns out to have been only a copy in the first place; thus it symbolizes, if anything, the futility of the postmodernist effort to break through to the uncontaminated cultural past. Having broken through one layer of simulacra, they find yet another layer. Bitov's novel is largely a comment on "the afterlife of culture,"[23] on the impossibility of spiritual freedom—of which Pushkin is the symbol—in the world of simulacra, and as such it is a pronouncement on his time.

An even more obvious and obviously failed attempt to apprehend the real Pushkin is the subject of Bitov's short story "Pushkin's Photograph. 1799–2099" (*Fotografiia Pushkina. 1799–2099*, 1985). Its protagonist, Lev Odoevtsev's descendant Igor Odoevtsev, embarks on a time-machine trip from 2099 back to 1836 to obtain Pushkin's photo for the official celebrations of the tricentennial of his birth. Igor fails to produce the photograph: the "real" Pushkin cannot be captured; history eludes Igor even as he attempts to participate in it. Igor's experience of the historical past is grounded in the already existing narratives of history: he can perceive only events he already knows about. By the same logic, his participation in Pushkin's life occurs only through Pushkin's texts: he inspires one Pushkin text ("God save me from losing my mind . . .") and lives through the events of another ("Little House in Kolomna"). He finally returns to his own time, mad and without Pushkin's photograph: what his camera captured was "only a shadow, like the wing of a bird taking off before the lens."[24] Igor's few meetings with Pushkin are preceded by several false starts: he first visits Mr. Apushkin and Mr. Nepushkin. In a house on the Moika he espies a scene described in one of Kharms's anecdotes about Pushkin: Pushkin's wife and children sitting around a table; all are cross-eyed and all fall off their chairs one after another. It turns out to be the family of Mr. Apushkin. When he finally finds the poet, Pushkin refuses to see him, forcing Igor to stalk him, and all he is left with is the impression described by Abram Tertz, that of "the indestructible sideburns, a cane, a hat, flowing coattails. . . ."[25] This, according to Tertz, is what one is left with after recovering Pushkin from both official laurels and popular anecdotes. Pushkin's historical context and Pushkin as a historical person cannot be known outside the history preserved and reconstructed by the documents available to Igor's times: "The barrier was insurmountable: he saw only that which HIS time knew."[26] Moreover, an effort to get through to the unofficial Pushkin brings Bitov to the authors who have gone this way before him, Kharms and Tertz. It is mostly their Pushkin that Igor follows around St. Petersburg, their reconstructed vision.

Bitov builds his account of a failure to actively know history on, not surprisingly, the impossibility of knowing the historical Pushkin. The idea of a photograph as a way of seeing and knowing, though faulty, points to another danger of trying to appropriate the past: mistaking reproduction for preservation. As Bitov's metaphor of Pushkin's broken death mask shows, a copy, whether smashed or revered, remains a mere simulacrum; it represents not reality but a cultural model of reality. Of course, a snapshot of Pushkin, made by order of the State, would be a triumph of the State's ideological reinvention and reappropriation of Pushkin. However, the fact that the official committee entrusts the mission not to a party bureaucrat but to a literary scholar and a "hereditary Pushkin scholar,"[27] emphasizes once again that the State, the intellectual community, and popular conscience, all participate equally in this project.

Bitov's and P'etsukh's awareness of the futility of the post-Soviet search for Pushkin becomes the subject of their stories. Both authors emphasize that the connection is desired and important, but both also produce a multitude of metaphors for the failure to connect. In the critique of their time, the authors are as successful in their task as their heroes are not. An effort to bring Pushkin into the late twentieth century results in the images of his sullen ghost, (a copy of) his death mask, a distorted photograph. In the story "Limpopo," Tatyana Tolstaya works through the same set of issues: her characters take the idea of reproduction to its extreme in going for not just a photographic likeness but an actual physical version of Pushkin.

Under the Monument

In "Limpopo" (1990), the *intelligent* Lenechka, a poet of the sixties (*shestidesyatnik*) and an ideological enthusiast to the point of absurdity, meets Judy, a black woman who has come from Africa to study to become a veterinarian (hence the title, "Limpopo," designating a river from "Doctor Aibolit," the children's story about a doctor who goes to Africa to heal sick animals). Lenechka becomes obsessed with the idea that the two of them can give birth to a new Pushkin. Most of the story's events, whether they occur or not (the new Pushkin never appears, in fact), verge on the absurd. There are the fantastic occurrences in the town of R: boiling waters surging beneath the asphalt, the arrival and killing of the delegation of the Greater Tulumbass Tribe, and a hellish account of a trip to Italy by one of the town's dignitaries. There is also the story of Lenechka's uncle Zhenia, who in order to be appointed to an embassy in Africa strives for extreme ideological and political purity only to be eaten by a wild animal soon after arriving. Against such a fantastic background, the idea that a black woman and an underground poet can give birth to Pushkin seems the least absurd of all. Judy's blackness represents for Lenechka more than the African blood in Pushkin; it also actualizes the saying "black as a stoker" (*kak kochegar*), where a stoker is the quintessential metaphor for the underground poet, and in general for those members of the intelligentsia who hole up in basements in order to "preserve the last candle, the last tear, the last letter of their dispersed alphabet."[28] Lenechka is a poet, but his vision of Pushkin is political rather than poetic; the fighter for the people, for "the insulted and injured," plans the rebirth of Pushkin as the triumph of the downtrodden:

> It therefore followed that the *intelligent* (Lenechka) and the black woman (Judy) should be joined in the bonds of matrimony and this union of the insulted and injured, the wounded and outcast, this minus, multiplied by a minus, would yield a plus—a curly-headed, plump-bellied, swarthy little plus: if our luck holds we'll get Pushkin right off; if not, we'll go at it again and again, or wait for our grandsons, great-grandsons—and going to the grave my blessing will I give!—decreed Lenechka.[29]

The Soviet myth of the poet as freedom fighter, which casts Pushkin in the role of revolutionary poet, is here blindly accepted by the contemporary poet, who envisions the new Pushkin as his own contribution to rebelling against the State. Lenechka's Pushkin is reduced to an abstract figure of "our last hope," but for the rest of the story's characters, he is even less: he is the monument on Pushkin Square. It seems that the only human feature uniting Pushkin, the other classics of Russian literature, the generation of the sixties, and Judy, is that they are always cold. Judy dies of pneumonia; that is, she is physically unable to cope with the cold, unwelcoming country; the medallion portraits of classic authors on the school's walls appear as "frostbitten profiles" (*obmorozhennymi profiliami*); and the Pushkin monument is seen through the cold and darkness of a Moscow blizzard. The nameless classics on the medallions in the school, the Pushkin monument, and Saltykov-Shchedrin's portrait in the school stairwell represent the school version of Great Russian Literature. In this version, "the melancholy of green walls" and the absurdity of the school textbooks' ideological reading of the classics—"This Saltykov was always either 'castigating ulcers' or 'revealing birthmarks'" (*Etot Saltykov to 'bicheval iazvy,' to 'vskryval rodimye piatna*)[30]—merge into a terrifyingly cold and dead image. The classics of the Soviet canon are reduced to objects on walls, on pedestals, on the pages of textbooks, unchanging, dead images with features forever fixed. But is not Lenechka's idea precisely to conceive and give birth to Pushkin the product of a fixed image, the portrait with curly hair and distinctly "African" features? Is not his idea of a new Pushkin as the creation and the voice of "the wounded and the outcasts" a product of the official myth of the socially engaged poet? The passion and the heat of his and Judy's "pneumonia-like mutual love " (*dvukhstoronniaia krupoznaia liubov'*)[31] fade in the face of the dead and cold concept of official culture, which Lenechka enthusiastically rejects, but the premises of which he nevertheless tacitly accepts.

After Judy's death, Lenechka loses his mind and disappears into the woods. Like Bitov's hero who, having failed to capture the image of the historical and real Pushkin, turns into one of his characters, Lenechka, too, failing to become Pushkin's creator, finally turns into one of Pushkin's creations. He is both the mad Eugene from "Bronze Horseman" and, as is clear from the last lines of the story, an embodied "misreading" of Pushkin's lines from "I have erected for myself a monument" (*"Ia pamiatnik sebe vozdvig . . ."*) (hereafter referred to as "Monument"): Tolstaya has "And the Slavs' proud grandson, and now grown wild . . ." (*i gordyi vnuk slavian i nyne dikii . . .*), while in Pushkin this is *"I gordyi vnuk slavian, i finn, i nyne dikoi / Tungus. . . ."* This misreading turns "the proud Slav" into a "now wild Lenechka," and so foregrounds the real tragedy of the story: the failure of memory in a people whose history and literature have been replaced by their official versions. Pushkin "the illegitimate babe" cannot come to the people who have no memory of him aside from the legitimized, final, and ossified image of the national hero. Tolstaya's story is permeated with intertextual references to Pushkin, Pasternak, and Chukovsky, but Lenechka's endeavor ignores texts in favor of biographical facts and ideology. Textual dialogue with a predecessor implies a synchronic view of history, one in which all texts exist simultaneously and which "entails the leveling of all temporal differences; history is suspended in favor of the co-presence of the past."[32] Lenechka shifts this textual practice onto the level of the human body and attempts to suspend history and time by recreating the body of Pushkin. The success of intertextual practice depends on the recognition of previous texts, that is, on their permanence in the cultural memory shared by the reader and the writer. Lenechka instead exploits the recurrence of biographical facts, their formal near-coincidence. In effect he reduces Pushkin's image in the same way it was reduced by the State in order to mold it for political purposes.

At the end of the story, the narrator and Lenechka's aunt bring flowers to the Pushkin monument, look up at the "blind" face as if expecting that Pushkin will hear and bless them "through the cold and gloom of his new, commander-like countenance."[33] Dialogue, however, is impossible. Pushkin's status as an idol-like figure excludes the very idea of dialogue as an interaction of individual consciousnesses. Instead, the story's protagonists offer the monument a kind of a prayer—the distorted line from "Monument" cited above followed by a failure of memory: "I don't remember another word." The story posits Pushkin's monument as another form emptied of meaning, like the ghost in P'etsukh's story, like the death mask in Bitov's novel, a form that means nothing but a failure to mean. The contemporary reader and writer have no access to Pushkin the poet and the man; he has been replaced by his multiple canonical and mythological images. When worshiping a poet does not prevent one from forgetting his texts, cultural memory loses its generative function: monuments do not produce texts, only other monuments.

In the Canon: From Pushkin to Chekhov

Tolstaya's 1986 story "The Poet and the Muse" (*Poet i Muza*) operates, at least at first glance, in the same way as "Limpopo": juxtaposing a contemporary poet to the ideal poet, Pushkin, and laying bare the mechanisms by which our cultural myths form our vision of a poet and our own historical, cultural, and personal experiences. However, the story's intertextual structure is more complex: it pits Pushkin and Chekhov intertexts against each other, intertwines issues of creativity and gender, and probes the historical roots of society's psychological dependency on cultural myths.

Tolstaya develops an ironic portrayal of a contemporary poet as presented through the eyes of a contemporary Muse, one quite unlike its Romantic counterpart. Both the Poet and the Muse of the story are products of a culture in which the nineteenth century is catalogued from Pushkin to Chekhov in strict alphabetical, chronological, and ideological order, and in the process is stripped of any context, leaving only the form of the myth. In this form it is available for everyday use, for simplification to the point of degradation, and this is exactly what happens in Tolstaya's story.

The story's title refers the reader to the Golden Age of Russian literature, when the Muse was a stock image of romantic poetry. Tolstaya's love story of a poet and his muse subverts societal gender stereotypes. Critics have commented on Tolstaya's debunking of stereotypes, how she reverses the cultural cliché of "woman as an inspirational Muse," and explodes these "cultural bromides."[34] I suggest a look at how Tolstaya puts the stereotypes she targets in the context of Russian culture. She is interested, first of all, in the sources of their power and longevity; when and if she does explode them, it is done from within, through their inner logic. In fact, Tolstaya's inquiry is into the literary origins of Russian cultural clichés, including gender stereotypes. This inquiry leads Tolstaya to the literary treatment of the theme of the Muse and gender relations in general. The story is framed by reference to the writers who exemplify both the literary canon and an unorthodox approach to the love theme—Pushkin and Chekhov.[35] The title and the last paragraph position the narrative between these two names, two poles, the before and after of the nineteenth-century literary treatment of all aspects of the male-female relationship according to the strict code of Victorian morals. While the story's title alludes to Pushkin and the Golden Age of Russian poetry, its plot follows, albeit in an altered form, the plot of a Chekhov story.

Pushkin's "Monument" serves as his referent text. From Chekhov, Tolstaya takes his portrayal of women whose behavior defies convention and who actively seek self-fulfillment in whatever form they imagine it. The particular Chekhovian intertextual source for "The Poet and the Muse" is "The Grasshopper" (*Poprygun'ia*), although the appropriation of Chekhov's plot is complicated by invocations of the whole of the nineteenth-century literary tradition. Thus, the story moves from Pushkin to Chekhov, painstakingly reversing cultural assumptions about the poetic vocation and gender, and dramatizing the conflict between poetic transcendence and material reality. It immediately overturns the oppositions informing the Pushkin and Chekhov texts, reverses the roles of the characters, and realizes their metaphors.

The story's first group of motifs revolves around the relationship between the poet of the story and his self-proclaimed Muse. Tolstaya undermines both figures in the traditional pair by questioning the basic assumption of the poet's gift and the Muse's ability to inspire. Simply put, the poet is not very talented and his Muse not very inspiring. Grisha, the poet, represents the twentieth-century version of the unrecognized genius—he is a realization of the quintessential metaphor for the generation of "janitors (*dvorniki*) and night watchmen." The combination poet-janitor, a cliché of the intelligentsia's discourse (and lifestyle) since the 1960s, surrounds him with the romantic aura of the intellectual underground: "Grisha, janitor, poet, genius, saint!" (*Grisha, dvornik, poet, genii, sviatoi!*).[36] Grisha hardly fits the twentieth-century image of a martyr, of a persecuted artist run underground by ideological conformists. Quite simply, he enjoys this way of life, the artistic disorder of his room and his company, and the physically uncomplicated task of clearing the snow from the pavement. Even less does Nina fit the role of Muse. Nina first comes to Grisha's room as a doctor when he is sick, and she falls in love with him before she discovers that he is a poet and she must assume the role of Muse after the fact. She is attracted first of all to his poetic, romantically vulnerable looks: "the sorrowful shadows on his porcelain brow, the darkness around his sunken eyes, and the tender beard, thin like a spring-time forest."[37] As Helena Goscilo observes, Tolstaya exploits the timeworn obsession of literature and the visual arts "with the moment when a male subject discovers (or perhaps uncovers) the female object of his libidinal drives as she is sleeping, or merely reclining, in a vulnerable pose particularly attractive to the voyeuristic/sadistic mentality."[38] The moment is one of many that signal the reversal of gender stereotypes. The story then proceeds to reverse the romantic stereotypes of the Muse's function.

In the traditional portrayal of the Muse, she is passionately awaited, even summoned, by the poet to raise him from mundane reality into a state of artistic inspiration. In Tolstaya's story, not only does Nina's cure initially take the poet out of a delirious state akin to the state of creativity—he speaks in rhyme while delirious—but she directs all of her future efforts to physically extracting Grisha from his poetically disordered dwelling and his artistically inclined circle of friends and followers. As a result, he is unable to write at all. She moves him into her clean, orderly apartment and provides him with an organized working space:

> [H]e would be moving to Nina's, where a sturdy, spacious glass-topped desk awaited him, with two willow switches in a vase on the left, and, on the right, from one of those frames that look as if they 'lean on a tail,' Nina's photo smiled at him, 'your face in a simple frame' so to speak. And the smile promised that everything would be fine, that he'd be well fed, and warm and clean . . . .[39]

The poetic function of the photograph in this description, indicated by the quotation from Aleksandr Blok[40] ("your face in a simple frame")—from a poem "Of Valor, Noble Deeds, and Glory" ("*O podvigakh, o doblestiakh, o slave . . .*") that is also about the tension between the Muse and her real-life embodiment—is undermined by the preceding mention of "the frame with an extended tail" (*otkliachennym khvostikom*), an unpoetic detail thoroughly unnecessary except for its function of ridiculing Nina's attempt to play the role of the Muse. In contrast to the traditional function of the Muse as the guide to the sphere of art unregulated by trite reality, Nina exemplifies regulations: from the number of the pussy-willow branches on the table to the position of the vase and the photo frame, to the paper on which to write, she organizes the poet's world, even affecting the shape of Grisha's poetry, since her goal is to "slice the muddy cake of Grisha's creativity into edible individual helpings."[41] Nina's obsession with material order interferes with Grisha's aspirations to transcendence. She is intent on bringing him back into the "real world" even if it means changing her beloved, beginning with the modification of his name from the neutral Grisha to the childish Grishunia, and ending with changing the nature of his poetry. And while affecting his poetry is directly connected to the Muse's traditional function, it takes a very untraditional form. The Muse becomes a censor: she insists that he write verses appropriate for publication: "you have to think about a book, we live in a real world."[42] She looks for concrete references behind his convoluted imagery and even throws away the poems that she deems unacceptable: "Once a week she checked his desk and threw out the poems that were indecent for a married man to compose."[43] In the discourse of the Golden Age, the Muse can be a lover or a sister. Nina adds both capacities to those other two, of doctor and censor: she gives him her heart and checks, "like a caring sister, what Grishunia has written today."[44] Thus, she usurps all of the poet's world rather than serving in the limited role of the Muse prescribed by the romantic tradition.

Nina's character is structured on the tension between the romantic image of the Muse that she is forced to assume and the concept of the "real world" that forms her identity. It is further complicated by the fact that for Nina there is no contradiction, because the notion of the romantic is built into her conception of the real world. Both of these conceptions are based on cultural clichés: Nina's idea of happiness includes not only a successful career and financial independence, but also mad love:

> a wild, true love, with tears, bouquets, midnight phone vigils, nocturnal taxi chases, fateful obstacles, betrayals and forgiveness. She needed a—you know—an animal passion, dark windy nights with street lamps aglow. She needed to perform a heroine's classical feat as if it were a mere trifle: to wear out seven pairs of iron boots, break seven iron staffs in two, devour seven loaves of iron bread, and receive in supreme reward not some golden rose or snow-white pedestal but a burned-out match or a crumbled ball of a bus ticket—a crumb from the banquet table where the radiant king, her heart's desire, had feasted.[45]

This long list mixes together (and compresses in one sentence) the marks of several discourses: from contemporary movie culture with car chases and night phone calls, to the "cruel romance" of urban culture, to the fatal passions of the nineteenth-century novel, to folklore;[46] in a word, it encompasses all of the cultural space that forms a woman's image of what love should feel like. Nina enters Grisha's room with a preformed image of romantic love and happily walks straight into the trap of cultural and literary clichés. For her, however, these clichés are not only real but form a significant part of the "real world" whose demands structure her behavior as Muse.

Tolstaya repeatedly stresses the ordinariness of Nina's vision and personality in general: she is an ordinary woman, and "everyone knows how it goes." This stands in opposition to another romantic prerequisite of the Muse: her uniqueness, exemplified, for instance, by "the unique look of her face" (*ee litsa neobshchim vyrazhen'em*) in Yevgeny Baratynsky's poem "Muse." Nina's failure to inspire either poetry or love is predetermined by the clash of her ordinary personality, living in and formed by the real world, with the vague but no less influential conceptions of love and happiness floating around her in the collective consciousness. Everything she has ever read or studied in school has taught her that everyone deserves to be happy and has to fight for happiness, that love means mad romantic passion and beauty has a value of its own. In her ordinariness, Nina exemplifies the collective consciousness that has been saturated through and through with cultural images that have lost their transcendent quality and have degraded into clichés.

Grisha's performance as a poet is undermined throughout the narrative as well. His verses, "thick, significant poems that recalled expensive custom-made cakes covered with ornamental inscriptions" (*gustye, mnogoznachitel'nye stikhi napodobie dorogikh zakaznykh tortov s zateilivymi nadpisiami*),[47] serve as a mere decorative detail at quasi-intellectual underground soirées. The description of the motley crowd in Grisha's room includes the first "intertextual signpost"[48] directing the reader to the ultimate symbol of a poet—Pushkin. It comes at the end of a long list of Grisha's admirers: ". . . unattached girls with spiritual aspirations in their eyes; philosophers with unfinished dissertations; a deacon from Novorossiisk who always brought a suitcase full of salted fish; and a Tungus who'd got stuck in Moscow . . ." (*. . . i nich'i devushki s zaprosami v glazakh, i filosofy-nedouchki, i d'iakon iz Novorossiiska, vsegda privozivshiy chemodan solenoi ryby, i podzaderzhavshiisia v Moskve tungus . . .*).[49] This *Tungus* is a puzzling element explainable only by connecting the text to the intertext in Pushkin's poetic manifesto, "Monument": "*i nyne dikii Tungus.*" The phrase "and a Tungus who'd got stuck in Moscow" (*i podzaderzhavshiisia v Moskve Tungus*), and later once again, "and the Tungus who came who knows why" (*i neizvestno zachem prikhodiashchii Tungus*), follows the form and the rhythm of the famous Pushkin line: it starts with the anaphoric "and" followed by qualifiers before the noun ("*. . . i nyne dikii Tungus*"). In Pushkin's famous list of the peoples who will know of him, the Tungus, a small Siberian ethnic group, is the only nationality one seems not to meet anywhere else in life or literature, including other *exegi monumentum* from Horace to Derzhavin. Neither Slavs, nor Finns, nor the Kalmyk, although mentioned by Pushkin, bring the poem to mind as immediately as does the Tungus. It is all the more ironic that this particular guest at Grisha's poetic gatherings "does not understand a word of Russian." Pushkin's prophesy is not wholly realized: the Tungus does not know his or any other Russian poetry. Tolstaya performs an ironic literalization of Pushkin's metaphor: she transforms a metaphorically distant people into a real-life Tungus who is present at literary fests but does not know Pushkin and does not participate in the consumption of Grisha's cake-like poetry—"he was afraid the capital's cuisine would spoil his digestion and so would ingest only some kind of lard, which he ate out of a jar with his fingers." The wild Tungus's function in the story is quite clear (despite the tongue-in-cheek "who knows why"). It directs the reader to Pushkin and at the same time casts ironic light on the contemporary poet who exploits his society's definition of a poet: "janitor, poet, genius, saint." Contemporary myth reverses the cause and effect between being a poet and leading the life of an unrecognized and persecuted genius. Grisha acquires the status of a genius because he fits the secondary criterion of living a poetic lifestyle: he is a janitor; therefore, he is a poet as all the other underground geniuses before him, whether real or fictional.

Throughout the story Grisha remains the more or less unresisting object of Nina's attentions. His final revolt, however, comes in the form of another realized metaphor: he finds a way to die not wholly, or die only in part, as in Pushkin's "Monument." He sells his body to the Academy of Sciences and happily explains to Nina that "his ashes he would outlast, and the worms elude" (*chto on svoi prakh perezhivet i tlen'ia ubezhit*).[50] This line from Pushkin's poem signals the end of Grisha's life as a poet, which from the beginning was a parody of the romantic myth of the poet. Grisha's version of living on and being cherished by the people (*liubezen narodu*) is reduced to the presence of his skeleton in a classroom, where students, "fun people" (*veselyi narod*), will play with him, slap him on the shoulder, "give him a flick on the forehead, and treat him to cigarettes" (*shchelkat' po lbu i ugoshchat' papiroskoi*). Thus Grisha's version of transcending mundane reality and his own mortality is achieved through literalizing Pushkin's lines, and in the process, he collapses the opposition between immanent and transcendent that is central to Pushkin's poem: his monument is "not made by hand" (*nerukotvornyi*) but "has ascended higher" than the real life Alexander Column. Grisha might aim at a very personal connection to Pushkin, but he can achieve it only in death and in unconscious parody. Grisha's skeleton joins the list of empty forms that symbolize nothing but the impossibility of personal connection to Pushkin: a ghost, a fake mask, an elusive photo, and an unborn new Pushkin. Thus ends the theme of the poet and the muse in their contemporary incarnations, their ironically confused relationship stripped of any vestige of a romantic aura. Both are products of the "real world" at the end of the twentieth century, in which the Muse is confused about her role, and the poet does belong to the people but only as "public property" and only as part of the "academic inventory."[51]

The story, however, does not stop with the end of this theme and offers one more "signpost," an inexplicable detail, in the last paragraph:

> And Nina also said that at first she was very upset about everything, but then it was all right, she calmed down after a woman she knew—also a lovely woman, whose husband had also died—told her that she, for one, was even rather pleased. The thing was that this woman had a two-room apartment and she'd always wanted to decorate one room Russian style, just a table in the middle, nothing else, and benches, benches all around the side, very simple ones, rough wood. And the walls would be covered with all kinds of peasant shoes, icons, sickles, and spinning wheels—that kind of thing. And so now that one of her rooms was free, this woman had apparently gone and done it, and it's her dining room, and she always gets a lot of compliments from guests.[52]

On the one hand, Nina continues to model her life on cultural clichés—the Russian-style peasant room is an ersatz version of old country life, as removed from reality as is Nina's activity as a Muse from the Romantic ideal. On the other hand, it is logical, albeit in a perverse way, that she should consider replacing her starved poet-husband with a dining room, where she, having failed to reform the "muddy cakes" of his poetry, might have better luck with real food. The substitution of real food for the poetic product provides yet another metaphor for the story's main conflict: an ersatz version of immanent reality takes over the realm of the transcendent, which itself was only a simulation.

Still more puzzling is the fact that the ending, one of the privileged places in a narrative, describes not Nina's actions, but those of some other woman, who is also very nice and who also lost her husband. The reader is driven to look for an external explanation, that is, for another text in which there is also a woman who lost her husband and had a dining room in the Russian style. Thus, even if the reader has missed the Chekhov intertext up to now, at this point, retrospectively, this discovery throws light on the plot parallels between Chekhov's and Tolstaya's stories. In Chekhov's "The Grasshopper," Olga Ivanovna is an amateur artist, musician, sculptor, and talent hunter. Her husband Dymov is a medical doctor, who dies before she discovers that he, whom she considered an ordinary and boring man, is a genuinely great person, the real thing. At the beginning of their marriage, Olga Ivanovna decorates the apartment: "In the dining room she hung cheap peasant-like prints, bast shoes, and scythes on the wall, and grouped a scythe and a rake in the corner, thus achieving a dining-room in the Russian style."[53] This seems to be the same room that is described at the end of Tolstaya's story. The roles of the main characters are reversed, however: the woman who in Chekhov is a pseudoartist in Tolstaya is a doctor, and the man, a doctor in Chekhov, becomes a parody of a poet in Tolstaya. The reversal of the occupational status further emphasizes the unchanged nature of the misconceptions that inform the characters' behavior.

Both women, Olga Ivanovna and Nina, fail to play the traditional role of a female companion: Olga Ivanovna deceives and ignores Dymov, which makes his life unbearable; Nina smothers Grisha until he can neither write nor live. Both men opt out of their unbearable family situations by committing a form of suicide: Dymov lets himself catch an infection, and Grisha starves himself. It would not be enough to assume that these similarities reflect merely the enduring tragedy of an unappreciated creative personality, whether that of a poet or a scientist; rather, they draw attention to and question the change in woman's role in the family and society at large. At the end of the nineteenth century, "the woman question" was among the central issues of the liberal movement. The multitude and diversity of Chekhov's female protagonists makes it hard to generalize about his approach to the question. Chekhov's attention to the plight of intelligent, educated women elicited appreciative responses from his liberal contemporaries. Some lauded him as an advocate of women's equality, while others, pointing to his cold, calculating seductresses or petty, limited housewives, labeled him a misogynist.[54] Most of the women in his stories who choose one of the very few professions open to them end up lonely, disillusioned, and ultimately unhappy. Most of the young idealistic women in Chekhov's stories see their future only in terms of love, their destiny that of accompanying their husbands through life as faithful and helpful companions. The negative portrayals, on the other hand, are based on a plot in which a woman's evil nature is revealed through her behavior toward a man. Like most progressive people of his time, Chekhov saw the root of the problem in the lack of equal education. One of the most quoted passages in the discussion of Chekhov's attitude toward women is the passionate speech of the protagonist in "Ariadna" who, lamenting the fact that a woman is brought up with the idea that her sole purpose in life is to capture a man, sees the solution in coeducation from early childhood: "it is necessary for girls and boys to go to school together, for them to be always together."[55] In Tolstaya's story, the heroine is a product of a society in which not only is coeducation a norm, but the assumption of gender equality is an ideological given, even if not always an everyday reality. She is a doctor, presumably satisfied with her work. Still, she perceives her life as lacking something essential, and she finds the definition of that essential thing not in the idea of marriage as a personal complement to professional fulfillment—as the cliché goes, happiness in work and in personal life (*v trude i v lichnoi zhizni*)—but in the abstract notion of romantic passion. Coeducation fails to produce real equality because the texts of the school's curriculum and popular culture still perpetuate the traditional idea of woman's role in family and society. While ideology teaches equality, classical literature teaches feminine idealization, and the clash of these two incompatible views produces a mindset, which, as in Nina's case, struggles with and fails to combine the transcendent and the immanent, the ideal and the "real world."

Chekhov's and Tolstaya's heroines long for something bigger than mundane reality. After all, Chekhov's Olga is not looking for love. Unlike those young women in Chekhov who, following a course prescribed by tradition, dream of love as the highest form of happiness, Olga Ivanovna wants artistic fulfillment and dreams of "success, fame and the love of the people . . ."[56] However, for her, creative success signifies not a truly great work of art but its tangible result, popular admiration. Like Nina, she too confuses the worldly with the transcendent. Romantic love, however, takes second place: note that she dreams of the love of the people, not of men. She chooses a lover based on his apparent artistic talents. Longing for the exceptional, she sincerely mistakes the second-rate painter Ryabovsky for a great person: "a truly great man, a genius, one of God's chosen." Her choice is predetermined by her upbringing: in her circle, as probably in all of Russian society, only an artist—a writer, painter, or musician—can qualify as a Great Person. How can it even occur to her that a doctor, a scientist, might have the greatness she is looking for? As unappealing as her character has been for readers and critics of Chekhov, she, in fact, is a version of Chekhov's favorite heroine, someone who wants more from life than the usual lot of a woman, someone who is not willing to settle for the prosaically limited life of a housewife. Granted, her aspirations take the form of a vulgar affair that destroys her husband. The obvious shallowness of her personality, as well as of her talents, places her among the ranks of the negative women-protagonists in Chekhov's works. Tolstaya's heroine, however, finds herself in the opposite situation: she is not denied professional choices and does not feel social pressure to be married. By all the standards of nineteenth-century liberals, she should be a happy model of women's equality. Nevertheless, she too feels that her life lacks purpose; she too acts under the pressure of social constructs—in her case, of the highly literary image of romantic love. Thus, what for Chekhov was a social problem becomes a cultural one for Tolstaya: it is not social conditions but rather cultural assumptions that form our aspirations. Living in different times, both women nevertheless respond to the lure of the extraordinary as it is posed by their different cultural situations. What has not changed in the hundred years between the two heroines is the status of the creative personality: an artist or a poet is still the only possible candidate for the position of genius or Great Person. The myth of the artist as "the elite"[57] is as strong as ever. Literary stereotypes prove to be stronger, more enduring, and at times more dangerous than the gender stereotypes they produce.

When asked about the writers who influenced her most, Tatyana Tolstaya gives a very traditional list: Gogol, Tolstoy, Pushkin. Like every educated and well-read person, she has her likes and dislikes: she does not like Turgenev's "beautiful novels" and feels that Dostoevsky's worldview is alien to her own. Gogol and Tolstoy, on the other hand, are brilliant writers. Speaking about Pushkin, Tolstaya displays the reverence common to all Russians: "he is the measure of all Russian literature" and "a Russian door to the universe."[58] As for Chekhov, she does not dwell on the subject: "I have my own view of Chekhov, not quite traditional. The shorter he wrote, the better it came out. All long Chekhov works are hideously boring; his plays are awful."[59] Critics, however, ignore the strongly worded disclaimer, and from the first press reviews of Tolstaya's stories to the first interviews in the Western press, Chekhov's name consistently surfaces in discussions of her style. In a 1989 interview a journalist suggests that "it is not Leo Tolstoy's but Anton Chekhov's melancholy spirit that seems to linger in Tolstaya's pages." Tolstaya protests: "His writing is different from mine, the principle is different."[60] She admits to a form of influence but only because of an unbroken line of tradition: "Chekhov influenced Bunin and Bunin in turn influenced Nabokov; there is a line."[61] Time and again, in different interviews, she talks about the importance of the nineteenth-century tradition for Russian literature, and in general about the paramount role of literature in Russian life. "No one can live without literature,"[62] she says simply. And literature in Russia "replaces religion."[63] She likens the contemporary "decline" of literature and its replacement by journalism to "the period when Chekhov was growing up and everybody wrote mass journalism."[64] Tolstaya herself regularly writes pieces for various journals and newspapers, which display her sharp opinions on subjects ranging from contemporary literature to the status of the intelligentsia to the anti-Semitism of the right-wing press. However, Tolstaya's "Pushkin" stories take her away from pressing contemporary problems into the realm of the absolute: the Poet, history, the nation's fate. When a Chekhovian intertext appears, as in "The Poet and the Muse," it raises more immediate concerns, such as woman's status in society and the family. The fusion of Pushkin and Chekhov's intertexts produces a blend of the immediate and the absolute, which unfolds in the minds of the characters who try to balance the everyday with the idealized images of cultural models. Tolstaya's characters attempt to live out literary clichés in their oversimplified, degraded form: the Muse takes control of the whole literary process; the poet takes Pushkin's metaphors as a set of instructions for achieving immortality. Tolstaya's narrator reveals their efforts through her own realized metaphors, thus producing a meta-metaphoric reality, in which the whole of Russian cultural history is precariously balanced between persistent cultural myths and ever-changing reality.

The fusion of Pushkin's and Chekhov's intertexts is symptomatic of their roles in the contemporary literary situation. Throughout its existence and especially in the twentieth century, the Pushkin myth has functioned as the bedrock of Russian culture. In the beginning of the twentieth century, the Silver Age self-image, grounded in the notion of "the circle of return" or "a centennial return," was based on its perceived connection to Pushkin's Golden Age of Russian Literature. During the Revolution, the Pushkin myth provided Russian culture with the "cultural constant" which it needed to assure its continuity, and, as Renate Lachmann puts it, "to satisfy the needs of a culture that has been split wide open and that had always been able to assure its own continuity by relying on the identification with cult figures."[65] Contemporary culture addresses the Pushkin myth in the context of the redefinition of Russian culture and the myth of Great Russian Literature as a whole. In this process, despite the attacks on Soviet metanarratives, Pushkin still remains the highest authority, "the main actor in a mythical story about the classical, a myth that is recounted time and again whenever it is a matter of reinterpreting culture."[66] The present-day reinterpretation of culture is directed against the ideological appropriations of the classics by Soviet criticism, but even the most destructive endeavors by contemporary authors unfold within the textual field of the classical tradition and make use of the mechanisms of cultural memory. The attack on the Pushkin of the canon is an attempt to uncover the Great Russian poet from under the layers of political discourse; in no way does this attempt entail undermining Pushkin's status within the national consciousness. The cultural heritage is still a constitutive element of the Russian national image, and contemporary literature in its increasingly intertextual form relies on cultural memory and its text-producing function in order to uphold the nation's wholeness and ensure the perpetuation of culture.

Tolstaya's connection to Pushkin is through the Silver Age: she has said that she sees herself continuing the tradition of modernism, working "in the place" of an unknown modernist writer from the beginning of the century.[67] This is a powerful metaphor in its emphasis on the need for continuity even if it involves "forgetting" or crossing out a whole period in cultural history. Cultural memory arranges received texts according to their importance for upholding the national image, and in this sense the Soviet literature of Socialist Realism did not contribute to this particular image of the great culture of the Word, nor did it replace the ideal standard of the nineteenth-century tradition. Contemporary authors return to pre-Soviet literature in search of acceptable ancestors. This search, like the modernists' search for Pushkin, has to do with the contemporary writer's own place in literary history. Tolstaya's envisioned "return" to the modernist age and the parallels it proposes highlights rather than downplays the difference between her dialogue with Pushkin and that of the modernists. Tolstaya's protagonists attempt to join the modernists in their active engagement with Pushkin, while the author steps back to observe their failure. The characters' world is that which Osip Mandelshtam described in 1921 as one with "so many glorious premonitions: Pushkin, Ovid, Homer"[68] and in which it is still possible for Mayakovsky to "literally" take Pushkin's monument down from its pedestal and start a conversation between two equals: "I need to talk to you while I am alive. I too soon shall die and fall silent. After death virtually side by side they will place us, you under letter P, and me under M" ("Anniversary Poem").[69] Mayakovsky's poem belongs to the tradition of "my" Pushkin: it envisions a personal connection and understanding. Hence the first- and second-person emphasis: "You, in my view, when alive, I think, rebelled too" (*Vy, po-moemu, pri zhizni—dumaiu—tozhe bushevali*). "Anniversary Poem" responds to the official Jubilee campaign of 1924[70] and attempts to counteract the effects of the canonization campaign. In the process, Mayakovsky inscribes his own name into the canon.[71] However, Tolstaya and other authors of the postmodern rather than modernist age are well aware that the Pushkin available to them cannot be approached with a simple "let me introduce myself," for he is mostly a political and ideological symbol. An intersubjective dialogue with him is impossible. While Mayakovsky has no trouble stripping the canonical gloss off the real Pushkin—"I love you but alive, not the mummy. Overlaid with anthological gloss! (*naveli khrestomatiiny glianets*)"—by the end of the twentieth century the gloss has thickened and become impenetrable. Yet, Russian culture is still as much in need of assuring its continuity during the post-perestroika period as it was after the Revolution. For the end of the twentieth century and the beginning of the twenty-first, the cult figure capable of guaranteeing this continuity is Chekhov, and he becomes the main addressee in the contemporary literary dialogue with the classics. Pushkin still rules the transcendent, the timeless, and history itself, but through textual engagement with Chekhov the person and the artist, the contemporary writer makes sense of his or her own time and art.

CHAPTER 3

The Chekhov Myth and the Mechanics of Centennial Return

> . . . as if between them there was nothing, neither Tolstoy, nor Dostoevsky, but just like this: suddenly Pushkin and right away—Chekhov.
>
> —Andrei Bitov, "My Grandfather Chekhov and Great-Grandfather Pushkin," 2004

> Behind Chekhov "the twilight bard" we discern the outlines of the other Chekhov: the joyous and powerful master of the art of literature.
>
> —Vladimir Mayakovsky, "Two Chekhovs," 1914

FOR THE MODERNISTS, the idea of centennial return provided a personal connection to Pushkin. In the same way, the perception of historical recurrence underlies the post-Soviet intelligentsia's identification with Chekhov's persona. The similarities between the dominant images associated with Chekhov's time, the end of the nineteenth century, and those of the end of the twentieth make Chekhov appear temporally close and relevant to post-Soviet times. In other words, recent cultural discourse has created another centennial return. As a movement with revolutionary aspirations developing in revolutionary times, in an effort to separate itself from its immediate predecessors (the realist school of the 1860s and 1870s), modernism was reaching back, over the heads of the preceding and therefore rejected schools, toward the purer past of the romantic period. Boris Gasparov writes on the cultural mythologies of Russian modernism:

> In its battle against Positivism and Naturalism—the reigning artistic trends of the late nineteenth century—the age of Modernism invoked many values characteristic of the Romantic era [. . .]. However, *both* Modernist strong ties with the pre-positivist era *and* its radically new self-consciousness—the prism through which these ties were experienced—found their fullest expression in the role played in Russian Modernism by Aleksandr Pushkin.[1]

Post-Soviet literature is engaged in a similar process of rejecting the reigning trends it has come to supplant and is busy deconstructing official canon and turning Socialist realism from a method of writing into its subject. The new Russian literature is also reaching back, over the heads of Socialist realism, intent on claiming its roots in the modernist past. There is an obvious historical irony in the fact that Chekhov, who for modernists was a figure in direct opposition to their project, becomes the central figure of postmodernist discourse, as significant to it as Pushkin had been to the modernists.

Chekhov, like Pushkin, belongs equally to the canon and to myth. In Russian cultural memory, their names are associated with two distinct time periods: Pushkin stands for the Golden Age, Chekhov for the "twilight of the [nineteenth] century." Bridging the time gap, critics have commented on the similarities between the two authors' attitudes toward art and its purpose and on their preoccupation with the problem of personal and artistic freedom. The growing field of Chekhov-Pushkin studies[2] includes analyses of the themes and images from Pushkin present in Chekhov's stories, and while some critics concentrate on parallels and others on differences between the two writers' artistic methods and philosophies—particularly regarding their perception of the writer's position in relation to society and the State—all reach basically the same conclusion: in Chekhov's art, Pushkin's artistic discoveries reach their fullest expression and become the foundation of his creative method.[3] The field already has its commonplaces, some of which have undergone a second round of scrutiny. Tolstoy's famous definition of Chekhov as "Pushkin in prose," for example, is reported differently in a range of memoirs and is consequently shaded differently in the scholarly literature, emerging in some studies as the somewhat ambiguous "Chekhov is a small Pushkin in prose." Most often, however, the two authors are set on a par, as in the lines from Boris Pasternak's eponymous hero in *Doctor Zhivago:* "What I have come to like best in the whole of Russian literature is the childlike Russian quality of Pushkin and Chekhov, their modest reticence in such high-sounding matters as the ultimate purpose of mankind or their own salvation. It isn't that they did not understand about these things, and to good effect, but to talk about such things seemed to them pretentious, presumptuous."[4] Nabokov too singled out Chekhov and Pushkin as "the purest writers that Russia has produced in the sense of the complete harmony that their writings convey."[5] A contemporary critic makes the connection between the two writers in similar terms: "Perhaps Pushkin's spirit of independence and the fullness of his perception of life—expressed first of all in his trust of its natural flow—were most clearly reborn in the works of Chekhov."[6] Both Pushkin's and Chekhov's status in the canon and in myth have been firmly established, yet variances in the extent of their canonization and the way they achieved it presents an interesting case of how myth and canon alike are informed by historical contingency.

Unlike the myths of Pushkin and other classics of the nineteenth century, Chekhov's myth has not solidified into a distinct concept. To an even larger extent than the Pushkin myth, it is characterized by interaction between official canon and cultural myth, the interaction which ensures its vitality and adaptability to historical change. An analysis of Chekhov's introduction into the canon—a relatively recent, halting, and controversial process—and of the peculiar dynamics at work between the canonical and mythical Chekhov will help one to understand how and why the literature of the end of the twentieth century keeps returning to Chekhov's persona, themes, characters, and techniques and in so doing marks its moment as Chekhovian time.

Chekhov's short stories, which are thought to have so captured the spirit of his time, are the prism through which writers and critics from his day to the present have perceived the end of the nineteenth century, and from which they have drawn their images for it. Among the literary expressions of the mood of the late nineteenth century, Aleksandr Blok's image of "the desolate years" (*goda glukhie*), and of the generation of the 1890s as the "children of Russia's terrible years" (*deti strashykh let Rossii*),[7] is one of the most memorable. Osip Mandelshtam picks up Blok's image in the opening of his "Noise of Time" (*Shum vremeni*), where he describes the 1890s, "the remote and desolate years of Russia" (*glukhie goda v Rossii*), as "the last refuge of a dying century" (*poslednee ubezhishche umiraiushchego veka*).[8] One may ask to what extent this retrospective look by early-twentieth-century poets was a manifestation and extension of the literary expressions of the period's outlook, rather than of historical reality. Historical accounts present the last decades of the nineteenth century as characterized by the rapid development of the sciences, theater, music, and other spheres of the art. Literature, however, in the view of literary critics, was going through a crisis. No great writer had come to supplant the giants of the Age of the Novel. The nascent philosophy of modernism derived its eschatological ideas from the same source: it seems likely that the titles of Chekhov's collections of short stories, *In the Twilight* (*V sumerkakh,* 1887) and *Gloomy People* (*Khmurye liudi,* 1890), were as much an articulation of the mood of his time as a source for later characterizations of it. The critic Aleksandr Bogdanovich, in his 1897 article, "Chekhov—the Talent of a Dead Period" (*Talant mertvoi polosy*), characterizes Chekhov's works as a truthful reflection of his time: "The twilight, gloomy mood of this life found in him its best spokesman" (*Sumerechnoe, khmuroe nastroenie etoi zhizni nashlo v nem luchshego svoego vyrazitelia*).[9] The critic's choice of epithets, echoing Chekhov titles, seems hardly accidental: since literary journals were the main forum for cultural, sociological, and political discussions, literary events seem to define social life as a whole. Chekhov, as is well known, did not share this view and ardently objected to being labeled the bard of a vanishing Russia. Despite this, as Simon Karlinsky points out, "a new generation of critics [from 1890 to the1900s] managed to reduce the complexities of Chekhovian concern and compassion to their own moaning and melancholy level and thus at last to co-opt him into the very tradition to which he was so alien and so opposed."[10] This view of Chekhov as a gloomy bard for gloomy times, superimposed on the photograph of a sickly, thin, bespectacled man gracing the title page of most twentieth-century publications of his work,[11] has forced out any other Chekhov, be it the young and still healthy six-foot-tall theater lover and ladies' man, or the able doctor, or the writer doubtful of his gifts. The way Chekhov's contemporaries imagined his person, and the image of his times, are both cultural constructs derived from one-sided readings of his texts. Chekhov, it seems, did not himself provide any other source: he did not create his own biographical myth.[12] This is in marked contrast to Pushkin, who actively shaped his own poetic persona and literary biography.[13] By withdrawing from the time-honored paradigm of the romantic poet-hero and/or realist poet-citizen, he put himself, quite deliberately, in opposition to an established literary tradition.

The modernists, who infused their philosophy with neo-romantic trends, reacted by creating their own Chekhov, a construct opposed to the romantic myth of the artist. Dmitry Merezhkovsky, a leading modernist critic, considered Chekhov a personification of the period of decline of Russian literature. In Merezhkovsky's view, Chekhov is the poet of the moment, a quality unacceptable to the generation that aspired to Pushkin-like transcendence. Thus, Merezhkovsky contrasts Chekhov's rootedness in his own time to Pushkin's universal and eternal presence. For him, Pushkin is a man of great wisdom effortlessly achieving harmony where others see dissonance. He celebrates life and joy and accepts death with the calm akin to the attitude of "those Russian peasants whose courage Tolstoy envies"; he embraces both the pagan religion of the rebelling "I" and the Christian philosophy of compassion. Paraphrasing Gogol and Dostoevsky, Merezhkovsky poses Pushkin's art and life as those of the ideal Russian man of the future and as harbingers of universal harmony.[14] In Chekhov, on the other hand, Merezhkovsky sees the spirit of destruction and the image of a present without a future. Chekhov is the voice of those who have lost all faith, whose only passion is boredom; he is the mirror of the spiritual destruction of Russia. Chekhov's art is simplicity in its final, ultimate form, at a point "from where one has no place to go. Here the last great artist of the Russian word meets the first, the end of Russian literature meets its beginning, and Chekhov meets Pushkin."[15] Merezhkovsky does not join these names to compliment Chekhov: his simplicity, unlike Pushkin's "lofty simplicity," signifies emptiness ("*prostota budet pustota*"). Where Pushkin symbolizes the future, Chekhov is a "present without past and future, one frozen moment, the dead stop of the Russian present day."[16]

Zinaida Gippius echoes Merezhkovsky: Pushkin is outside time, eternal and contemporary at the same time, "was—and is,"[17] but Chekhov is the end of time. His moment is the moment of "here and now, forever ossified."[18] It is both ironic and significant that Merezhkovsky and Gippius do not hesitate to pair Chekhov with Pushkin in their criticism: there is a tacit and reluctant acknowledgment of Chekhov's growing importance. Chekhov's popularity was becoming incontestable as they wrote and, in their view, indicative of the spiritual crisis of Russian art. Gippius sees the Moscow Art Theater's first productions of Chekhov's plays, with their attempt to erase differences between art and life, as leading to the death of art itself. She describes the plays as moments when the author, the actors, and the crowd are "all united in one desire—the desire for immobility, dull stupor, and death." Here again Gippius appeals to Pushkin as the highest authority on the relation between art and life, and someone who would surely be appalled by Chekhov's art: "I think, had Pushkin lived till our day, he would not have wanted to go on living. Because he did not want to die while he had hope [. . .]."[19] The realism of the Moscow Art Theater symbolizes, for Gippius, the end of art as transcendence. Chekhov's belonging to the moment, which excludes movement forward and the potentiality of creation, ultimately signifies mere vulgar banality (*poshlost'*).

The nineteenth-century idealization of the artist explains Gippius's aversion to the ordinariness of Chekhov. Other Chekhov contemporaries had similar difficulty placing his persona in the paradigm of the great writer. Both the liberal nineteenth-century view of the writer as a teacher and a political leader and the modernists' ideal of a spiritual leader and a higher being could not be reconciled with Chekhov's earthiness, with his clear-minded skepticism of all "philosophy of the great men of this world,"[20] and with the multitude of contemporary testimonials portraying him as an ordinary person. The same Silver Age thinkers who actively sought to claim "my" Pushkin, and credited Pushkin with a personality as unique and as poetic as his art, deplored the "normality" of Chekhov. Writers of "my Pushkin" tradition—Akhmatova, Tsvetaeva, Mandelshtam—disliked Chekhov as a lowbrow writer, the bard of the ordinary. The modernist project of building parallels between Pushkin's life and their own was an integral part of the construction of their identities.[21] Chekhov's personality, on the other hand, defied this modernist attempt at life creation as a form of art creation. "'Universal genius,'" Merezhkovsky exclaims sarcastically, "'Sage! Giant! Supreme Ruler! Teacher' etc. [. . .]. Of course not a universal genius, of course not a supreme ruler, not a teacher. He is our equal, standing next to us, an ordinary person. . . ."[22] For Merezhkovsky, Gippius, and Khodasevich, Chekhov's life and personality were unforgivably like theirs; no elaborate creative effort was needed to emulate him. Like other critics of all camps, Merezhkovsky and Gippius admitted Chekhov's talent and considered him among the most important writers of their time. The contemptuous tone of their accounts pertains primarily to what they perceived to be incompatible with their notions of the creative personality: Chekhov's art neither "taught [one] to believe in the triumph of progress, science and the human mind"[23] nor engaged the reader in a metaphysical quest; even his personality and life challenged their notions of the true artist. In the modernists' interpretation, Chekhov becomes a negative personification of immanent reality, at odds with their idea of a centennial return to Pushkin. However, reevaluated in a positive light, this very notion ensured, somewhat paradoxically, Chekhov's continuous relevance throughout the twentieth century.

The modernists were well aware that to most of Chekhov's readers not involved in the modernist project, his "standing next to us" was among the most appealing features of both Chekhov's art and his personality. "Chekhov's Russia," writes Vladislav Khodasevich, "fell in love with Chekhov, the characters applauded the author—for the fact that he excused their existence through his lyricism, that in his loving description they saw better and more beautiful versions of themselves, that they were pitied and embraced: after all, since Gogol's times they had been endlessly flogged."[24] The energy of a myth-in-the-making was enough to transform Chekhov's very ordinariness into a positive feature. Provincial teachers, small clerks, and landowners saw Chekhov as their writer, one of their own, someone with whom one exchanges letters and develops a friendly relationship.[25] "In Chekhov," notes Vasily Rozanov, "Russia loved itself. No one else expressed her collective type (*sobiratel'nyi tip*) the way he did, not only in his works, but also in his very persona, face, figure, manners, and, it seems, his conduct and way of life." Rozanov here praises Chekhov, no doubt, but he also passes judgment on his time and his Russia: "a mediocre (*seren'kaia*) and unpretentious public" learned from Chekhov's "silent and dumb" Muse how to survive their "un-heroic epoch."[26] None of the modernist critics were willing to allow for the possibility that Chekhov, without ever viewing his work in the ambitious terms of life and art-creation, was conscious of the groundbreaking nature of his story-writing techniques and his theatrical innovations. Most also missed the fact that Chekhov's art, for them the apogee of raw realism—"the ordinary expression of ordinary life"[27]—had approached and surpassed the limits of the realist method.

This position outside of accepted paradigms is typical of Chekhov with respect to most issues that defined a writer's status in the critical and public view. In the same way that he did not side with a political camp, when drawn into discussions of artistic movements he replied, in his own words, by nodding "to everything uncertainly and answer[ing] in banal half truths."[28] While Chekhov spent innumerable hours providing young authors who sent him their work with serious and detailed analyses, when prompted to generalize about art, he replied rather unenthusiastically: "I divide all works into two categories: those I like and those I don't."[29] Chekhov's views on the woman question, or the Jewish question, or even—most important in the tradition of writers as religious thinkers—his religious beliefs, are still the subject of intense critical debate. The problem is not a lack of material to suggest a definite position one way or another, but rather the number of different and equally convincing statements found both in Chekhov's letters and in his texts. Chekhov consistently individualizes every character in accordance with his or her worldview; his characters' voices reflect their reality and philosophy; they are engaged in making sense of their lives, not in making extratextual statements for their author. The author's own statements, abundant in his letters, also defy categorization: "I am neither liberal, nor conservative, not gradualist, nor monk, nor indifferentist. [. . .] That is why I cultivate no particular predilection for policemen, butchers, scientists, writers or the younger generation. I look upon tags and labels as prejudices."[30] This apophatic definition—explaining oneself through what one is not—puts Chekhov in a neither/nor, borderline position, one that is the source of constant perplexity for critics but that also assures Chekhov's persona and artistic influence continuous relevance to the Russian cultural tradition, particularly in times of major paradigmatic shifts—political, ideological, and cultural turmoil such as those shared by Chekhov's own time and the closing decades of the twentieth century.

Chekhov connects the nineteenth and twentieth centuries of Russian literature and stands on the borderline of realism and modernism. From the outset, Chekhov's realism challenged critics' vocabulary: something was obviously peculiar about his way of telling an "ordinary story about an ordinary event." Thus Rozanov, in the article quoted above, admits that Chekhov's story "testifies, like every apogee and peak, that we have approached the edge, beyond which 'a pass to another [peak]' begins. . . ." Thus, Korolenko calls Chekhov's realism super-realism, and Gorky asserts that Chekhov is "killing realism" by taking it to extremes. Andrei Bely claims Chekhov for symbolism, and Merezhkovsky defines Chekhov as an impressionist, although this term, accurate as it is when applied to Chekhov's techniques, to his "light touch" as Nabokov phrases it, does not explain the underlying philosophy of art and the worldview that create what we know as Chekhov's world.[31] Chekhov did not participate in the discussion of symbolism and did not ally himself with the new theories of art. Nevertheless, he defies the realistic imperatives of social relevance and in effect presents a thoroughly modernist vision of a world in the midst of existential crisis. Vladimir Kataev offers an astute analysis of Chekhov's stories in which people fail repeatedly in trying to orient themselves in the world. He sees the epistemological theme as pivotal in Chekhov and defines the "organizing center of Chekhov's world" as "the pathos of the unknown but definitely existing truth, 'the real truth,' and the skepticism toward all of its known interpretations."[32] The epistemological, questioning nature of Chekhov's method and worldview is ironically paralleled by the confusion his work produced for contemporary critics who found it difficult to reach a clear understanding, "the real truth," about Chekhov's method and philosophy. How are we to orient ourselves in his texts? Why has his "vulgar ordinariness" produced passionately engaged responses from realists, modernists, and "mediocre" readers alike? The liberals wanted a socially engaged artist and bemoaned Chekhov's lack of interest in the issues of the time while, on the other hand, modernists demanded transcendence and saw him as engaged too deeply in the everyday. Both of these views continued to play major roles in forming both the canonical and the popular image of Chekhov throughout the new century.

This tension between the ideological and the aesthetic influenced the formation of the Soviet canon and Chekhov's inclusion in it. Continuing the civic trend of nineteenth-century criticism, Soviet critics performed a selective interpretation of all the classics, including Chekhov. The form and the function of the official view of Chekhov, that is, his canonical image, went through several stages of development. During the years after the Revolution, Chekhov languished on the margins of critical attention. At that time, the principles of the new culture were being formulated and expected to be radically different, both aesthetically and ideologically, from those of pre-Revolutionary culture. Most living modernist writers found themselves forced into what they thought was temporary emigration; others, with more or less sincere enthusiasm, accepted the Revolution as an extension of revolution in art. The 1920s produced an exciting but short-lived explosion of new trends and movements. By the early 1930s, however, the doctrine of Socialist realism had established its reign. Throughout the 1920s the demand for new forms and new heroes, for large-scale portrayals of epic events, made Chekhov's characters seem trite, insignificant, and simply not worthy of attention. The Revolutionary theater excluded most of Chekhov's plays from its repertoire as unsuitable to the heroic epoch.[33] A left-wing newspaper insisted that it was "time to abandon to their own era the down-in-the-mouth, grief-stricken Chekhovs [. . .] The theater must now present bright gripping spectacles, joyful and powerful experiences, and not staged funerals."[34] However, as expectations for a proletarian literature, made for and by the new ruling class, quickly proved to be inflated, the importance of the classics of the nineteenth century came to be appreciated anew. The State's use of the classics followed the process already started in the last decades of the nineteenth century. Jeffrey Brooks outlines the gradual, and at first reluctant, acceptance of the great nineteenth-century writers into the official pantheon of national heroes. The nineteenth-century authorities, reluctant to accept the idea that writers who were often perceived as opposed to the State should be honored along with "the traditional symbols of Russian nationality, the tsar and the church," attempted to dissociate the images of the writers from the notion of opposition. After the Revolution, however, the process went in the opposite direction: the new State, seeking "symbols of national unity independent of church and autocracy,"[35] used the authority of the classics for the purpose of legitimizing the new order, emphasizing and at times exaggerating the older writers' democratic and antigovernment views.

Chekhov's much-discussed apolitical stand would seem to have been an obvious obstacle to his acceptance into a new, post-Revolutionary version of the canon, but it also could be turned into a positive factor by a sympathetic critic arguing for the latent presence of a revolutionary impulse in Chekhov's humanistic portrayals of common people. Such a sympathetic critic was Maxim Gorky, Chekhov's friend and admirer, who brought to the "fight for Chekhov" not only his highly positive view of Chekhov's art but also the authority of his own eminent status as "the father of Socialist Realism." Gorky's views on Chekhov as a great realist talent who exposed the vulgarity of bourgeois society and portrayed simple folk with the love and honesty of a great humanist determined in many ways the future reading of Chekhov by Soviet critics. Promoting Chekhov's democratic and realist art, Gorky urged writers to study Chekhov's works and learn the techniques and style of the great master. He insisted on the publication of individual Chekhov stories and small thematic collections that included stories exposing the ills of life in pre-Revolutionary Russia. His choice of stories would determine the content of short popular collections for years afterwards.

The authority of Gorky's voice, enormous as it was, was not enough to secure Chekhov's inclusion in the canon. In 1924, the Commissar of Popular Enlightenment, Anatoly Lunacharsky, in his article "What Can A. P. Chekhov Be for Us?" still considers it necessary to explain why he offers the readers his thoughts on "one (*kakom-nibud'*) Chekhov." "Perhaps," he writes, "it is clear to everyone that to disown (*otkreshchivat'sia ot*) Belinsky, Gogol, Nekrasov, and Pushkin is shameful, but it is not clear to everyone how we can find a use for Tchaikovsky and Chekhov. It is not clear to everyone whether we should even recognize artists of this type as harmful."[36] At the end of the article, Lunacharsky arrives at the conclusion that despite his ideological weaknesses, Chekhov undertook the heroic task of "announcing in every line of his work that life was ugly and vulgar, and that an honest person, when faced with this life, could only be melancholy or declare ruthless war on it."[37] He concludes, somewhat unexpectedly, that Chekhov's works should be placed "somewhere in the closest proximity to Gogol's masterpieces."[38] This high praise notwithstanding, four years later, in his 1929 article "A. P. Chekhov in Our Day," Lunacharsky still asks, "Do we need him?" His answer: we need Chekhov as a master. We need him also because Chekhov's enemies, the remnants of the old regime, are still alive; therefore there is a need for Chekhov as not only a "big writer, but first of all as a fighter."[39] It is safe to conclude that Gorky's and Lunacharsky's efforts to rehabilitate Chekhov bore fruit: in as early as 1921 Chekhov's house in Yalta was declared a memorial museum, with Mariia Chekhova, his sister, as the first and most devoted director; and a small Chekhov museum was organized in Moscow at the Public Library (later the Lenin State Library). In 1914 the Chekhov house in Taganrog was declared a museum. In 1935 it was designated the Chekhov Literary Museum. Cherry trees were planted in the yard, while the street was renamed Chekhov Street—the first of a multitude of Chekhov streets to appear throughout the Soviet Union in the years to come.[40] Massive amounts of publications, newspaper articles, and lectures marked the anniversaries in 1924, 1929, and 1934 of Chekhov's death, and in 1930 and 1935 of his birth. Moreover, the 1934 Great Soviet Encyclopedia (*Bol'shaya Sovetskaya Entsiklopediia*) included a long detailed entry on Chekhov including a full-page portrait.

To what extent did Gorky's and Lunacharsky's efforts play a role in the establishment of Chekhov as a canonical writer? Most probably, their authority—Lunacharsky's status as Commissar of Popular Enlightenment and Gorky's as a forerunner of Socialist realism—lent great weight to their opinions, including those on the classics of pre-Revolutionary literature. It is also possible that being, like most of the first generation of Party leaders, members of the intelligentsia, they were guided by their own literary tastes, and political considerations could not make them denounce one of the intelligentsia's favorite authors. The critical problem of positioning Chekhov on the ideological and aesthetic axis takes second place to the feeling of class unity, the common sense of identity Chekhov provides for the intelligentsia. Vladimir Lenin, whose traditional taste in literature is well known, also played a role in forming the State attitude toward the classics of the past. Lenin, and Stalin after him, used classic literary images in their polemics with political enemies. Soviet critical studies of the classics never failed to quote passages from the leaders' speeches that related to literary figures and their creators. Chekhov criticism routinely included phrases by Lenin, such as "pitiful men in cases," and most often his passionate comment on Chekhov's story "Ward no. 6" that the whole of Russia was a ward number six.[41] Thus, Chekhov's place in the official pantheon of national heroes was secured by the 1940s. At the beginning of World War II, Stalin put Chekhov next to Pushkin, Tolstoy, and the classic of Socialist realism, Gorky. Stalin's speech of November 6, 1941, on the eve of the anniversary of the Revolution and six months after the beginning of the war, appeals to the patriotic feelings of the Soviet people, reminding them that Hitler's troops are striving to destroy the great nation "of Plekhanov and Lenin, Pushkin and Tolstoy, Glinka and Tchaikovsky, Gorky and Chekhov, Sechenov and Pavlov, Repin and Surikov, Suvorov and Kutuzov. . . ." The list combines the names of political leaders with those of writers, painters, and military victors of the past. In the face of the approaching enemy, all of them, including Lenin's political enemy Plekhanov, serve as symbols of the great country and nation in need of defense.[42]

The Party leader's awareness of the political potential of classic literary names shows itself very early: already in 1918, a few months after the Revolution, the state declares a monopoly on the publication of Russian classics. Chekhov is on the list. The history of Chekhov's publication over the next few decades offers valuable insight into the dynamics of his canonization. During the following years, according to Maurice Friedberg's study, the number of printed copies of Chekhov's works was among the highest: he was first on the list from 1918 to 1923, and second from 1924 to 1933. On the whole, from 1918 to 1957, Chekhov ranks consistently among the most published classics, close to and sometimes exceeding in numbers the print runs of Pushkin and Tolstoy.[43] The most frequently published of Chekhov's stories were those that presented "a sad picture of Russia [. . .]—a picture of ignorance, poverty, prejudice and suspicion":[44] "Van'ka," "Sleepy," "The Chameleon," "The Criminal," "Sergeant Prishibeev," "Women," and "Peasants." While the Bolshevik press deemed Chekhov's plays unsuitable for the Revolutionary theater, which was still well attended by the public, those of his stories that portrayed the lives of the lower classes were easy to incorporate with the current ideological reading. The very subject matter of these stories assured Chekhov a place in print while the critical debate about Chekhov's technique and ideological standing continued. After the Second World War, the total print run of Chekhov stories was still among the largest. At that time, the publication of multivolume editions of the classics proliferated. Political considerations determined which of the classics were honored with such productions. As a rule, multivolume editions were accompanied by forewords and commentaries by noted literary critics, which were meant to guide the reader in approaching the works. Combined with the forewords of smaller popular editions and with interpretations in school textbooks, these critical analyses formed the generally accepted image of the classics and facilitated their assimilation into the whole of Soviet culture. Friedberg remarks on the list of labels used by Soviet criticism to distinguish classics from one another within the otherwise homogeneous group of progressive nineteenth-century writers. The number of available qualifiers was extremely small: "Griboedov was 'progressive,' and so were Saltykov-Shchedrin and Belinsky; Turgenev was a 'patriot,' and so were Nekrasov and Lermontov; Chekhov was a 'humanist,' and so were Leskov and Pushkin; Goncharov was a 'realist,' and so were Tolstoy and Gogol."[45] Soviet criticism, of course, served ideological ends and paid little attention to the individual characteristics of the classic authors. However, the print runs of certain classics—Tolstoy, Chekhov, and Pushkin—outnumbered those of writers who, albeit with less artistic value, were significantly more amenable to ideological criticism. As Friedberg concludes, "these [authors] are no longer subject to political metamorphoses; they are a part of the country's ethos."[46]

Inclusion in a literary canon, as the contemporary debate about the means and the politics of canon formation shows,[47] reflects much more than a work's aesthetic value. Other forces in modern capitalist societies influence the status of literary works, such as the authority of educational institutions, the social impact of the literary work, and its market value. Some scholars concentrate on a canon's conformity to the ruling ideology and political climate; criticize its social, racial, or gender exclusivity; and call for the reevaluation and expansion of the canon. Others point out that exclusivity is the nature and function of the canon, and however unfashionable this view might be in the contemporary discourse of cultural diversity, one cannot open and reevaluate the canon on demand by simply changing the school curriculum. Harold Bloom formulates this view with characteristic deftness: "The Western Canon, despite the limitless idealism of those who would open it up, exists precisely in order to impose limits, to set a standard of measurement that is anything but political or moral." Canons, he adds, are "not unified props of morality, Western or Eastern."[48] As is often the case with literary and political issues, the Russian situation does not fit neatly into either side of the canon argument, at least not until the post-Soviet decades. In a situation of total government control over publishing, disseminating, teaching, and interpreting literary works, the literary canon does indeed reflect the ruling ideology. And in a culture that endows literature with scripture-like importance, its classics are first and foremost "props of morality." "Classical literature," a Soviet writer muses in post-Soviet times, "gives us a boundless wealth of notions that feed the self-conscience of the nation and allow us, the readers, to orient ourselves in the people and in life around us."[49] Vladimir Vysotsky, the popular poet, actor, and singer, insists in his "Ballad about Fighting" (1975) that the ability to live and fight with honor comes from reading the right books as a child.[50] The Russian literary canon has reflected the government's manipulation of the classics' authority and the use it makes of popular validation of their works. It has provided a politically neutral ground where official ideology and popular consciousness coexist in a peaceful compromise: both sides agree on the paramount importance of the classics of the canon, while choosing to concentrate on different aspects and to offer different interpretations of them. The official ideology and cultural myths share space in the popular consciousness and in the classroom.

School textbooks express the Party line on the interpretation of pre-Revolutionary literature in its most straightforward form. The changes in the textbook presentation of Chekhov reflect fluctuations in the official attitude. In the 1926 textbook for adult schools, *The History of Russian Literature of the Nineteenth Century,* Chekhov is included in the chapter, "The Populist-Intelligentsia Period." The chapter includes other writers of the period, although it is apparent that the list of 1880s authors to be included in textbooks and in the canon had not yet been finalized. The nine pages devoted to Chekhov are titled "The Poetry of the Intelligentsia's Melancholy." Following Chekhov's pre-Revolutionary critics, the textbook's author describes the "melancholic, aching poetry of A. P. Chekhov" as born of the gloomy atmosphere of the 1880s. He enumerates the social classes portrayed by Chekhov—peasants, merchants, landowners, and the intelligentsia—and concludes that all groups are presented in an equally negative light. "For Chekhov," he writes, "all of life was a steppe, where people lived without goals, without desires, without passions."[51] The short chapter concludes with a negative verdict on Chekhov's social significance for the new State: "If only this big idea [of Chekhov's] expressed the struggle of the classes for a better life, we would be able to admit the great social significance of Chekhov's art, but Chekhov himself knows that in his art 'something is missing.'"[52] The form of the statement is peculiar: not an outright rejection but a syntactic play on "if" and "would," as if the author is not quite sure how far he can go in either direction. The official position on Chekhov in the mid-1920s is close to the position of N. Mikhailovsky, A. Bogdanovich, and other liberal critics among Chekhov's contemporaries: his apolitical stand prevented him from becoming a real writer, and his great talent was a wasted gift.

The situation changed quite noticeably in the next ten years. The 1935 ninth-grade textbook *Russian Literature of the Nineteenth Century* introduces Chekhov as a strikingly different writer. Unlike the 1926 textbook, it presents only two of the large group of writers of the 1880s: Uspensky and Chekhov. The chapter on Chekhov concludes the book; it is longer—fifteen pages long—and more detailed, and offers analyses of several short stories and two plays. The author defines Chekhov as the most significant writer of the 1880s and an unsurpassed master of the short story. His tone is characterized by a reverent attitude toward the "great master." The author emphasizes Chekhov's lyricism and humor, "a special, soft, lyrical humor, sad, full of compassion for those at whom it is directed." The analysis of *The Cherry Orchard* (which according to the 1926 textbook is a harsh verdict on aristocratic culture) concentrates on the "new people," Trofimov and Ania, as they leave at the end of the play to start "a new, pure, genuine life." The end of the chapter, and of the textbook, is straightforward praise: "Chekhov is a genuine, great artist, [. . .] that person with 'a little hammer,' who stood at the doors of the calm and the satisfied." The very last paragraph uses a famous image from Chekhov's story "Gooseberries" (*Kryzhovnik*) included in school syllabi throughout the twentieth century, and it outlines in condensed form the way Chekhov would be read in schools for years to come: "Subjectively defending 'reforms,' 'progress,' 'culture,' Chekhov objectively revealed all the bankruptcy of the liberal-reformist hopes, all the absurdity and impossibility of trying to reach the 'radiant future' by non-revolutionary means. In this lies the great artistic and socio-political importance of Chekhov's art."[53] Thus, this textbook finally manages to resolve the problem of that "something missing" in Chekhov's art: it implants the missing political message by government fiat. Chekhov the person is forgiven for being a Russian liberal; Chekhov the writer is praised for being a revolutionary, albeit unconsciously. A 1949 teachers' handbook, *Chekhov in School,* urges teachers to elucidate Chekhov's life and works in ways that would draw students' attention to his patriotism, his interest in the lives of simple people, and the democratic nature of his works. The teacher, says the handbook, should also point out the limitations of his political position. With time, however, all mention of the apolitical nature of Chekhov's works disappeared from textbooks and the introductory pages of popular editions.

The choice of Chekhov's works for school curricula differed in each period, but at all times the nineteenth-century literature selections for the school program concluded with Chekhov. Literature lessons took up about 30 percent of all class time.[54] The humanities were, of course, the most obvious venue for ideology in the schools; thus, history and literature teachers carried the full weight of the socialist upbringing of the younger generation.[55] The distribution of class time among particular authors reflects not only the length of the works but also their ideological significance. Class time allotted to the analysis of "Ionych" and *The Cherry Orchard* was twelve hours, the same as that devoted to Turgenev's much longer *Fathers and Sons* and Dostoevsky's *Crime and Punishment.*[56] From the 1950s on, the other writers of the 1880s were no longer included even in the recommended reading list.[57] Throughout the Soviet period, critics portrayed Chekhov as a fighter against bourgeois values and a herald of the new revolutionary generation. He was praised for the humanism and realism of his works, and for his truthful representation of pre-Revolutionary life. The Soviet school system worked to bring up loyal and nonquestioning citizens, and the standard interpretation of Chekhov's style clearly favored the image of the writer "with a little hammer" over the far more violent image of Dostoevsky's hero with an axe.

As a master of the craft of the short story, Chekhov was held up as an example for every prose writer, a model seemingly easy to imitate but, in fact, unattainable in its perfection. One of Gorky's dicta to young writers was to learn from the masters. In a 1929 article, Gorky instructs young writers to learn the secrets of the craft from the classics and then develop them further.[58] "Read Chekhov, read Tolstoy" became a persistent critical imperative that for many writers resounded as a statement on their inadequacy. This official endorsement of influence imposed upon writers from above produced a peculiar kind of anxiety driven by a contest not with the older masters' art but with their fixed canonical status, aimed not so much at artistically surpassing them as at clawing out a place in the hierarchy. Vladimir Voinovich, in his novella "The Fur Hat" (*Shapka,* 1987), presents just such a struggle for inclusion, one with social rather than artistic issues at stake. His hero, the second-rate writer Yefim Rakhlin, is infuriated by the constant comparison with Chekhov imposed on him from all sides:

> As for Chekhov, Yefim read him often and closely. And did not understand a thing. Each time he read Chekhov, he . . . He would never confess this to anyone, of course, but . . . but each time he read Chekhov he felt that there was really nothing special about the writing. He, Yefim Rakhlin, wrote just as well. Perhaps even a little better.[59]

Interestingly, the novella itself is structured around the plot of Gogol's "Overcoat": Rakhlin becomes obsessed with acquiring a hat made from expensive fur, while the writers' organization offers him a hat made from cat fur because, apparently, it better suits his status as a writer. As with the Gogolian clerk and his overcoat (with a collar made from the best cat fur), a piece of clothing comes to symbolize social status. As in Gogol, striving to acquire it brings the hero to his death. Why, then, does Voinovich introduce Chekhov into his modern version of Gogol's tale? Most probably because his protagonist is not a clerk in a nameless department, but a writer; and the comparison with Chekhov, clearly unfavorable to Rakhlin, makes his position on the lowest step of the creative, as well as the social, ladder quite apparent. Were Voinovich to make his hero an engineer or a junior researcher in a nameless research institute, he would have to use another model. The writer, however, is cursed with having to write himself into the list of authoritative names by constant comparison with the canonical figures.

Abram Tertz's story "Graphomaniacs" (*Grafomany*, 1960) presents a similar struggle for the social status signified by publications, respect, and a place on a library shelf. The hero-writer also bitterly complains: "'Read Chekhov, read Chekhov!' people kept on at me all my life, tactlessly suggesting that Chekhov wrote better than I. . . ." He rambles on that the classics "stole vacant places and I was faced with their competition without possessing one-hundredth part of their inflated authority."[60] This outburst is brought on by the hero's trip to a publishing house where he suffers yet another rejection of his novel. The scene highlights another aspect of Chekhov's function in the official canon—as a model realist—and involves him in a discussion of literary style and the use of tropes. While the hero argues with a secretary, he hears the editor lecturing another "graphomaniac" on the inadequacy of his plot, language, and style. Singling out the sentence "The sun sweated in the clouds," the editor asks, "Do such things really happen? Can the sun really sweat? And in the clouds at that? Study Chekhov!"[61] The mention of Chekhov's name in this context—as an argument against an unfortunate metaphor—seems unwarranted, since Chekhov's style can hardly be described as a standard for the use of tropes. Most probably, the editor makes his remark automatically, out of the habit of referring writers to Chekhov every time he needs an exemplary model. This automatism calls attention to the hollowness of the "official" Chekhov, an empty signifier. Neither the editor nor the poor graphomaniacs can or wish to really read Chekhov—that is, to form a personal view that might be at odds with the officially prescribed one. It is then ironic that the editor's remark echoes Chekhov's own in a letter to Gorky in which Chekhov chastises the younger writer for getting carried away with anthropomorphism in his descriptions of nature: "when the sea breathes, the sky looks on, the steppe basks, nature whispers, talk, grieves, etc. . . ."[62] However, the editor's remark strips down Chekhov's statements on the value of simplicity to the parodic "Read Chekhov!" His name functions as a sign, a signifier of artistic perfection with no real content attached. The missing content can be formulated, although not by Tertz's character. Nabokov, for example, does so in explaining how and why Chekhov is a model for writers: "Chekhov is a good example to give when one tries to explain why a writer may be a perfect artist without being exceptionally vivid in his verbal technique or exceptionally preoccupied with the way his sentences curve."[63]

The readers are free to disagree both with the editor's evaluation of the metaphor and with his alleged expertise in Chekhov's style. He is a Soviet editor, interested more in ideological purity than in purity of style, yet he might be a man of genuine literary sensibility. In that case, his reference to Chekhov would present a typical combination of the official and popular uses of Chekhov's name: without straying from the official line about emulating the masters, he at the same time announces that he is a member of the intelligentsia, the circle in which Chekhov has served as a kind of a litmus test for belonging. As Nabokov reminds us, "[I]t was quite a game among Russians to divide their acquaintances into those who liked Chekhov and those who did not. Those who did not were not the right sort. [. . .] Chekhov himself was a Russian intellectual of the Chekhovian type."[64] The telling paradox—of Chekhov being a Chekhovian *intelligent*—is a crucial part of Chekhov's myth. In Chekhov's works, for the first time in Russian literature, the middle-class intelligentsia, already the principal reader of Chekhov, became the principal character. Images of the intelligentsia, this most peculiar Russian "class," presented in Chekhov's works, have in many ways grounded the intelligentsia's image of itself. However, the intelligentsia's Chekhov and the Chekhov of the canon are two drastically different personae: the canon poses him as a model of unattainable perfection; the myth constructs him as "one of us." Reading Chekhov and being like Chekhov serve to identify someone as a member of the intelligentsia. Viktor Erofeev defines Chekhov as "the prophetic workaday routine of the Russian mentality" (*prorocheskie budni russkoi mental'nosti*). In his usual provocative manner, Erofeev outlines

Chekhov's status as a symbol and the essence of the intelligentsia's image of itself: "We are the intelligentsia. Chekhov is the same as us, only a little better. In order to understand the Russian intelligentsia's consciousness, our norm—read Chekhov. Pushkin, Lermontov, Gogol, Dostoevsky, Tolstoy—all this is the extreme. One cannot be a Gogol, and who would want to be anyway, but it is possible to become a Chekhov if one tries hard enough."[65]

Erofeev is referring to the image of Chekhov the person, an image immensely appealing to the twentieth-century intelligentsia, as appealing as it was objectionable for the modernists one hundred years earlier. In the post-Soviet period, in reaction to the Soviet State-sanctioned idea of the writer's higher role, this image of a person whose very ordinariness made him unique in the ranks of teachers and prophets acquires new appeal. A contemporary writer and critic joins Chekhov's and Pushkin's names together yet again to extol Chekhov's accessibility:

> In my opinion, Gogol's words about Pushkin as an extraordinary phenomenon apply in full measure to Chekhov: "this is the Russian man in his development as he might appear in two hundred years." Two hundred years proved unnecessary, Russian nature and culture created the type of man any comparison to whom can be flattering. It is precisely in Chekhov that the Russian soul, Russian language, and Russian character are reflected with crystal clarity and fullness. Pushkin is god; he is unapproachable; imitating him invariably turns into farce and caricature. Chekhov is a human being in the full meaning of the word, and to imitate him is not easy but possible.[66]

This statement operates with the same elements as the modernist formula but reverses its values: Pushkin is a god and therefore outside any possible zone of contact; Chekhov is human, perfect but human nevertheless and should be imitated. In the post-Socialist realism context, the contemporary writer is glad to be relieved of the burden of curing the ills of society and answering the unanswerable questions thrown at him and his reader by social and economic forces. The modern intelligentsia, unlike its predecessors, finds it agreeable to be ordinary, exactly like Chekhov.

Chekhov's time, the end of the nineteenth century, is perceived as similar to the end of the twentieth in the spirit of dissatisfaction and disappointment, revolutionary stirrings and uncertainty. It is of little importance to the mythological nature of this perception that nothing comparable to the scope of the disintegration of the socialist system and the Soviet Empire took place during the 1880s and 1890s. It is enough that the popular consciousness sees the periods as similar in mood and spirit. The end of the nineteenth century was a time of growing disapproval of the regime, dissatisfaction with the insufficient reforms of the 1870s, and demand for more-radical reforms. The liberal circles of Russian society united in proclaiming the monarchy the wrong form of government and in anticipating and demanding social change. The statement that "it is impossible to live like this any more" expresses the overall mood in the society of the time.[67] The end of the twentieth century witnesses a similar level of extreme dissatisfaction with the social system, expectation of change, and a sense of hope for mixed with distrust in the possibility of peaceful transitions. The short-lived hopes of the mid-1980s, at the beginning of perestroika, gave way in the 1990s to a deep sense of disappointment and to a perception of events as chaotic and tragic, portending the disintegration of the society as a whole.

Among the signs of disintegration were the changes in the existing system of social values, a shift in the notions of what constituted socially acceptable and prestigious occupations, and the assignment of market value to life choices that had previously been determined by inertia and/or tradition. Changes in the social status (and financial situation) of the intelligentsia were among some of the inevitable outcomes of this process; the diminishing status of literature and the writer was another. It is not surprising, then, that the discussion of these issues keeps going back to Chekhov, as, first, the "creator" of the intelligentsia, and second, a writer who refused to see himself as a teacher of the nation. Contemporary literature displays "skepticism toward even the possibility of a social ideal"[68] and refuses "to go in for rallying cries because it doubts the power of the word and the right of art to attempt to rally and instruct."[69] Whereas Chekhov did not participate in ideological and political debates because he did not believe that it was the writer's mission to preach to the reader (even if the reader demanded a sermon), contemporary authors find themselves in a situation where a sermon simply irritates the reader. What for Chekhov had been a personal choice is for the writers working in the post-Socialist Realism period the only way to avoid the moralizing that permeated Soviet ideological discourse. The well-known attacks on Chekhov by his contemporaries, the accusations that he lacked principles, that he was "killing peoples' hopes," and creating "from a void"[70] of indifference sound strikingly similar to the complaints in recent Russian criticism that "present-day literature does not heal society by pointing the way to possible recovery, but only accompanies it to its spiritual, political, and material end."[71]

Contemporary authors, according to recent criticism, have lost the modernist belief in an ideal world order hidden beneath layers of mundane reality. However, this assumption seems unwarranted for most contemporary writers, except the self-conscious postmodernists, who have made the game of meanings their principal technique. Most present-day writers are unwilling and/or not ready to give up the search for meaning and value and to embark on the postmodernist project of creation from a void. They sidestep the principles of Socialist realism only to find themselves in its immediate past—the modernist era—and their works appear as at least partly "a reclamation of the lost or repressed impulses of Russian and European modernism."[72] Chekhov's innovations in the theory and practice of writing, especially in the genre of the short story, are the closest available model for a writer who is caught between the rejection of rallying cries and an unwillingness to turn his art into a play of signifiers. Chekhov's skepticism toward the possibility of providing explanations and rationalizations is close in nature to what Alan Wilde calls modernist irony, which "expresses a resolute consciousness of different and equal possibilities so ranged as to defy solution."[73] Yet this skepticism, this unwillingness to provide a solution to a range of human problems, enables rather than excludes a constant search for one. Fending off accusations of being apolitical and indifferent, of not having a definite platform, Chekhov was forced to turn an admission of not having a platform into a declaration of one: "and if an artist in whom the crowd has faith decides to declare that he understands nothing of what he sees,—this in itself constitutes a considerable clarity in the realm of thought, and a great step forward."[74] Chekhov's techniques, especially his structural choice of an open ending, represent an expression of the modernist realization that to strive toward a resolute and resolving ending means to see the world as a well-made fiction and to attempt to deal with the anxiety of contingent existence by taking hold of it and bracketing it between definite beginnings and endings. As William Spanos argues, such endings-as-solutions are no longer acceptable to the modern writer.[75]

Thus, it is only logical that throughout Soviet times Chekhov provided a model for a humanist but socially disengaged (or much less engaged than the Socialist realism doctrine demanded) literature, and that in the post-Soviet period, he has become the central figure in the discussion of literature's role in society. As a recent critic points out, "[I]n Soviet literature much that was opposed to the aesthetics of Socialist Realism either consciously or unconsciously harkened back to Chekhov, starting with Zoshchenko and Dobychin, and ending with Trifonov and Makanin."[76] Chekhov's artistic innovations were not further developed by the writers of the first quarter of the twentieth century because the most influential artistic schools of that time were within the scope of high modernism and its preoccupation with form. The advent of Socialist realism brought back the notions of "humanistic ideas" and "social types" directly related to nineteenth-century realism. Thus, in mainstream Soviet literature there was really nothing between Chekhov, on one hand, and the "young prose" of the 1960s and the "other prose" of the 1980s, on the other, that could provide a model for a nonideological yet not avant-garde discourse.

Chekhov represents precisely this mode of discourse, and in this sense his aesthetic is the modernist aesthetic that in Lyotard's words "allows the unrepresentable to be put forward only as the missing content, but the form because of its recognizable consistency continues to offer to the reader or viewer matter for solace and pleasure."[77] The missing content of his stories is the idea of a norm that no one can grasp, but deviations from which cause everyone suffering. Chekhov refuses to formulate it: "the norm is unknown to me," he wrote in 1889, "as it is unknown to all of us."[78] Defining the norm equals posing a positive ideal, a model to imitate, something the nineteenth-century realist tradition had done countless times. Chekhov's aesthetics, on the other hand, incorporate the idea of the missing norm into the very fabric of his realist method. In the attempt to "show life truthfully and, by the way, to show how much it deviates from the norm," as he put it in the same letter, Chekhov modified the realist method to the extent that it became a peculiar, Chekhovian kind of realism. It stands on the borderline of realism and modernism because it offers innovative aesthetics in seemingly traditional forms. "Showing life truthfully" is a constitutive part of nineteenth-century realism, but Chekhov's emphasis is on the method ("truthfully") rather than the content (truth): to show life truthfully is not the same as to show the truth about life; to enable the search for the norm is not the same as to champion one definite idea of it. Chekhov operates with adverbs rather than nouns, with *how* rather than *what,* and develops a mode of discourse that is true to life but breaks the tenets of the realist method: it represents life without social types and general truths, and it poses questions, the answers to which are missing and left to the reader to find. Chekhov's poetics thus might be called a *heuristic poetics:* he poses his questions correctly and thus enables the readers to search for their own answers. This method shows Chekhov's awareness of, and his reaction to, the tradition of viewing writers as teachers, a tradition out of which he emerged; he chooses, however, a method of teaching that puts maximal emphasis on the process of arriving at the answers rather than on offering the answers themselves. In this way, too, Chekhov represents the borderline between the nineteenth-century positivist worldview, with its belief in the power of reason and analysis, and the modernist's attention to the unknowable. This borderline position ensures Chekhov's continuous centrality in post-Soviet culture, which has undergone a similar cultural shift: a struggle against realism and for new art forms.

Neither canon nor myth reflects the full complexity of Chekhov's poetics and worldview. The official, canonical image of Chekhov disregards his apolitical stand and the peculiarities of his creative method, while the Chekhov of the myth is discussed in the same terms of type and norm with which he refused to operate. The canon coerces Chekhov into the great realistic tradition; the myth molds him as a type, or rather a prototype, for a large social group, the intelligentsia. From Rozanov praising Chekhov for expressing Russia's "collective type," to Nabokov calling Chekhov an *intelligent* of "Chekhovian type," to Erofeev designating him as "our norm," to Soviet editors setting Chekhov up as the standard for literary style, all operate with constructed images of Chekhov—all infuse their own meaning into the empty form that is myth. For the intelligentsia, the idea of Chekhov as "our norm" is crucial to its positive self-identification; thus the myth transmogrifies the images of those flawed but lovable intellectuals created by Chekhov, and the images of his own person as the first *intelligent,* into a positive type. The cultural myth of Chekhov as the creator of the intelligentsia functions quite independently of the fact that Chekhov's own view of the intelligentsia is extremely critical and despite the fact that his portrayals of teachers and lawyers, students and artists, professors and bankers, are for the most part unflattering and often harsh. The intelligentsia ignores the harshness just as Chekhov's first readers had when, as Khodasevich put it, in Chekhov's "loving description they saw better and more beautiful versions of themselves"; it keeps applauding their author.

Both the cultural myth of Chekhov as a "Chekhovian *intelligent*" and the official canonical image of Chekhov as the writer who unmasked bourgeois society and predicted a socialist future became the subject of reevaluation in the journalism and criticism of the 1980s and 1990s. Chekhov's status as an artistic model, however, is still a part of the Russian ethos, and writers routinely cite Chekhov as an influence in interviews. His status with the intelligentsia is also intact. The continuous reworking of Chekhov's themes and techniques has turned into an intense dialogue with the classic, going far beyond problems of influence and into the sphere of reinterpretation of the whole cultural tradition. The following chapters outline the modification and reevaluation in contemporary texts of three main thematic elements of the Chekhov myth represented by three distinctly Chekhovian images: the Chekhovian *intelligent* figuring in most discussions of the intelligentsia's identity crisis; the cherry orchard as metaphor for loss and nostalgia; and the lady with a dog representing the theme of the power and mystery of love.

CHAPTER 4

The Chekhovian *Intelligent*

The Burden of Being a Hero

So, who gave birth to whom? The intelligentsia to Chekhov or Chekhov to the intelligentsia?

—Viktor Erofeev, *"Lia Sofi a dorme dezha"*

I have no faith in our intelligentsia; it is hypocritical, dishonest, hysterical, ill-bred and lazy [. . .] I have faith in individuals . . .

—Chekhov, letter to I. Orlov, February 1899

IN THE EARLY 1990S cultural critics announced the "leave-taking of the intelligentsia"[1] because its "last effort," its last heroic feat to open the flood of forbidden texts and to mobilize active social forces for democratic elections, wrecked the system with which the intelligentsia was more vitally connected than it realized. In the following decade the "Agonies of the Russian Intelligentsia"[2] have been described as (to sample just the titles) "Double Suicide" in Natalia Ivanova's article and as *Dead Again* in Masha Gessen's 1997 book.[3] Stanislav Rassadin, a popular journalist, asserts in the very title of his essay that "The Intelligentsia As a Conciliar [*sobornyi*] Concept Does Not Exist. It Has Played Out Its Role, Been Crowded Out, Destroyed, Leaving Us with Intellectualness,"[4] while in 2003 Evgenii Ermolin proclaims, "The intelligentsia is immortal!"[5] The uncertainty implicit in these statements indicates a need and a search for a new plot and a new narrative in which the intelligentsia can once again entrench itself and redefine its image.

Defining the intelligentsia has been difficult for sociologists and historians alike, yet while scholars agree that it is almost impossible to define the intelligentsia in terms of class structure or its ideologies, there is a prevailing sense that the intelligentsia *is* an identifiable category and, moreover, that everyone knows what the intelligentsia is and can, intuitively if in no other way, recognize its members. However, in discussing the matter, one enters the realm of subjective attempts to grasp the intelligentsia's self-perception. This subjectivity relies on cultural assumptions and thus engages in the discourse of cultural myths. I suggest that this is precisely the kind of discourse most suitable to address the problem of the intelligentsia. The terms and methods of history and political science prove inadequate in dealing with this fluid group because they ignore its mythic dimension, the way in which it is socially and culturally constructed.

The Russian intelligentsia is the milieu in which major Russian cultural myths originate and develop as distinct sets of concepts. The most impressive and most enduring myth the intelligentsia has produced is of itself, because it is best understood in terms of myth, that is, as a set of ideas about itself. The discussion of the concept, like that of most cultural myths, is perpetuated first of all by the intelligentsia itself. This is essentially a literary and/or journalistic discourse in which the names of the Great Russian Writers figure as characters in the plot of the group's struggle to define itself and its place in society. The narrative aspect of the myth relies heavily on the plot of self-definition through contact, contrast, or overt struggle with other identities. The distinguishing feature of the Soviet intelligentsia's identity was its reliance on culture, rather than on ideology and philosophy, for self-description.[6] In many ways this testifies to the limitations of the Soviet intelligentsia—in particular to its inadequate education in comparison to the educational scope of the pre-Revolutionary intelligentsia. Given a limited access to world literature, especially philosophical texts, the very act of gaining access to and reading those philosophers who formed the worldview of the old intelligentsia became a manifestation of nonconformity, sometimes even of social protest. In other words, what for the nineteenth-century intelligentsia was the means sufficed, for the majority of their twentieth-century heirs, as the end. Russian literature and foreign classics approved for translation and publication by the government formed the cultural education of the rank-and-file Soviet *intelligent*.[7] His main feature was therefore his sense of being the agent and/or the object of cultural production. This and/or quality, the ambiguity over his own agency, led the *intelligent* to put an enormous emphasis on his affiliation with Great Russian Literature. Since literature is among the fundamental components of Russian national identity, the repository of aesthetic and moral riches, the act of attaching itself to it and thus appropriating its status helps the intelligentsia to justify its perceived position of spiritual leadership.[8] As other features of the old intelligentsia—specific social origins, a thorough education, and political nonconformity—were becoming less central, the keeping of the cultural heritage and its moral values gained a hypertrophied importance.

The intensity of the intelligentsia's discourse of self-definition differs at different moments in Russian history. When society undergoes crucial changes, we witness its intensification. During the first decades of the twentieth century, this discourse addressed the intelligentsia's role in the revolutionary process. The famous *Vekhi* (*Landmarks*), a collection of articles published in 1909, subjected the intelligentsia to severe criticism for its isolation, spiritual impotency, and political blindness. The ensuing heated polemics, involving most of the prominent political and cultural figures in Russia, and unfolding during the critical revolutionary period, demonstrated how seriously members of the intelligentsia regarded their role as leaders of the people. The authors of *Vekhi* proclaimed the intelligentsia's failure to fulfill that role, while the revolutionary camp saw in their position a betrayal or at least a misunderstanding of progressive ideals. The debate, continuing well into the post-Revolutionary period, stemmed from the conviction, shared by both sides, that the ideas and actions of the Russian intelligentsia have a direct effect on Russia's political development.

A very similar debate has been taking place in Russia during the 1990s and the first years of the new century. Once again, revolutionary changes in the political and economic spheres have triggered an intense discussion about the intelligentsia's role in bringing about these changes, and about its place in the newly forming society. A close look at the many essays addressing these questions reveals that most authors deal with the concept of the intelligentsia in terms of myth. The image of the intelligentsia that emerges from the pages of the thick journals and *Literaturnaia Gazeta* comprises precisely a mythical set of attributes, subjectively defined in an emotionally charged discourse which either condemns or validates the self-definition of a large and amorphous group of individuals. However, the content of the contemporary discussion demonstrates how much the intelligentsia has changed over the last century. The authors of *Vekhi* seemed to be addressing a very different phenomenon. Nikolai Berdiaev chastised the intelligentsia for its shallow and utilitarian approach to philosophy,[9] while Sergey Bulgakov denied it true religious feeling.[10] These are no longer the most important issues in the contemporary discussion. The main issue today concerns the intelligentsia's reaction to and its role in the cultural crisis in post-Soviet Russia. The intelligentsia feels that during the years of the Soviet regime, it preserved the liberal, humanitarian values of Russian culture, that in fact it preserved the culture itself. Culture, therefore, has provided members of the intelligentsia with both a model and a justification for their way of life and worldview. Their (often benign) political antagonism to the authorities was merely a byproduct of their way of life. If most of the contemporary debate about the problem of the intelligentsia has a slightly hysterical tone, it is because the intelligentsia feels cheated: it strove to bring about the demise of totalitarian rule only to be ignored and discarded after this goal was achieved. It has envisioned itself as the protagonist in the mythical narrative of the struggle against totalitarianism, and now it faces the question whether the myth can survive the end of the struggle and the narrative.

Literary texts reflect the crisis of the myth of the intelligentsia as prolifically as the thick journal articles. A number of works of the 1990s take up the demise of the intelligentsia: there are the semi-*intelligenty* of Lyudmila Petrushevskaya and Igor Iarkevich; Vladimir Makanin's underground heroes; "family chronicles from the life of the intelligentsia" by Andrei Dmitriev, Vasilii Aksenov, and Liudmila Ulitskaia; and Pelevin's poets and critics turned advertisement writers. Their characters range from lonely intellectuals to such traditional intelligentsia figures as doctors and teachers, to the proverbial junior researchers (*mladshii naucnyi sotrudnik*); their common feature is their sense of loss, of spiritual shallowing and demoralization.

Many a discussion of the state of the intelligentsia today turns to Chekhov as the absolute standard against which the modern *intelligent* falls short. Andrei Sinyavsky (Tertz) contrasted Chekhov's moral principles with the intelligentsia's materialism and conformity to the new capitalist order, and he blamed equally the intelligentsia and autocracy for the general cultural degradation and his own lost illusions. He criticized Bulat Okudzhava, a writer, a singer, and the voice of the intelligentsia from the 1960s forward, for his complacent indifference to the Russian cultural catastrophe in exchange for personal gains: the chance to travel and publish. "Chekhov would not have said that!" exclaimed Sinyavsky.[11] Viktor Erofeev's assertion that "Chekhov is the same as us, only a little better"[12] works on the same principle. Stanislav Rassadin relies on the same standard describing how Ivan Bunin behaved improperly due to hunger and assuring the reader that it is impossible to imagine "under any, even worse conditions, the *intelligent* Chekhov acting this way."[13] Rassadin refuses the twentieth-century *intelligent* the right to identify himself with the great concept, making an exception only for Chekhov. Even Chekhov, however, stands at the limit, "balancing, having accumulated in himself the typical signs [of the intelligentsia] but already looking on them with ironic cruelty."[14]

The image of Chekhov as "the first Chekhovian intellectual" is so pervasive that, like every myth, it contains the seeds of its own deconstruction. It does not take much effort to point out that some of the most-quoted definitions of the *intelligent* in Chekhov's stories come from the mouths of questionable characters. Chekhov's own harsh opinions about the intelligentsia, abundant in his letters, are hard to ignore. One must not disregard, however, that while condemning the intelligentsia as a class, Chekhov juxtaposed to it individuals, "be they *intelligenty* or peasants," who move knowledge forward, and in whose minds societal and moral questions "take on a more disturbing character."[15] If Chekhov was skeptical about the intelligentsia's class role as the conscience of the people, he did not deny that role to individuals in whose minds the unsettling questions take precedence over everything else. Not as a class but as particular people Chekhov's most memorable characters are *intelligenty.* This is why the modern-day intelligentsia chooses Chekhov as its "founding father," ignoring the skepticism of his own view as it concentrates on the positive part of the myth.

Chekhov's personality is the most appealing part of the myth: to those who aspire to be "the same as Chekhov," this image offers a very flattering reflection. It is an image of a truly self-made person, someone of humble origins who refused to feel inferior because of it, someone who possessed the clearest sense of personal freedom and calmly but firmly opposed this ideal to the ones generally and unquestionably accepted by all around him. It is a person in possession of a wry sense of humor and serious convictions, a professional always dissatisfied with his work, a loving brother, friend, and husband. He could have been a saint had he not been so much "the same as us." He does not ask too much of his characters—only that they not settle but continue to search for truth and meaning in life. He forgives these characters—the inadequate doctors, teachers, writers, actors—their inability to "orient themselves in this world," and he allows the reader to love them, however weak, ineffectual, and passive they may be. There are no heroes in his world, only personalities burdened with unsettling questions. Chekhov's heuristic poetics put forward, in a positive light, the characters who, even if they do not rebel against the ruling norm, at least continuously question it. This model is ideally suited for the intelligentsia in both Soviet and post-Soviet times: its opposition—to the totalitarian state for the former and to the new capitalist order for the latter—consisted wholly of pressing on with unsettling questions.

The intelligentsia of the 1990s, the times of changing cultural paradigms, is reluctant to give up this flattering self-image. To give up modeling one's life on literary examples is to be left with no satisfactory model. With literature losing its status, the intelligentsia's heroes find themselves stranded in a postliterary word. Yet, before they can start creating a new plot, they must deal with the weaknesses of the old one. Vyacheslav P'etsukh does just that: he builds his narratives on the specifics of the intelligentsia's worldview and self-definition. P'etsukh probes various aspects and consequences of the intelligentsia's relationship with culture, and does it in literary terms, that is, in intertextually constructed texts.

Vyacheslav P'etsukh remains one of the few contemporary writers, the only one perhaps, who, amidst the announced crisis of the Word, seems to be unaware of literature's predicament, and states repeatedly that "we believe in literature as absolutely as our great grandfathers believed in the Last Judgment."[16] Far from accepting or even acknowledging literature's grave condition, P'etsukh proclaims literature's primacy over life, its unique ability to "tell more about life than life itself,"[17] and asserts that "without literature a human being cannot fully become a human being."[18] P'etsukh's narrator's view of literature is essentially romantic: literature reflects not life but a higher ideal of life; talent, a mystical category, allows the writer to refract objective reality (*prelomit' bytie*) and create an ideally meaningful reality from life's raw material—the multitude of nonsensical details of everyday existence. One of the conclusions of his novel, *The New Moscow Philosophy,*[19] is that

> literature is, after all, life, in other words, the ideal of its construction, the model of all measures and volumes. So-called life is a sketch, an approach, a half-finished product, and in the most happy cases—a version. No, honestly, it seems most plausible that literature is the clean copy, while life is a rough draft, and not even the most sensible one.[20]

The novel closes with a directive: "people must live looking back on literature like Christians on the Lord's Prayer."[21] This view is so excessively emphasized, so unfashionably romantic, especially in the present cultural climate, that it is easily recognized as a strategic device. The hyperromanticism of P'etsukh's narrator is the key to his analysis of the intelligentsia's condition, the first step toward deconstructing its dependence on literature in every aspect of life.

P'etsukh is a writer's writer: many of his stories are about Russian authors of different epochs. The loosely defined cycle "Stories about Writers" includes stories devoted to Tolstoy, Kuprin, Chekhov, Babel', and Shukshin. P'etsukh presents a peculiarly old-fashioned image of a writer as someone revered above mere mortals. This romanticized image is perhaps best exemplified by the passage from the story about Vasilii Shukshin, "The Last Genius": "in Russia the very position of the writer coincides with the rank of genius and denotes his belonging to eternity, just as sainthood and belonging to eternity is indicated by a halo painted above a saint's head."[22] P'etsukh is equating literature with religion, writers with saints, and thus pushes the myth of the intelligentsia as cultural agents and/or objects to its limits. He turns the danger of the overvaluation of literature inherent in Russian cultural myths into the subject of his stories.

At a time when postmodernist discourse enables critics to announce the breakdown of traditions and the end of history, P'etsukh's insistently hyperromantic view of literature and the literary calling might seem outdated. It might even appear ridiculous if not for the fact that he has made the glorification of Russian literature into one of his techniques, a device that he consistently lays bare. P'etsukh the author may be very well aware of the fact that literature, especially its school textbook version, has been the target of increasing skepticism in post-Soviet society. P'etsukh's narrator is under no obligation to face this reality: he addresses the reader while creating him. In other words, he provides the reader with the set of assumptions needed to proceed with the story. P'etsukh's reader of choice is the mainstream Russian *intelligent,* someone who shares with him the cultural grammar of the Russian intelligentsia. However, the average *intelligent* of the 1980s and 1990s is overwhelmed by the infusion of Western culture and the rapid development of domestic popular culture. He is dealing with major shifts in the cultural situation, including the preponderance of visual images over verbal ones, of pulp fiction over high literature, and of market demands over artistic value.[23] P'etsukh's narrator performs a kind of exorcism on the confused and dispirited post-perestroika *intelligent:* holding up the scripture of high culture, he calls upon the part of him that still believes in literature as in "the Last Judgment." Whether the reader agrees with the narrator's view of literature or not is irrelevant as long as the reader is put in the position that any reading of the story is impossible unless he accepts the narrator's point of view as his own point of departure. P'etsukh's humor disguises this rather aggressive tactic, and his aggression is also softened by the fact that the view he imposes on the reader is merely an exaggeration of the otherwise common notion of the logocentric nature of Russian cultural identity.

The Russian reader is defined by the belief in the preeminence of the Word. During the last decades of the twentieth century this old belief found peculiar sustenance in postmodernist discourse that, stressing the literary origins of literature, finally took reality out of the definition of literature altogether. For the intelligentsia, who has always defined itself through literature, this is an easily acceptable notion. It may seem a mere reversal of the old metaphor of literature as a mirror reflection of life, but such a reversal of course subverts basic assumptions about literature's role in society. The intertextual fabric is made of reflections, in which reality has no place. This is why intertextuality is indeed a postmodernist phenomenon despite the fact that it is a very old practice. It became the principal technique at a time of complete recognition and acceptance of the fact that every text grows out of previous texts and is not an emanation of reality. P'etsukh's reader, the *intelligent,* is quite accustomed to measuring life by the standards of literature, and even if he is presently deeply disappointed with literature,[24] he cannot help recognizing familiar notes in assertions like this: "since olden times, Russian people have been living under the domination, one could even say under the yoke, of their native literature" (*russkaia lichnost' izdavna nakhoditsia pod vladychestvom, dazhe igom rodnogo slova*).[25] Since most of P'etsukh's stories are set in Soviet times, the time of political totalitarianism, the interchangeability of power agents in such statements emphasizes how closely the yoke of literature resembles other kinds of domination; it can be as powerful and harmful as any other.

Since P'etsukh consistently creates his own reader and provides that reader with the appropriate amount of information about the referent work, he rarely employs literary works that are out of the average reader's reach; rather, he ensures that the "reader's recovery," as Riffaterre puts it,[26] of an intertext is instantly triggered by transparent references to well-known texts. In the 1992 story "Ward No. 7" (*Palata no. 7*), such a reference is the title itself, immediately followed by another direct and somewhat superfluous reference to Chekhov's story "Ward No. 6": "As it becomes clear from Chekhov's story about Doctor Ragin, a madman through misunderstanding, through mistake, people in Russia cannot be sure to avoid not only poverty, prison, and the city of Paris, but also madness through misunderstanding, through mistake."[27] The city of Paris, the ultimate "pleasure place" in Russian cultural tradition, offsets the list of misfortunes and stresses the arbitrariness of either turn of fate. Yet, the fate of the Russian people, P'etsukh has already emphasized, is dominated by their literature. In this case, the fate of P'etsukh's character is sealed by the plot of Chekhov's story.

"Ward No. 6" has been one of Chekhov's best-known stories since its inclusion in the school syllabus. At a minimum, this guarantees common knowledge of its plot. The Soviet school textbook presents a thoroughly political reading of the story: Ward No. 6 with its terrible suffering, humiliation, and despair is a symbol of tsarist Russia. In this reading, when Chekhov's protagonist, Doctor Ragin, finds himself in the ward, he is punished ultimately for not fighting against the regime while he still had a chance. The metaphor of a madhouse is widely used in anti-Soviet literature as well. The Soviet practice of incarcerating dissidents in psychiatric institutions is exposed in a number of texts, including Valerii Tarsis's autobiographical "Ward No. 7" (1963), based on the author's experience in a psychiatric clinic following the *samizdat* publication of his political satire.[28] Both the ideologically approved readings of Chekhov's story and the dissident writings stem from the assumption, shared by both camps, that a member of the intelligentsia must be socially engaged. However, while the fictional Doctor Ragin in Chekhov's story is punished for his failure to take political action, the real-life dissident writer Tarsis is incarcerated for his protest. Tarsis's doctor, a namesake of Chekhov's Ragin, reflects on the fact that while a Soviet hospital is cleaner and more comfortable than the one in Chekhov's story, it is still a prison: "Well, I guess we moved from Chekhov's ward no. 6 to ward no. 7, a more comfortable one."[29] P'etsukh has not read Tarsis's story;[30] otherwise his much later story (still, however, set in Soviet times) would have to move forward with the improvements, and with the numbering—his "ward" then would have to be no. 8. As it is, we get the same number, the same image of a prison masquerading as a hospital, and, most important, the same path into it—through political protest. P'etsukh's story establishes a direct link between Chekhov's and his text to develop his inquiry into both the relationship between reality and fiction and Chekhov's role in creating this reality. While P'etsukh conspicuously ignores the contrast between the actions of his and Chekhov's characters, he makes ample use of a contrast that he himself sets up, between the fictional, albeit prophetic, nature of Chekhov's narrative and the alleged reality of his own story. Several times in the course of his narrative, the narrator stops to exclaim in wonder: "This is what a great artistic talent means: that which in the twilight of the nineteenth century could only transpire in a mighty imagination, has become today sorrowful reality, the sign of our everyday life, like mental idleness or mass theft."[31] The story bluntly announces itself to be a true account of certain events, basing this assertion solely on the dichotomy of imagination and reality it sets up.

Contemporary Western scholarship is more interested in a philosophical reading of "Ward No. 6" than an ideological one: it is read as Chekhov's response to Dostoevsky[32] or as an inquiry into the validity of Tolstoy's teachings; as a critique of the philosophy of the stoics, Marcus Aurelius and Schopenhauer; and as bearing echoes of ecclesiastical motifs. It has been analyzed as an inquiry into the cathartic nature of fear and pity[33] and even as a statement on the "wisdom of pain."[34] P'etsukh, from the beginning of his story, uses both political and philosophical interpretations in order to lead the reader toward yet another theme—social protest as madness.

P'etsukh's announcement of his intertextual intention points the reader to Chekhov but at the same time delimits the scope of the reader's intertextual inquiry to one aspect of Chekhov's story. Both characters, Chekhov's and P'etsukh's, are unsettled by certain events to the point of madness. In both stories, the protagonists are medical doctors outraged by the state of their respective hospitals. Both, in the course of the stories, engage in long philosophical discussions. At the end, both evoke suspicion in their colleagues, who declare them mad, and both end up as patients in their own hospitals' psychiatric wards. There is, however, a crucial difference that P'etsukh conspicuously ignores throughout the story: the way the two doctors react to the terrible state of their hospitals. Chekhov's Doctor Ragin makes no protest and deals with the surrounding misery by resorting to philosophical abstractions. It is only when he becomes a patient in the psychiatric ward that he realizes he was able to contemplate suffering and happiness as relative and subjective states because he did not experience suffering. P'etsukh's character, on the contrary, finds himself in the psychiatric ward *because* he attempts to improve the conditions in his clinic. P'etsukh's narrator insists on the parallels between his and Chekhov's doctor as if unaware of the entirely opposite nature of their actions. He also ignores another remarkable difference: the fact that the dwellers in Ward No. 7 enjoy much better treatment because they are of a privileged sort—former high-ranking government officials. This fact makes Ward No. 7 seem almost a parody of Ward No. 6: its patients are those who formerly held the power to imprison the patients-dissidents of other psychiatric wards. Somehow this glaringly obvious difference between Wards 6 and 7 does not seem to bother the narrator: he goes on presenting his story as an almost literal repetition of the events of Chekhov's story.

The fusion of literature and history, of fiction and reality, begins in the story's first paragraphs with P'etsukh's insistence that his story is a realization of events imagined by Chekhov. The account of the history of the building housing the clinic gives equal prominence to literary and historic facts: the house is connected both to Pushkin and to the events of the Russian Revolution. It used to belong to "the Hannibals, the descendants of Peter's favorite, and ancestors of 'the sun of our literature' [. . .], and in nineteen eighteen, General Nikolay Yudenich[35] stayed there."[36] P'etsukh's narrator seems unable to address his reader without the help of literature, as if his only excuse for telling the story is the fact that it has a literary precedent, and Doctor Krutov's fate is worthy of attention only because it mirrors the fate of Chekhov's doctor. His characters, in turn, rely on literary examples to formulate their views and sometimes see themselves as literary characters. As much as P'etsukh insists on the factuality of his story, he openly constructs it from literary rather than extraliterary material. In short, P'etsukh is consistent in promoting the view that life is merely a poor draft or copy of literature; and his narrator as well as his characters really live "looking back on literature like Christians on the Lord's Prayer." Yet, if his story is a copy of Chekhov's, the portrayal of pain, madness, and social protest is distorted and diminished in size and effect—a poor copy indeed.

The key to P'etsukh's use of Chekhov's intertext lies in this distortion, in the difference between Krutov's actions and worldview and that of his alleged prototype, Chekhov's Doctor Ragin. Krutov combines the main features of two Chekhov characters: on the plot level he submits to the doctor's fate, but his philosophy is close to the madman Gromov's impulsive reaction "to baseness—with indignation, to abomination—with aversion."[37] Doctor Krutov engages in social protest where doctor Ragin attempted to transcend it. The transcendence that in Chekhov results in passive acceptance is relegated in P'etsukh to the clinic's director, Grigory Illich. The director reasons: "why look for trouble if we have no power to change anything," and he insists that happiness is in "the peace within oneself and freedom from fools."[38] His thoughts echo Doctor Ragin's conclusions at the beginning of Chekhov's story that "his will is not enough"[39] to change the state of the clinic, and the highest satisfaction is in free inquiry into the depths of life and "complete contempt toward the silly vanity of the world."[40] Despite the fact that Krutov combines some of the features of two Chekhov characters—madman and doctor—his function is not merely to counter or support the others' ideas. He is an autonomous character who poses an independent inquiry into the problem of madness as a social phenomenon.

Krutov's character emphasizes another trait common to both Doctor Ragin and the madman Gromov, one ignored by critics: these two highly individualized characters are typical representatives of the intelligentsia in their passion for reading and philosophical discussions. The topic of their conversations are invariably on "violence trampling the truth" (*nasilie, popiraiushchee pravdu*),[41] on a beautiful and just future, and on the "coming together of all the forces of the intelligentsia" (*splochennost' intelligentskikh sil*). Gromov delivers his "clumsy potpourri of old but still unfinished songs" in a state of unhealthy agitation; Ragin talks with sad resignation about his yearning for "an intelligent and interesting conversation" that even the town's intelligentsia cannot provide. But it is this yearning for intelligent conversation that brings the two together; Ragin is driven to Gromov's hellish dwelling by the desire to satisfy his passion for philosophizing. Their conversations center on the reaction to suffering and evil; what they ultimately talk about is the extent not only of human responsibility generally, but in particular of the intelligentsia's responsibility to react to social evil. Thus, P'etsukh goes deeper into Chekhov's story than his recap of its plot suggests: his characters, the intelligentsia a hundred years after Chekhov, explicitly link the intelligentsia, social engagement, and madness. What starts as the director's slight annoyance at Krutov's truth-searching, which can only be construed as social protest, leads the two toward a serious inquiry into the nature of heroism. P'etsukh's story is as philosophical as Chekhov's, and in both stories the events test the validity of the characters' philosophy. P'etsukh puts a character whose actions and views are directly opposed to those of Chekhov's passive doctor into a similar situation and lets him end up exactly in the same place—in the psychiatric ward. Action and inaction seem to produce identical results, or rather lack of results, thus challenging the reader to come up with his own answer to the question the author leaves unanswered: is social protest heroism and is it a form of madness?

In a conversation that the narrator characterizes as "the same" as the one between Chekhov's Doctor Ragin and the madman Ivan Gromov, the director reasons that no sane person would go against the basic instinct of self-preservation. He therefore considers Doctor Krutov's proclivity toward truth-seeking, "that sin that is called truth-seeking, a sin fairly common in Russia, but one that nevertheless evokes a vague antipathy,"[42] as a sign of madness. Thus the heroic *intelligent* is defined as insane first because he goes against nature, and second because he goes against the inertia of Russian history. Chekhov's *intelligent* and the genuine madman Gromov had already posed this question: "should I be considered an idiot if I suffer, disturbed, and appalled by human baseness?"[43] P'etsukh's Krutov is, at least clinically, sane, but in the opinion of the director, a sane person knows that his efforts will change nothing: "would a healthy person put himself in danger, would he look for troubles when it is common knowledge that in this country nothing can be changed?!"[44] The director offers a historical perspective, urging Krutov to take history "after Chekhov" into account. He would like to base his argument on historical examples, just as Chekhov's Ragin referred to the historical stoics, yet he refers Krutov to literature: "this mess is ineradicable in our country of the Soviets. However, it was ineradicable in tsarist Russia as well—read literature."[45] The director, like the narrator, has no other system of reference at his disposal except Russian literature. Incidentally, the director's comments link the state of the psychiatric hospital to that of the country in the same way it had been linked by the Soviet critical interpretations of "Ward No. 6."

Although Krutov's actions are contrary to those of Chekhov's character, whose fate he is ostensibly reexperiencing, he does belong to the literary tradition inasmuch as he is obsessed with the same "cursed" questions as the Russian classics, and he represents the fate of the intelligentsia in the twentieth century. P'etsukh's narrator keeps reminding the reader of the story's relationship with the Russian literary tradition: "This is a great artistic talent for you: that which in the past came to life in a mighty imagination, a hundred years later became incarnated in our malignant reality, that is, let's say on the British Islands both Chartists disappeared without a trace and about Whigs one hears nothing interesting, but with us, still the questions are the same, and the answers are the same, as if someone preserved us in alcohol."[46] Yet, P'etsukh's question is not exactly the same as Chekhov's. He shifts the focus when he poses the problem of social engagement not just alongside but *as* the problem of madness. Since the intelligentsia is the main protagonist in the cultural narrative of social engagement, this leads P'etsukh to question, first, how effective it has been in this role and, second, what price it had to pay along the way.

To widen the scope of the problem, P'etsukh brings world history into the discussion of the social and philosophical nature of madness. He includes the names of historical heroes, the proverbial names of Giordano Bruno and the Archpriest Avvakum, the revolutionary group "The People's Will," and dissidents in general. The last conversation between Krutov, already a patient in Ward 7, and his doctor explores this question:

> "Listen, Grigory Illich," asked Krutov somewhat childishly, with trust in his voice, "Aleksandr Matrosov's exploit—is it pathology or heroism?"

The chief, evidently embarrassed, turned his head to look around and lowered his voice: "Between you and me, my dear, of course pathology."

"Well, then I am at peace. Thank God. Because, you know, this thought keeps on bothering me: someone who acts against the law of self-preservation, what is he, a hero or just a madman?"

"This is the whole point, a madman!"

"Well, then I am at peace. Thank God."

"I will elaborate on this now: you see, the normal psyche always bases itself on the law of self-preservation, and all those jordano brunos, archpriests avvakums, 'people's will' members, and other dissidents are to some extent psychos, who are obsessed with themselves. Not with the idea, not with justice, but precisely with themselves! Simply, they cannot reconcile their feverish 'I' with our absurd ways of life, while a normal person can, because he knows: 'there is no happiness in the world, only peace and freedom,' that is peace inside oneself and freedom from fools."

"Wait a moment! What about Jesus Christ?"

"Come on! This is clearly a clinical case, your Christ!"

"Well, then I am at peace. Thank God."

Grigory Illich never visited ward 7 again.[47]

This discussion mentions various types of heroes: a war hero, political rebels, a scientist, and two religious figures. We leave aside for the moment the question of hierarchy, lest we need compare the relative value of Christ's deed to that of Aleksandr Matrosov.[48] All four figures are commonly perceived as having committed a selfless sacrifice in the name of their beliefs. Grigory Illich, however, asserts that they "are obsessed with themselves"; in other words, he challenges the basic assumption of heroism and heroic sacrifice—its selfless nature—and attributes it to narcissism.[49] Krutov, however, had not acted in the interest of self-promotion: he had made his complaints because he did not know how else to improve the state of the hospital, not because he had consciously chosen the path of a dissident. At the end, however, the only way for him not to be the abuser is to become one of the abused. Still, there is an ambiguity to his fate that relates to the ambiguity of the intelligentsia's role in the narrative of resistance against totalitarian rule, as well as this narrative's paradoxical reliance on Chekhov who emphatically refused this role. Krutov ends up not in the crowded corridors of the main block, but in the ward for privileged patients, so not only is his sacrifice pointless, but his heroic feat is undermined. Accordingly, the end of his story is not nearly so tragic as Doctor Ragin's death: only part of Krutov dies, albeit the constitutive part of his personality, that which made a hero out of a decent but weak man. Even more ambiguous is the implication of his mentioning Christ: is it a comment on the intelligentsia's illusions of grandeur, its self-perception as the nation's saviors? Chekhov's madman mentions Christ too: as an argument that no one is or should try to be immune to human suffering. His interlocutor does not reply, and Gromov suddenly laughs, it seems at his own words, at his attempt to bring the ultimate authority to his side of the argument. P'etsukh's characters are serious in both bringing up and then dismissing the authority of Christ. The story's ideas come to their conclusion at this point: if literature is a religion and social engagement is the intelligentsia's holy calling, then it has also become its curse. P'etsukh's character might not realize how predetermined his actions are, but he is thrown into the plot of the intelligentsia's narrative of self-definition and thus forced into the role of a hero.

The constitutive part of Krutov's personality is his love for literature: reading used to be his definition of happiness. Not surprisingly, literature plays the defining role in forming Krutov's conceptions of social engagement; his "madness" is entirely literary, with Chekhov's story its prototype. Tarsis's "Ward No. 7" is a genuine Soviet-era narrative about an *intelligent*-dissident who produces a document about the injustice of the system, thus setting his readers on the path of engagement through moral indignation. The link between Tarsis's and Chekhov's stories is straightforward reversal: Chekhov's protagonist, at least in Soviet readings, is punished for attempting to transcend social problems; Tarsis's hero is rewarded at the end by having survived the incarceration and being able to tell his story and thus continue his engagement in social protest. If P'etsukh's story, ending with Krutov's incarceration, had not made Ward No. 7 a privileged ward, it would have produced the same effect. However, the ending leaves the reader slightly bewildered. "Unlike Chekhov's Ragin," Krutov does not die, but he becomes a different and less appealing person: he does not read anymore, and his eyes have a blank expression of "concentrated dullness that one sees at rush hour in the eyes of mass transit passengers."[50] Krutov's heroic engagement is undermined: it comes as a result of the inescapable juncture of reality and literature in Russian culture. Krutov has taken on the traditional role of the *intelligent* and stepped into the plot that forced him along the path of social protest. No matter how "real" the narrator insists his story is, it follows the plot prescribed by literature or rather by the overvaluation of literature in the life of the Russian intelligentsia. The futility of P'etsukh's narrator's attempt to distinguish the reality of his story from the imagination of Chekhov's and thus break free from the domination of literature over life shows how this hold remains strong and destructive still.

P'etsukh employs the plotline and setting of one of the best-known of Chekhov's stories to activate the reader's memory of this plot and of the traditional political reading of the story. Certainly, employing a famous intertext allows the writer to set the parameters of his story in a very economical manner. Thus, P'etsukh's very short story benefits from the parallel with Chekhov's story by presupposing its setting and plot without the necessity of justifying either of them. In other words, the events of the story cannot go any other way but to make a patient out of the doctor. However, the plot is merely a part of the import that an intertext brings to the new text. An intertextually constructed text balances on the border between two texts; its meaning is found in the semantic field created by the interaction of the old text and the new. Such a field is a stasis between the differences and the similarities of the old and the new, and it always points to whatever it attempts to contrast or parallel. P'etsukh's story replaces Tarsis's text in the semantic field around Chekhov's story and highlights the philosophical and political impact of Chekhov's story over the last century. He pits the reader's knowledge of the story's political message as set by the school textbook—one has to protest social evil—against the historical experience of the same reader—the tragic consequences of protest—to pose the question: what makes one go against personal interest and sacrifice one's life for the benefit of others and/or for one's beliefs? His conclusion is that a great part of one's ideas of social responsibility depends on literary and cultural prototypes. The point P'etsukh continuously tries to get across is a familiar one: that Russian literature is a social and political, and only secondarily an artistic, phenomenon. The kinds of questions addressed by the characters of "Ward No. 7" are typical of the intelligentsia's thinking. It has perceived itself as the mind, the conscience, and the cultural laboratory of the Russian people, its function to find solutions to and answer the cursed questions of Russian life. Addressing these questions, or rather the fact that, as P'etsukh phrases it, "with us, the questions are the same, and the answers are the same, as if someone preserved us in alcohol," is best done through the texts of the only classic writer who made a conscious effort not to answer the questions that he posed. Not only did the intelligentsia fail to find the answers for the benefit of the masses; it suffered from its own rigid view of its role as a truth-seeking hero.

Whereas the story "Ward No. 7" develops the theme of the intelligentsia as the conscience of the people, the protagonist in the grand narrative of social engagement, an earlier cycle of three stories, "Chekhov Is with Us" (*Chekhov s nami*), written in 1988–89, approaches the same theme from a slightly different angle and concentrates on the intelligentsia's reliance on literature-for-life models. In other words, while "Ward No. 7" is about the intelligentsia and society, this cycle is about the intelligentsia and the Word. For the intelligentsia, the present-day reevaluation of Russian cultural heritage amounts to an inquiry into its own self-perception. Chekhov has been central to this inquiry not only because he provides the intelligentsia with its modern image, but also because he bridges realism and modernism, the end of the nineteenth century and the end of the twentieth, and poses questions about the relationship between literature and life that are most relevant to the contemporary moment of cultural crisis. In the cycle, P'etsukh addresses the consequences of the intelligentsia's dependence on literature to define both reality and itself. Since in his inquiry he too operates with the material of literature, his contradictory "critique" of the intelligentsia's dependence on it turns into a doubly ironic metaliterary endeavor.

The cycle's title is a mocking distortion of the Soviet cliché "Lenin is with us" (*Lenin s nami*). On the one hand, it activates a host of associations with Soviet *Leniniana:* like Lenin, Chekhov is forever present in our lives; his work lives on; and so on. On the other hand, it emphasizes the tension between canon and myth in our vision of Chekhov (and other Russian classics). By invoking the image of the intelligentsia which is created and already undermined in many ways in Chekhov's works, P'etsukh examines the tension between Chekhov's vision of the future—his wistful invocations of what life would be in a hundred years—and the politicized Soviet school textbook version of it.

Calling attention to the myth highlights the constructed nature of Chekhov's image in twentieth-century cultural memory. After all, the intelligentsia's myth of Chekhov as the first "intellectual of the Chekhovian type"[51] does not coincide with the Soviet school textbook vision of a fighter against bourgeois values and the herald of a new revolutionary generation. Both the myth and the canon function independently of reality. P'etsukh utilizes both: in his hyperromantic narrator's view, Chekhov is very much with us, because, as the three stories of the cycle show, his themes, characters, and artistic methods are continuously relevant. On the other hand, his reader is consistently reminded that in the past hundred years, life should have changed enough for them to cease to be relevant: the political and sociocultural situation is, after all, different. Putting together the names of the highest political and literary authorities, Lenin and Chekhov, emphasizes once again the crucial role literature plays in Russian history and makes the reader wonder whether Chekhov has dominated and shaped the turbulent history of twentieth-century Russia as much as Lenin did.

Two stories of the cycle, "Our Man in a Case" (*Nash chelovek v futliare*) and "Uncle Senia" (*Diadia Senia*), refer by their titles to two of Chekhov's best-known texts: "The Man in a Case" (*Chelovek v futliare*) and *Uncle Vanya* (*Diadia Vania*). The third title, "R.D.C." (*D.B.S.*), is an abbreviation for "Really Defenseless Creature" (*Deistvitel'no bezzashchitnoe sushchestvo*), a modification of the title of Chekhov's story "A Defenseless Creature" (*Bezzashchitnoe sushchestvo*). The stories' protagonists range from a quintessential *intelligent,* a literature teacher, to an impoverished actor who barely fits the intelligentsia's standard, to an old woman who cannot be called an *intelligent* at all. The parallels to specific Chekhov texts also diminish within the cycle: if the first story is based on a clearly posed contrast with "The Man in a Case," the third does not allude to any specific text but rather focuses on Chekhov's literary techniques. Throughout the cycle, the intelligentsia hero becomes disembodied, while literature itself moves to the foreground and its "domination" over Russian life becomes P'etsukh's main subject.

"Our Man in a Case," set in the Soviet period, begins with a direct contrast of the two "encased" men, Chekhov's Belikov and P'etsukh's Serpeev:

> The teacher of Greek Belikov actually did not know what he was afraid of and died from an insult; the teacher of Russian language and literature Serpeev knew perfectly well what he was afraid of and died because he did not survive the fear.[52]

Thus, an opposition is created between the nineteenth-century teacher of a dead language and his twentieth-century colleague, a teacher of Russian literature. In "The Man in a Case" Belikov is a social anomaly; P'etsukh's Serpeev is a product of his time and social order, and hence he is indeed "ours," included among us rather than an absurd or dangerous Other like Chekhov's hero. Belikov is terrified of breaking (mostly imagined) rules; he dies when an outsider, oblivious to his fear or, for that matter, to any rules or regulations, sends him flying down the stairs, to the ridicule of the assembled spectators. Imagining the mockery, caricaturing, and perhaps even the forced retirement that would follow, Belikov goes home, gets into bed, and dies. Serpeev's fears are not only real but also symptomatic of every Soviet man's fears: he is afraid that there will be no food in the stores, that women will force him into marriage with the help of the Komsomol organization, of bad news on the phone, of being summoned to a court or a venereal clinic, and of anonymous informers among his colleagues. Belikov's "case" is more or less symbolic: Chekhov's narrator makes it clear that it is his attitude toward life that makes him a man in a case, rather than his galoshes and umbrella. Serpeev's "casing" is physical and spatial:

> At the end, Serpeev became saturated with dread of life to such an extent that he undertook a number of constructive measures in order to shut himself up in a case completely, so to speak. He put a cast-iron bar on his door, and covered the walls between his and neighbors' apartments with old blankets that he had been gathering for a long time from relatives and acquaintances. He got rid of the radio and TV, fearing that his shell would be penetrated by some apocalyptic information, put cotton cloths on the windows to let just enough light in, and at work wore glasses with a weak prescription so that he could not discern anything frightful in others' faces.[53]

At this point, however, the story takes a turn toward emphasizing significant differences between the two teachers' personalities. In Russian literature of the twentieth century, the teacher usually represents the intelligentsia and stands in for the whole image of the class as the "nation's conscience" and progressive force. However, Chekhov's nineteenth-century teachers were for the most part emphatically irreconcilable with this idealized image. Whereas for Belikov the Greek language is another form of a case where he hides from real life, for Serpeev "the radiant books (*svetlye knigi*) written in the past century" provide more than an escape. It soon becomes clear that Serpeev's love for literature is all-consuming and that he cannot imagine his life without it. In the classroom and in his quilted room, there is not a glimpse of Serpeev's personal life, past or present. As becomes clear when Serpeev joins the battle against the system, literature is his life and he will fight for his right to teach it. After the description of his all-consuming fear, his actions seem somewhat unexpected. The reader cannot help wondering whether Serpeev's heroism is that of desperation or, in other words, whether he fights not for his job but for his whole existence. This exaggerated dependence on literature highlights his function in the story: Serpeev is the embodiment of the quintessential Russian *intelligent.* As a member of the intelligentsia, he finds in literature the models on which to base his behavior, and as a teacher he provides models; he thus has no choice but to fight for progress, culture, and, of course, literature.

The plot hinges entirely on literature and its role in Serpeev's life. First, he does not change an unauthorized topic for discussion in class when an inspector comes in unannounced: "Serpeev was not the kind of person who could immediately change his course of action. Besides, he did not want to change it in front of the whole class. . . ."[54] Again, such bravery and constancy of convictions, on which the reader is given no information, could be explained only if Serpeev's actions are seen as typical of the idealized image of the *intelligent,* someone possessing "intellectual decency." He conducts a lesson on obscure nineteenth-century poets, displaying admirable knowledge but terrifying the inspector with his choice of subject. Soon he is ordered to resign from his position. The "ethical side of his retreat"—note the sudden appearance of the military term 'retreat'—is ensured when he begins to teach at home: "and he continued to teach them—if one can put it this way—the soul, basing his instruction mostly on the radiant literature of the nineteenth century."[55] Obviously, this cannot last: the children are ordered to report on him as an ideologically alien element, and Serpeev's worst fears come true: he spends three days waiting for arrest and dies from a heart attack. The sudden death seems to relate Serpeev to Belikov once again, but the relation is superficial. The reader still bears in mind the reminder placed by the author at the very beginning of the story: "Belikov died from an insult." It is also clear that Serpeev's fears are not phantoms of his imagination, and people have been arrested for lesser transgressions. His death from a heart attack is not that of Chekhov's famous "civil servant," who imagined the danger and "lay down on the divan and died," but a result of fear brought on by real danger. The danger, reality itself, enters Serpeev's "case" and his home through and because of his hypervaluation of literature. The theme of histrionic living and its dangers is common in Chekhov's texts, especially in his drama, and has been analyzed in depth.[56] Living one's life as if it were a literary plot and refusing to accept reality if it does not stand up to standards imposed by such a perception causes heartache to many Chekhovian characters; yet in this story P'etsukh complicates the case by externalizing the danger: Serpeev does indeed impoverish his life by subordinating it to literature, yet his punishment is external and real and comes from the outside nonliterary world.

Apparently, the similarities between the two teachers are misleading and are used only to emphasize the differences. The story's conclusion is ambiguous:

> [A] hundred years ago people escorted the teacher Belikov to his final rest with great pleasure because they took him for a harmful anomaly, while at the end of our century everyone pitied the teacher Serpeev. No, whatever you say, life does not stand still.[57]

A teacher of dead languages, Belikov, who lived in a case of rules and fears and somehow managed to impose his fear on the whole town of Chekhov's story, does not elicit pity. Yet, Serpeev, one of us, a teacher and a high priest of Russian literature, does because the close relationship of reality and literature, in his case an equation, is real for the reader as well. The last darkly ironic statement, "life does not stand still," leaves the reader with the question: "where is it going?" or, "where has it taken us?" If the author indeed intends to show historical progress, is it not fair to say that Serpeev's fate is no better than Belikov's and that the story in effect challenges Chekhov's characters' hopes for happiness in the future, "in a hundred years," the famous phrase that recurs in a number of his stories? The contemporary reader, living almost exactly a hundred years after Chekhov, is tempted to view those hopes as real and to feel entitled to bitter disappointment.

If P'etsukh poses Serpeev's death as the no-longer-postponed future of the Russian *intelligent,* then the parallels between two teachers risk breaking down entirely. Serpeev is miles apart from Chekhov's Greek teacher; there are definite ties, however, between him and the best-known literature teacher in Chekhov. In fact, what shifts the story's focus from the traditionally political interpretation of Chekhov's Belikov as a symbol of the deplorable way of life in tsarist Russia, to the problem of the intelligentsia posed by P'etsukh, is the intertextual presence of Chekhov's story "The Teacher of Literature." Its protagonist, Nikitin, is significantly more relevant to P'etsukh's argument despite the professed connection between Serpeev and Belikov. The main theme of P'etsukh's story is the fate of an intellectual in the twentieth century, and "The Teacher of Literature" functions as an interpretant, which, according to Riffaterre's principle of the third text, is a necessary additional link between the text and its intertext. The two teachers of literature present an inverted pair: Nikitin's personal crisis is intensified by his realization that he is not a good teacher, does not know or even like children, and has no understanding of his subject; Serpeev, on the other hand is an articulate, passionate, and beloved teacher. Nikitin's story ends with the hero at a turning point, choosing between roads, while Serpeev's seems to play out the conceivable end of one of them. Nikitin's awakening starts him on the path to "a new life of unrest and clear sight which is incompatible with peace of mind and personal happiness."[58] Serpeev's life, devoid of peace and happiness except for the moments when he is alone with the "radiant" literature of the nineteenth century, is a possible denouement of the path on which Nikitin is starting. Serpeev differs from the false intellectual Belikov in the extent to which he allows his fears to control his life; he differs from the awakening intellectual Nikitin because he has the purpose in life for which Nikitin longs. Serpeev's passion is Nikitin's hated job—teaching literature. What brings all three together and lays out the semantic field for reenacting archetypal literary conflicts and modes of behavior is that Serpeev's passion arms him with the strength to overcome his fear and forces him into civic heroism in opposing the authorities.

In line with his view of the paramount role of literature in the life of the Russian individual, P'etsukh makes it into a calling and a cause for his Serpeev but offers no illusions to the reader as to the outcome of the age-old struggle of a lonely intellectual against the crowd or the state. Perhaps Chekhov's vision of the future is one of the reasons why his works are alluded to time and again by present-day writers. His consistent referring to a hundred, two hundred, a thousand years after, a detail that Soviet criticism unfailingly interpreted as testifying to his belief in the bright future, is most probably a manifestation of another Chekhovian feature—his unwillingness to provide solutions to the problems he depicted. Postponing the solution to the distant future is only slightly different from admitting its impossibility. However, this slight difference is enough to draw a sharp distinction between Chekhov's modernist worldview and the contemporary postmodernist one. Chekhov does not know the answers, but his art is imbued with the hope that the solutions, while unknown to him, are possible; the contemporary Russian writer, still without answers, no longer looks for them. Unlike Chekhov, P'etsukh does not leave his character on the threshold of a new life, and he is not willing to postpone either gloom or happiness for "a hundred years." Standing at the end of the next century, P'etsukh closes the circle of return with the death of his character. Still, the intertextual nature of his text, his choice of an openly dialogical stand, testifies to an underlying belief in and reliance on the validity of the cultural archetypes that he evokes. Intertextuality demonstrates and reinforces culture's vitality and activates the reader's cultural memory so that in the very process of reading and writing, the culture continues and emerges. The story "works" because it generates the reader's "compulsory response" (in Riffaterre's terminology), making him recognize the traditional conflict; sympathize and side with the lonely teacher in his struggle to keep pure his only source of happiness, culture; and thus accept the premise that this cause is one worth fighting for. It also "works" because it operates intertextually with the material of culture: the life of a teacher fighting for Russian literature of the nineteenth century is presented in the framework of a nineteenth-century writer's texts. P'etsukh's intellectual hero cannot exist without Russian literature, while P'etsukh's reader may not be able to follow the author's argument if it is not played out within the semiotic system of Russian literature. The content of the story, the enduring worth and relevance of nineteenth-century literature, and its form—intertextual reliance on that literature—become one and enact P'etsukh's premise.

"Our Man in a Case" presents the tragic aspect of the *intelligent*'s dependence on literature. It even manifests the classic tragic apparatus: there is pity for the protagonist and there is fear. But here something shifts and goes wrong: the fear is the protagonist's, not the reader's. Thus the story offers no catharsis; "our" man in a case remains outside our reality, too engrossed in literature, too enslaved by it to function.

The second story of the cycle, "Uncle Senia," also shows the effect of this enslavement: it presents a character who, while not quite an *intelligent,* still completely depends on literature for self-expression. "Uncle Senia" is the most straightforwardly dialogical of the three stories: its referent text is a play, and the character, uncle Senia, who plays Voinitsky in Chekhov's *Uncle Vanya* in a provincial theater, at one point addresses Chekhov's characters directly with a speech of his own. Uncle Senia is peculiarly related both to literature and to the intelligentsia: he stands on the border between the two because he articulates literary texts but does not willingly internalize them. Yet, he has no defense against these texts and reluctantly enacts their archetypes.

Uncle Senia's story begins with an unpleasant incident: he loses consciousness on the street and finds himself in a prison cell. Apparently he has been taken for a drunk. Uncle Senia is offended at the thought and on his way to the theater goes to the town hall to protest. There he is insulted again. The elderly actor is quite distraught when he finally gets to the theater. He goes through the motions of preparing for the play: "he mechanically put on makeup, mechanically put on his character's costume."[59] His actions remain automatic even when he comes onstage: "he pronounced his lines again mechanically, because he knew them by heart."[60] Up to this point, the story does not employ Chekhov's text as intertext, for there is no similarity with Chekhov's characters in uncle Senia. Rather, his misfortunes are those of a little person trying in vain to regain some of his dignity. The actor's dealings with officials make him more like a Gogolian little clerk: his coat was stolen while he was unconscious, and the Important Person, the tired-looking woman in a uniform to whom he presents his complaint after waiting in line for two hours, dismisses him abruptly, although without the outburst that befell Akaky Akakievich in "The Overcoat."

Uncle Senia is indeed a little person in the system's eyes: poor, old, living "in other people's corners."[61] Even so, he is an actor and gets to live another's life onstage. Unfortunately, his mechanical performance does not allow that to happen until he "for some reason as if wakes up" (*no otchego-to kak by ochnulsia*) during a performance of *Uncle Vanya* while saying the following lines: "In a minute or two the rain will be over, and everything in nature will be refreshed and sigh with relief. Only I shall not be refreshed by the storm. Day and night I feel suffocated by the thought that my life has been irretrievably lost. I have no past—it has all been stupidly wasted on trifles—while the present is awful because it's so meaningless. . . ."[62] Up to this point, our hero had resorted to silence, paradoxically, to express himself better: he "fell significantly silent" (*znachitel'no zamolchal*) in a conversation with a policeman, and silently, although "not without some artistry" (*ne bez artistizma*), refuses a colleague's request for money. Clearly, the fact that these particular lines correspond so closely to what he might have said about his life if he had had a gift for expressing himself explains why he "comes to" at this point in the play. This may be one of the story's implications: literature may not help explain life, but it can provide one with the uniquely right words to express one's feelings, to transform the rough mess of one's thought into the clean copy of literary expression. It has certainly been the case in Russia. Like Serpeev, who embodies the intelligentsia's view of literature as a model for life, uncle Senia is a metaphor for the intelligentsia's dependence on literature to define its identity. He literally has no voice outside of the lines he has memorized for his roles—in this particular case, Chekhov's lines. His life is devoid of stability and comfort; he has neither family nor home; he does not function outside the theater. Every night he takes on a role prescribed by a classic, Russian or foreign, and recites the lines of his character. Significantly, the reader is presented with this particular night and author: Chekhov provides uncle Senia with the words to express his despair.

The story, however, does not end here, and before the evening is over, uncle Senia must suffer through a ritual invented by the play's director, "a raving avant-garde artist from Vologda" (*neistovyi vologodskii avangardist*) who changes Chekhov's plot. Uncle Senia "wakes up" for the second time to hear Astrov's monologue: "The people who will come in a hundred years or a couple of hundred years after us and despise us for having lived our lives in so stupid and tasteless a fashion—perhaps they'll find a way to be happy. . . . As for us. . . ."[63] After that he goes to the back of the stage, and there, following the director's modifications, Voinitsky commits suicide. Uncle Senia dutifully "performs" his death and falls down on the stage. It would seem that the verdict has been pronounced on Russian literature: verbalizing one's problems merely intensifies them and in effect kills the little person whose interests it supposedly keeps so close to heart. At the end, as in the beginning, of the story, the little person is "down," but this time he does not lie unconscious. On the contrary, he seems to have found his own voice. Lying on the dirty floor, the actor mentally delivers a long speech:

> Whiners, scum, life was not good enough for them! Most likely you wore excellent coats, gorged on caviar with Vorontsoff vodka, kept company with fairies, and talked philosophy from morning to night for lack of anything else to do . . . and still, you see, life was not good enough for them! You should try the claws of the planned economy, you sons of bitches, you should be offered to the attention of the town hall—they would show you the cherry orchard! Oh, what a life you had let go to pieces, you bastards, a fairytale of a life.[64]

Could there be a more striking misreading of Chekhov's work? Even the "raving avant-garde artist" director does not so distort the classic. Uncle Senia indeed "despises" the intelligentsia of the previous century, but not for the reasons predicted by Astrov. He blames them for not holding on to the fairy tale and the cherry orchard and thus precipitating his own grim reality. Ironically, he perceives his fate as much worse than theirs, while he has just identified himself with the suffering of the Chekhov character.

This sudden attack on classical literature and on the intelligentsia is symptomatic of several features of contemporary thought. One is the fashionable revival of Vasily Rozanov's ideas, assigning blame for the Russian Revolution to the classics. In *The Apocalypses of Our Time* written in the year following the October Revolution (but not published or widely read in Russia until the 1980s), he devotes almost as much attention to literature as to religion and repeatedly comes to the conclusion that "there is no doubt that it was literature that killed Russia. Those elements that effectively 'devastated' Russia all had literary origins."[65] Another trend is the no less fashionable postmodernist attack by a number of contemporary authors on the concept of Great Russian Literature as it was exploited by the official ideology.[66] While writers such as Vladimir Sorokin, Igor' Iarkevich, and Viktor Erofeev employ parody and farce in their deconstructive endeavors, the speech of P'etsukh's actor may be read as a parody, in turn, of these writers' efforts. In both cases the official ideology is undermined, but P'etsukh goes a step further and uses the ideology to add a second level to the deconstruction: uncle Senia simplemindedly parrots the Soviet official critique of the decadent bourgeois pre-Revolutionary lifestyle—"caviar with Vorontsoff vodka"—while at the same time envying and valuing it. In his own language, derived in part from the official ideology, he reacts against the myth of the progressive intelligentsia (shared by the ideology and cultural mythology) and poses himself a victim of the nineteenth-century progressive movement that resulted in the Revolution. He is also the victim of the contemporary *intelligent,* the play's director, who murders his (Chekhov's) character. Russian writers of a similarly deconstructive trend refute the concept of the progressive literature that, according to this same myth, led the nation to the radiant future. Yet, the openly hostile nature of their texts cannot be written off as a feature of parody. Unlike parody, these texts are independent literary works for which the classics are not targets but tools. In the attempt to involve the reader in making sense of their historical and cultural situation, they employ the cultural language that they share with the reader. All parties can verbalize the dissatisfaction with their times only by recycling classic literary imagery. All are locked in a dialogue (or a quarrel) with the classics.

The first two stories, "Our Man in a Case" and "Uncle Senia," use their referent texts in order to comment on and argue with their premises. Moreover, both stories operate with some of Chekhov's storytelling techniques: compressed discourse and the seemingly random but in fact carefully chosen detail. The third story of the cycle, "R.D.C." ("*D.B.S.*"), operates with the kind of intertextuality that is least susceptible to interpretation because it is based on generic and technical borrowings and does not overtly thematize the issues of literature and the intelligentsia's relationship to it. The title's abbreviation for "Really Defenseless Creature" revises Chekhov's title, "A Defenseless Creature." Whereas Chekhov's title is ironic because his defenseless creature turns out to be an aggressive woman who comes to the protagonist with an absurd request and manages to bully him into fulfilling it, P'etsukh's character is a "really defenseless creature": she cannot get anything from anyone. If it were not for the title and the fact that the story is a part of the cycle, one would be hard-pressed to find any reference to Chekhov's texts in the story. It is, nevertheless, an integral part of the cycle because in it P'etsukh utilizes most the literary devices that came to be known as quintessentially Chekhovian; and, moreover, continuing the analysis of the intelligentsia's entanglement with literature, he gives the reader a look at the thin line between reality and literature from the other side, so to speak, from the side of the character who does not belong to the intelligentsia.

The story's main character, "old Sophia" (*babka Sof'ia*), has a peculiar aversion for acronyms and abbreviations, one mixed with fear, because abbreviations were the "last straw" that broke the tender mind of the then-young Sophia during the years following the Revolution.

This is why the title itself is an abbrreviation. Sophia, who despite her name is considered by everyone a complete and hopeless idiot, does not seem to be able to comprehend Soviet reality, and this fact not surprisingly makes her life very difficult. Sophia's problem with Soviet reality is of a semiotic order: the condensed encoded signifiers of that reality have the power to terrify her but hold no meaning. Her tragicomic story hinges on her inability to either comprehend the signs or manage without them. One day old Sophia needs to go from Ochakov, a town on the Black Sea, to Berdiansk, a town on the Azov Sea. Oblivious to the fact that the two seas are quite far from one another, she comes to the seaport and asks for a ticket to Berdiansk. The ensuing conversations with the cashier, with an onlooker, and finally with a policeman who is called to the scene by the outraged cashier is a short condensation (about a page and a half) of complete but nevertheless fully believable absurdities. Old Sophia is repeatedly told that "there are no tickets to Berdiansk," and "tickets to Berdiansk do not exist in nature" (*ikh dazhe i ne byvaet*), while no one bothers to explain to her that the towns are on the shores of different seas. An onlooker drops the unfamiliar word *aquatoria*, "area of water," but old Sophia takes it for an abbreviation and dismisses the explanation as something beyond her comprehension and therefore useless—a *sovietism.* Finally the policeman escorts her away from the port, but looking at the small figure exuding misery, he takes pity on her and writes on a piece of paper the three words "Ticket to Berdiansk." Happy old Sophia, having finally gotten a sign she can understand, rushes to the pier and tries to board a small boat. She is stopped there by a sailor who good-humoredly tells her that on the policeman's orders he would take her even to the moon, but not to Berdiansk. The sign, as clear as its code seems to be by linguistic standards, turns out to have no relationship to reality. Old Sophia sits down in weary disbelief, and she cries not so much from hurt but from bewilderment. Then comes P'etsukh's punch line: "God who all this time had been observing the old woman's misadventures from the distance of ten light years looked away in helpless compassion. He could not do anything for old Sophia. For a long time now he had been unable to do anything with this country and its people."[67] Such is the short story that does not have a plot in any conventional sense and manages to tell old Sophia's life story in a matter of two paragraphs. At the end, it leaves the character almost exactly where it found her or even worse off—without a ticket, but also without any hope for one.

P'etsukh does not attempt to create a contemporary version of particular Chekhov plots; rather, he makes use of some of Chekhov's principal ideas and techniques. He intertwines the tragic and the comic, as is often the case in Chekhov's stories; he withdraws authorial judgment and, most significantly, undermines the traditional notion of the event as something worth telling in a story. P'etsukh employs the quintessential Chekhovian technique of questioning readers' assumptions, including assumptions about the significance of events.[68] If an event is something unexpected, something that changes the order of things, then there are very few events in Chekhov. However, there are very few events in contemporary prose as well (except in pulp literature). The postmodernist event has been described as a non-event, when "the only change of state would in fact consist of our being aware that nothing at all has happened."[69] An account of how a slightly crazy woman tries to buy a ticket from one small town to another can hardly be considered an event in the sense of a transgression of boundaries.[70] P'etsukh, however, concentrates on another kind of boundary, one between text and reality, two parallel universes that in this story, unlike the other two, do not intersect. Since the boundary between the two systems is not crossed, no event is possible. All three stories of the cycle hinge on this line between reality and literature: whether it is obliterated or overemphasized, the characters' fate depends on their position in relation to it. Serpeev lets his passion for literature turn into a mission which in turn makes him a tragic hero who dies for his cause; uncle Senia by the nature of his profession articulates his emotions through words of literary characters even while being a parody of these characters; and old Sophia suffers because she cannot even comprehend the power of the word over her reality. In all three cases, the reality itself is formed by Chekhov's word. The story "Ward No. 7" and the cycle "Chekhov Is with Us" demonstrate the dependence of the contemporary short story on Chekhov's techniques and of contemporary prose in general on the ways Chekhov's images and themes were appropriated in Russian cultural memory. P'etsukh concentrates on the dangers of dependence on literature that informed and formed the Russian intelligentsia. Not surprisingly, Chekhov becomes the central figure in his inquiry: central to the intelligentsia's self-perception, the Chekhov myth determines the validity of his texts in cultural memory.

The missing event of "R.D.C." stems from a semiotic disorder: one sentence, "Berdiansk stands on another sea," would resolve the problem and there would not be a story. However, no one says it. P'etsukh evokes one of Chekhov's recurring motifs, that of the lack of human communication. Moreover, he intensifies his point by following Chekhov's technique of withholding a climaxlike ending that would provide the reader with a moral. Instead, the reader is expected to guess the missing event. This narrative practice reflects a change in the way literature positions itself in relation to the reader brought up on the cultural paradigm of ideologically and morally charged literature. A traditional event creates the possibility for a character to undergo a mental change; in other words, it implies a lesson of some kind, and contemporary literature avoids lessons. As the contemporary text gives up the mimetic impulse and becomes a phenomenon of language, when working intertextually with cultural memory, its need for a plot in the traditional sense diminishes. Charles Newman observes that "the form of such fiction is what used to be called content."[71] Contemporary authors have to deal with uncensored life in all of its absurdity and harshness. One of the most difficult tasks, one that they understandably avoid after the experience of totalitarian ideology, is to give answers to the questions posed by this reality. Thus, for P'etsukh, as for many others, a non-event serves nonideological discourse most fittingly. Chekhov's heuristic techniques were the source and the model for nonideological authors of a humanistic bent long before the emergence of postmodernist discourse[72] and merely gained in relevance in the postmodern period. As Irving Howe asked American writers, "how can one represent malaise, which by its nature is vague and without shape? It can be done, we know. But to do it one needs to be Chekhov, and that is hard."[73]

P'etsukh's narrator's hyperromantic view of literature's ability to transform life goes against the postmodern much more skeptical view of literature as disconnected from reality altogether, yet both stem from the same source, that is, the deep concern with "the domination, one could even say [. . .] the yoke" of literature over Russian culture and history. This concern can be voiced and worked out only in the material of this very literature. Russian writers working in the postmodern period attempt, like the modernist neoromantics before them, to distance themselves from the dominant culture and its metanarratives. Yet, they have no other material for creating new texts than what is stored in their and their readers' cultural memory. Intertextuality, a mechanism for transforming memory into text, is especially productive in creating texts that do not aspire to have a source in reality and are quite content with their openly and insistently literary origins. Utilizing and thereby reaffirming the authority of the Russian classical tradition in cultural memory, such a text in effect works for the continuation of culture and puts intertextuality to work in its main function—as a positive defense of cultural memory.

CHAPTER 5

The Cherry Orchard

Paradise Abandoned

All Russia is our orchard.

—Chekhov, *The Cherry Orchard,* Act 3

His [Ivanov's] past, like that of most Russian intellectuals, is wonderful. [. . .] The present is always worse than the past.

—Chekhov, letter to Suvorin, December 1888 (Karlinsky 76)

CHEKHOV'S PRESENCE in cultural memory is a compound of several easily recognizable, distinctly Chekhovian images. It includes the images of "the Chekhovian *intelligent*" that blends with a black-and-white photograph of an intelligent face with a goatee and a pince-nez.[1] There is also the image of "someone with a little hammer," from the story "Gooseberries," knocking on the doors of those who are tranquil and happy in their ignorance, and trying to infect them with yearning for a more meaningful life. There is the lyricism of the doomed-but-beautiful love story in the image of "the lady with a dog." A classic writer and his myth attain this high level of cultural presence through a process of cultural familiarization, a process whereby a work of art becomes a part of everyday discourse. Cultural familiarity may be limited to a particular and rather short period of time, as is often the case with popular texts and films. A whole generation might use phrases from these popular texts and films as idioms in everyday speech, but with time they move to the periphery of cultural memory, and their referential potential diminishes. This kind of familiarity is especially conducive to parody: parody thrives in the here-and-now of culture. "Parody's motto," writes Yuri Tynianov, "is the living and the contemporary."[2] With parody, even if it attempts to go beyond a literary joke, the text can't escape being secondary in nature, existing only as a comment on the parodied work. A truly classic work of art continues to be a part of cultural discourse through decades and centuries; thus we might speak of canonical, as opposed to cultural, familiarization, which is "an historical process resulting from the continual reproduction of works in multiple contexts, as well as from the social confirmation across a range of variably influential institutions."[3] Intertextual engagement with these works transcends parody: it activates cultural memory of the reader in order to create a new meaning out of the interaction of texts. It creates a synchronic view of cultural history by temporarily bringing together old and new texts. In the case of most parodic works, however, both texts do belong to the same time: to the present.

Both myth and canon regulate the mechanism of familiarization; mostly without tension or even clear demarcation, both ensure that a classical author and his works remain actively present in cultural memory and production. Educational institutions play a major role in this process: they ensure the availability of classic works to the general public through school curricula, popular editions, and biographies. A number of government agencies regulate the process of cultural production through organized literary jubilees, literary prizes, the naming of streets, the erection of monuments, and so on. The literary (and more generally artistic) field reflects and advances canonical familiarization by quoting, alluding to, arguing with, or, in other words, constantly rewriting a canonical text. When a writer engages in a dialogue with a classic writer, when a novel is turned into a feature film, or a play is produced with a new interpretation, a canonical text is made again. According to Pierre Bourdieu, it is made "hundreds of times, thousand of times, by all those who have an interest in it, who find a material or symbolic profit in reading it, classifying it, decoding it, commenting on it, reproducing it, criticizing it, combating it, knowing it, possessing it."[4] *The Cherry Orchard* is a text that has gone through a process of both cultural and canonical familiarization: it has been reproduced in multiple contexts, literary and theatrical; confirmed by social institutions and venerated in public consciousness; studied in schools; and turned into films. More than any other Chekhov text, it has become a source of metaphors,[5] or rather of one powerful metaphor, that of the cherry orchard itself.

The metaphorical cherry orchard (*vishnevyi sad*) is an object of nostalgic love, a beautiful, albeit useless, thing that belongs to the past and is therefore irrecoverable. Over the course of the twentieth century its meaning has become proverbial. The fact that Chekhov designated *The Cherry Orchard* as a comedy does not undermine the nostalgic value of the orchard, both the real one and the one each character constructs in his or her mind. In fact, the question of the play's genre is at the heart of the history of its reception. Konstantin Stanislavsky and the Moscow Art Theater's uneasiness with Chekhov's generic designation for the play and the public's reaction to it are testaments to the strength of the melancholy layer of this last Chekhov comedy. From the beginning, the public responded to the elegiac impulse in *The Cherry Orchard* and perceived the play as drama, if not tragedy. The director and the troupe of the Moscow Art Theater, for whom Chekhov wrote his major plays, interpreted it as drama and even advertised it as such, to Chekhov's great consternation. Chekhov's repeated claims that *The Cherry Orchard* is comedy, at times even farce, were uniformly ignored. The Moscow Art Theater's production is responsible for setting up a model for the play's interpretation throughout the century, yet it did not create, but merely emphasized, the melancholy overtones of Chekhov's last play.

The motif of change, especially the change in social and economical circumstances, is the plot's driving force. As the aristocratic owners of the estate get older and poorer, the merchant Lopakhin becomes wealthier and buys the estate. Even the orchard, we are told, has changed from a profitable enterprise to a useless object of beauty. Most characters' view of the past is colored nostalgically: from Ranevskaya to Firs, all miss and mourn it. In the end, all except Firs rush off into their future. The action of the play is but a moment suspended between everyone's memories of the past and their mixed expectations for the future. The orchard disappears at the sound of an axe in the last seconds of the action. There is a sense of inevitability in every speech and every in-action by the characters. And yet, Chekhov insisted, this is a comedy. The audience is asked to part with its past with a laugh. Although the social and economic factors are central to the plot, Chekhov does not present them as tragic forces; neither does he join his characters in singing praises to the past. His interest is in the human reaction to change. The audience, however, has always refused to join the author in his detachment and cannot help sympathizing with the owners' loss, seeing the destruction of the cherry orchard as symbolic of the broad drama of human life.

The ideological interpretation of the play has changed over time, especially after the Revolution and again after perestroika, but this has not affected the connotations of the cherry orchard image. As the ideological climate changes, Trofimov and Ania are hailed in turn as future revolutionaries or impotent chatterers, and Lopakhin as a sensitive man or a ruthless predator, but the cherry orchard has always represented ethical and aesthetic values. Several times in the course of the play this point is stressed: the orchard does not bring profit and, unlike the splendid and profitable apple orchard in Chekhov's "The Black Monk," holds only nostalgic value, symbolizing memory and beauty. While writing the play, Chekhov most probably had in mind the biblical image of the Garden of Eden (*raiskii sad*), as well as Milton's *Paradise Lost,* but these concrete references did not explicitly find their way into the play. It is important that the Russian word *sad* means both *garden* and *orchard.* For the Russian twentieth-century consciousness, therefore, Chekhov's use of the garden in *The Cherry Orchard* has supplanted those older, potent symbols of loss.

There is another "literary" orchard that might have contributed to the idea of *The Cherry Orchard* and that helps illustrate Chekhov's approach to the dynamics of change. In *Anna Karenina,* Tolstoy has Levin contemplate his lot as a landowner in post-serfdom times. In Part six, chapter 29, Levin wanders around the scene of provincial elections. He understands neither the process nor its purpose. The only meaningful conversation he has is with an old landowner who shares his skepticism about the nobility playing election games. This scene, uniformly ignored by critics of *Anna Karenina,* may have provided a source for the plot of Chekhov's play,[6] and it helps clarify the discrepancy between Chekhov's designation of the play as a comedy and the public reaction to it.

The two landowners, the young Levin and the old man, castigate the new sort of nobility who owns the land but does not respect it: "they are landlords (*zemlevladel'tsy*), and we are landowners (*pomeshchiki*). As nobility, they are committing suicide." The old man then defends the idea of nobility during a time when the institution seems to be on its way to becoming obsolete. His argument is the force of tradition: "good or not, we've been a thousand years growing." To stress his point he uses the metaphor of a garden or orchard (*sad*): "when you want to make a garden in front of your house, you have to lay it out, and there is a hundred-year-old tree growing in that spot. . . . Though it's old and gnarled, you still won't cut the old-timer down for the sake of your flower beds. . . ."[7] The garden metaphor immediately becomes the center of the conversation. It so happens that the old man has just planted a garden on his estate even though there is no one to carry on his work. The futility of his effort is obvious to all, including himself:

> I had a merchant for a neighbor. We took a walk around my farm, my garden. "No," he says, [. . .] "If it was me, I'd cut those lindens down. Only the sap must have risen. You've got a thousand lindens here, and each one would yield two good pieces of bast. Bast fetches a nice price these days, and you can cut a good bit of lumber out of the lindens."

Levin predicts the next phase of the merchant's project: "and he'd use the money to buy cattle or land for next to nothing and lease it out to muzhiks. [. . .] And he'll make a fortune. While you and I—God help us to hang on to what's ours and leave it to our children." There is enormous pride in both men's words, pride in belonging to an age-old class, of ignoring the new and base economic reality, and of being therefore morally superior. Levin even offers a metaphor of his own, one that shows the extent of his pride in his land: "as if we've been appointed, like ancient vestals, to tend some sort of fire." "Why don't we do as the merchants do?" he asks rhetorically. He already knows the answer the old man will give: because "it's no business for noblemen."

A number of motifs crucial to Chekhov's play are at work here. Most important is the tension between the old classes and the new economic and social reality: the cherry orchard's owners react with proud contempt to the merchant Lopakhin's offer to cut down the trees and lease the land out for dachas: "Dachas and summer people—forgive me, but it's so vulgar." The garden in Chekhov's play, at the beginning of this new twentieth century, is doomed; its vestals have neither the strength nor the desire to tend the fire. What Tolstoy's characters discuss with the solemn emotions of moral responsibility and proud sacrifice, Chekhov's characters accept partly as punishment for their sins—"we have sinned, and sinned greatly,"—and partly because they have no moral energy to stop the inevitable. But to follow Lopakhin's advice is to honor the rules of the new, capitalist mentality, and that would be, using Tolstoy's formula, "no business for noblemen." The garden planted by Ranevskaya's ancestor, a relative perhaps of Tolstoy's nameless landowner, is finally cut down. The crucial difference in Tolstoy's and Chekhov's treatments of the metaphor is in their tone: Tolstoy admires Levin's and the old man's dedication to the tradition, their determination to leave the garden intact to their children; Chekhov smiles, somewhat bitterly, at their heirs' inadequacy to the task. Ranevskaya's child, Ania, is full of excitement at the prospect of leaving the orchard and her home behind on her way to a new and beautiful life. The mother leaves Russia altogether. The main source for the public's resistance to the comic impulse of *The Cherry Orchard* is its inclination to see the events in Tolstoy's vein. In this view, the moment of change, central in Chekhov's play, is a moment of rupture and loss. Tolstoy, with his heroic vision of continuity at any cost, would not accept this moment as anything but tragic. Chekhov, the poet of the present, does not engage the historicist perspective, but his audience does. Stanislavsky's reluctance to stage the play as comedy stems from the same inclination. The editor of the influential *New Time,* Alexei Suvorin, virtually echoes Tolstoy's characters in his reaction to the play: "something important is being destroyed, destroyed perhaps according to historical necessity, but still, it is a tragedy of Russian life, not a comedy or a joke."[8] Throughout the twentieth century, readers, directors, and audiences alike continued to perceive the cherry orchard as an elegiac symbol and to ignore the comic element of Chekhov's play.

An inevitable question presents itself: how strong is the play's comic element if it consistently remains hidden for generations of readers and critics? After all, the majority of characters and scenes unquestionably make the stuff of comedy: Charlotte's antics, the manservant Yasha's ridiculous Europeanism, Yepikhodov's clumsiness, and Gaev's incongruous speeches. Only the orchard, the main protagonist, remains removed from the comic plane. Its function is simply different: it highlights and brings into focus the other characters' human essence. Yet its symbolism casts shadows across the whole stage, enveloping the play in an elegiac mood. The comic penetrates this elegiac shield only if the audience accepts the moment of change as at least potentially comic, but it consistently equates change with loss, and the problem of the play's genre persists. Critics and directors are still at work to solve it, often by defining Chekhov's views on, and techniques of, comedy as different, uniquely Chekhovian. Donald Rayfield sees the play as comedy capable of incorporating tragedy, that is, a comedy "cruel enough to deal with tragic situations."[9] Harvey Pitcher considers *The Cherry Orchard* a comedy of the absurd; and Richard Gilman views all of Chekhov's comedies as containing, unlike his dramas, a concept of a future, of a possibility for something new. In this very specific and limited view, comedy does not have to follow the classical rules or even be funny; it merely has to be open "toward time to come."[10] Mikhail Gromov deals with the problem of reconciling the play's genre with the tears of its audience by proposing a curiously Chekhovian solution: he postpones the solution into a distant future when people will no longer respond to the elegiac connotations of the image. "Perhaps," he writes, "*The Cherry Orchard* is addressed to other generations, [. . .] and then the main content of the comedy—that which makes it a comedy—will come to the foreground and people will laugh where we have not been laughing, and smile with compassion where we secretly wipe away our tears."[11] *The Cherry Orchard* is indeed a comedy for the future: the future figures in it as a possibility, the open road of the last act; and only in the future, when enough changes have occurred, bringing other cruelties and losses, will the sadness of this particular moment of change cease to affect the audience.

Gromov enumerates the symbolic qualities of the cherry orchard and stresses the highly positive meaning of the very words *cherry orchard:* "the peculiar quality of the juxtaposition 'cherry orchard' lies, apparently, in the fact that it does not hold any negative meaning in our language; it is the pole of absolute meaning (*smyslovoi polius*) of our vocabulary."[12] This is certainly what the cherry orchard has become for the Russian reader in the course of the twentieth century. However, the garden that the characters in *The Cherry Orchard* leave behind has less absoluteness. For each character it symbolizes different, yet specific, things: for Ranevskaya, her childhood and innocence; for Ania, the burden of the old life; for her mentor, Trofimov, serfdom and exploitation. However different everyone's view, all accept the orchard's metaphoric nature. Since none of the characters see the orchard as land and trees, the practical, monetary approach offered by Lopakhin has no meaning to them. But even the practical Lopakhin cannot resist the force of its symbolism: in his "victory speech" delivered between purchasing the orchard and taking his axe to it, he acknowledges the symbolic nature of his act: "if my father and grandfather could only rise from their graves and see what happened, see how their Yermolay [. . .] bought this estate, the most beautiful place in the world. . . ."[13] This is the function of the "cherry orchard" motif in the cultural memory of the twentieth century: a metaphor of beauty and loss.

While the cherry orchard is a victim of change, Lopakhin is the character who might be called its agent.[14] Changes in the ideological interpretations of Lopakhin and his role in the destruction of the orchard reveal how easily the metaphor of the orchard lends itself to the dominating discourse of a historical period. The first Moscow Art Theater production of 1904 presented Lopakhin as a complex character, and, as different actors chose to emphasize either the peasant/merchant or the artist/gentleman in him, the complexity was reinforced. After the revolution, when Chekhov returned to the stage in new, ideologically approved guise, *The Cherry Orchard* appealed to the revolutionary critics and audiences as literary proof of the inevitability of the Revolution and its purifying storm.[15] Surprisingly, it is Lopakhin, rather than Petia Trofimov with his speeches full of revolutionary rhetoric, whom the communist press claim as their own. In 1924, a Kharkov newspaper "Communist" claims kinship with Lopakhin's hatred for the estate where his father and grandfather were serfs:

> Having bought the cherry orchard, he remembers how his grandfather and his father cringed before the now destitute Ranevskys. He knows his worth even though he seems to be ashamed of his own strength. His axe is already hitting the Cherry orchard, demolishing the beauty created by slavery. In place of beauty he gives usefulness (*pol'zu*), granted, now only for himself, but soon the new beauty will come to replace the Cherry orchard and the new Lopakhins will finish what he has started.[16]

By the logic of this interpretation, in October of 1917 it was the Lopakhins, not the Trofimovs—men of action not of words—who reformed the country and "cut down" the old world, paving the way for the new garden. Lopakhin is now Chekhov's man-with-an-axe: the violence of this image is emphasized or suppressed according to the ideological ruling trend.

By the mid-1920s, even Stanislavsky attributes—retrospectively certainly—a revolutionary impulse to Chekhov's play. Chekhov, Stanislavsky insists in *My Life in Art* (1924), foresees the "inevitability of the revolution." Chekhov's cutting down of "the beautiful blossoming Cherry Orchard"[17] testifies, in his view, to the fact that Chekhov was willing to accept the inevitable. During the 1930s Stanislavsky's conception of Petia Trofimov undergoes a radical change: Petia, "the seedy-looking gent" (*oblezlyj barin*), ridiculously impractical and given to verbosity, becomes a young revolutionary with the future in his hands, akin to the Soviet youth of the 1930s. This Trofimov is portrayed as the mouthpiece for Chekhov's belief in the bright future and as the precursor of the many now gray-haired Trofimovs in the audience. In this interpretation there is no room for Lopakhin the revolutionary: in this production, Lopakhin has become a capitalist devoid of all human features, a predator circling around Ranevskaya and the orchard, interested in nothing but profit.[18]

By the 1940s, the cherry orchard image was fixed in its metaphorical form, and the metaphor has since been manipulated to suit the ideology of the time. Olga Knipper, Chekhov's widow, played Ranevskaya for forty years. In a 1939 interview she expressed the new approach to Chekhov's last play in appropriately metaphoric terms: "I disliked the people who came to us in order to cry over the cut down Cherry orchards. But I love with all my heart the contemporary audience who stand under the footlights with their fiery shining eyes and give us rapturous applause because they are that young growth which is destined to grow into a beautiful orchard."[19] The plural "Cherry orchards" and the mix of the ideological and the aesthetic in Knipper's speech suggest an opposition between two distinct meanings of the metaphor, one individualist, the other collectivist. Whereas for the pre-Revolutionary audience the cherry orchard symbolized an object of personal loss and nostalgia, during the Soviet period, with its emphasis on the collective over the individual, the metaphor loses its elegiac shading and becomes the utopian symbol of the collective future orchard. Not until the end of the Stalin era was a different interpretation of *The Cherry Orchard* possible. Unsurprisingly, as the political climate became more tolerant, a shift occurred back to the individual.

The minor liberalism of the Thaw of the 1960s allowed directors to eschew the sociological and political readings of Chekhov. In 1965, the Soviet Army Theater's production of *The Cherry Orchard* concentrated on the theme of loss and the human inability to accept it. Director Maria Knebel wrote: "It seemed to me that in this last of his plays Chekhov understood very well what it means to lose something infinitely beloved. . . . Each of us has lost and will lose our own 'cherry orchard.' Each of us is trying to hold on to it." Most productions of this period display renewed attention to psychological complexity and the individual subject, an undoubtedly positive shift from the political point of view. At the same time, this new wave of Chekhov productions solidified the perception of *The Cherry Orchard* as a play about loss, and thus a drama, if not a tragedy. The Tallinn Youth Theater in 1971 placed a special emphasis on the characters' illusions about the orchard and all it stood for.[20] Anatolii Efros's production at the Taganka Theater in 1975 was a play about "doomed people who cannot hear the footfall of fate and will not face reality."[21] Ranevskaya, in this production, is a "broken wanton," while Lopakhin, "elegant, intelligent, was the only spiritual aristocrat among them, and the sale of the orchard looked to be his tragedy, not hers."[22] Not coincidentally, Lopakhin was played by the immensely popular actor and singer Vladimir Vysotsky. Efros's production centered on the spiritual void created by the pragmatism of the new Soviet society, and it attempted to foreground the psychological over the sociological in Chekhov's play. The complexity of Lopakhin's character is brought forward as a reaction to the rigid black-and-white arrangement of Socialist realist standards. Efros's and other productions of the 1960s and 1970s attempted to put forward the ageless aspects of *The Cherry Orchard* rather than the ideologically approved and temporally rooted political interpretations. Yet, this approach was perceived as innovative only in light of its implied opposition to the politicized interpretation of the play during the Stalin era. Playwrights in this period endeavored to reproduce this depth and moral ambivalence in the best Chekhovian tradition. Aleksandr Vampilov's play "Duck Hunting" (1970) is the first and best-known of a number of plays centering on a hero who is "Chekhovian in his messy mixture of aspiration and pettiness."[23] Such plays concentrated on the symbolic value and the ambiguity of Chekhov's treatment of the themes of time, loss, nostalgia, spirituality, and change.

The period's attention to Chekhovian themes, and the renewed wealth of interpretations, were ideological in nature, an attempt to set the individual before the collective at a time when the collective was still the main ideological focus. Vladimir Arro's 1979 play *The Orchard* is typical in this respect: it emphasizes the psychological aspect, and yet an undercurrent of sociohistorical concerns endows the play with real depth. *The Orchard* picks up the Chekhovian characters and themes and is steeped in Chekhov's symbolism. It has a very real orchard, of apple trees in this case, which is in danger of being destroyed. Some of Arro's characters seem to be repeating lines from Chekhov's plays, while others gain moral and psychological complexity because they do not fit into the familiar set of characters.

Arro's orchard is set in a Siberian town built around a new electrical plant. The product of the enthusiasm and romanticism of the young revolutionaries who built the town, this is the new orchard promised by Petia Trofimov sixty years earlier. The romantics, now no longer young, are well aware of the symbolic nature of their past undertaking. The orchard's apples are sour and too expensive to grow. Importing apples from warmer climates makes better financial sense. Yet, when the town builders first planted the orchard in their spare time, they were making an important statement that had nothing to do with financial profit. One of them recollects those harsh but exciting times: "The bright times have come! It is a never-ending celebration. This is what being young means, I thought. We are celebrating and at the same time building the bright future for Anka."[24] Another, a school teacher, puts their personal experiences in the broader terms of symbolic values:

> An orchard (*sad*) is not just fruit trees on a picturesque mountain side. . . . Our famous kilowatts, the cheapest in the world, no argument there, they give light. . . . But the orchard, it gives warmth. It exudes a different kind of energy. The most expensive and rare kind! You must understand that every person has to a have a place where he can at any moment escape from life's bustle[;] . . . don't you see, there must be such a place! The orchard is where one is cleansed by unselfish labor . . . and a place of communion. . . . And confession! And repentance! . . . The orchard is the town's soul.[25]

This passionate speech is addressed to the character who appears to represent the destructive forces, the city official who sees the orchard as a financial burden on the town and favors a proposal to turn it into an agricultural co-op—that is, to divide it into smaller individual plots. This agent of change is thus another negative version of Lopakhin—this time neither a merchant nor a capitalist, but a soulless bureaucrat called Matushkin. The bureaucrat is an approved antihero of Socialist realism, one who stands in the way of the hero's efforts at improving the workplace, the production process, and the whole town. Matushkin, however, is not a one-dimensional villain. Arro endows this character with considerable complexity: he is not motivated by politics, nor is he merely following orders; rather, he sincerely considers the co-op a better use for the land and a real service to the townspeople. Like Lopakhin, who draws a bright picture of the country house dwellers multiplying and enriching the land, he considers garden plots as the first step toward bringing about the well-being of this young town in the middle of nowhere. He passionately lashes out against the romantics who feel no respect for those seeking elemental comforts:

> There was the time when you sang songs and recited poetry. You walked through the city you have built on the stilts of your own excitement. But the reality you created has turned out to be much more complex than your songs and your fantasies. [. . .] But you insist and insist! In spite of facts! In the face of common sense! Your vision is consistently distorted! That is why you consider comfortable life, life without troubles petty and vulgar. An orchard co-op for you is the sign of spiritual decline.[26]

As in Chekhov, the participants in the discussion about the orchard's fate might as well be speaking different languages: behind each argument there is a radically different set of values. Moreover, the conflict between the city official and the old romantics is further complicated by the fact that they too are tired and disillusioned; they too are not as opposed as they would like to be to the security and domesticity of having their own little plots of land. With strained affectation, the same woman who remembered planting the orchard as the best days of her youth now declares: "I'll cut down the trees and plant potatoes! What are you looking at?! [. . .] I have a daughter. And no illusions! That's it. Finished. And she too won't have any."[27]

The young generation in the play, Anka and Valera, do not participate in these discussions. They feel that they have heard it all: "these lie, those denounce." But they are far from having no romantic illusions. Valera dreams of going to exotic places, and Anka is in love with the archromantic character in the play, the gardener (*sadovod*), and leaves with him at the end to plant a new orchard in an unspecified place.

Before she leaves, she addresses her mother (who had thought that the orchard was Anka's "bright future") with a monologue mirroring Ania's monologue at the end of *The Cherry Orchard:* "Mama! Mommy! Come with us! My dearest! (she kisses her hands) Come away! Everything will be there!"[28] Like Chekhov's Ania, who implores her mother, "come with me, dear, come away. We shall plant a new orchard . . . ," Anka has already turned away from the doomed orchard and dreams of a new life where "everything will be" (*vse budet*). She too has no clear plan for the new life she so passionately welcomes. And as in Chekhov, those who cannot and would not join her say in unison, "Our youth is gone." The young and the incurably romantic will go on planting and building. The gardener insists that he has no choice: it is spring, time to plant the trees. He seems to be guided by some unseen but irrefutable force: when asked "what are you going to do . . . plant another orchard?" he replies simply: "How can I not?" (*a kuda zh devat'sia*).[29] But the young will, presumably, grow up and will someday want stability and comfort in their lives; their orchards will be once again replaced by garden plots, and the cycle will go on.

Arro's orchard is as much a symbol as Chekhov's cherry orchard. The play's intertextual focus is on the inevitability and the complexity of the forces that bring about its destruction. Unlike *The Cherry Orchard,* however, Arro's play is a drama: it seriously and thoughtfully outlines the complexity of the problem. Comedy must have an externalized foe, but here the dynamics of change unfold within the consciousness of the characters, and no one external to the conflict represents historical change. The conflict of generations, a potentially comic clash, is also internalized: the young and the old are the same people. This is the main difference between Chekhov's and Arro's treatment of the motifs of change and loss, and it is the reason why Arro's play concentrates not on the agent of change but on its symbolic victim, the orchard. Change is not embodied in a character in Arro's play; the moral is that romantic enthusiasm does not survive its own limits—the characters' youth. Moreover, its demands on people become a burden as they get older and can no longer function on enthusiasm and hopes alone. There are no villains in Arro's play, no man-with-an-axe. Yet, the orchard's destruction is once again inevitable because the people themselves have become agents of time and change. This is why when Arro rewrote the play into a script for television in 1988, he changed the title from *The Orchard* to *Forgive Us, Orchard.*

The fact that Arro's *The Orchard* is so openly Chekhovian actually highlights the differences between the two plays. The play's message comes into view out of its departure from the established readings of Chekhov. The young protagonists' indifference to the orchard acquires special significance through the parallels with the traditionally ideological interpretation of Trofimov and Ania as new revolutionaries set on turning the whole of Russia into an orchard. The fact that the people who planted and lost the orchard are not the gentry, rightly deserving of their fate, but young communists, further complicates the issue and emphasizes the universal aspect of the conflict over the sociohistorical. This complexity was for Arro and his audience an aim in itself, a welcome deviation from the strictly ideological classing of characters according to positive and negative types. The complexity of human emotions, goals, and motivations, shown with compassion and without judgment, was the play's most Chekhovian feature. It was, however, another Vladimir Arro play that prompted critics to look for specific links to *The Cherry Orchard.* His 1981 play *Look Who's Here* (*Smotrite, kto prishel*), which has no obvious intertextual pointers to *The Cherry Orchard,* immediately started a discussion on the relevance of Chekhov's characters and conflicts for the reality of the 1980s. If *The Orchard* internalized the motif of change, in *Look Who's Here,* change has a properly external agent, a character who represents the changing social reality. The critics and the audience immediately picked up on this parallel with *The Cherry Orchard;* it is significant, moreover, that all traces of the comic in Arro's play, in the same way as occurred with Chekhov's play, were ignored in favor of a solemn sociohistorical interpretation.

In *Look Who's Here,* the center of the conflict is a summer house, the dacha that seemed so vulgar a concept to Ranevskaya. Ranevskaya's orchard and house—her estate—is a typical nineteenth-century image. Dachas, by contrast, even though well in existence before, are a predominantly twentieth-century concept.[30] An estate signifies the aristocratic, old landowners' culture, a dacha—that of the growing middle-class. It is ironic that the sharp estate/dacha dichotomy, so crucial for Chekhov's characters, has become an equation in the twentieth century. Within the parameters of the Soviet time frame, the dacha is as much a family gathering place and symbolic link to its past and stability as the estate had been. It has become a symbol of rank for the class that supplanted the aristocracy in its privileged status, the *nomenklatura* and the artistic and scientific elites. In *Look Who's Here,* the late owner of the dacha was a writer; his family pride themselves on belonging to the intelligentsia. But now the writer's widow is selling the house, and the family is forced to leave the place they came to consider their home. What pains them most is that the prospective buyer is neither a general nor a professor, but a hairdresser.

The new owner is, at first glance, as unacceptable as Chekhov's Lopakhin. Yet Arro again complicates the potentially easily definable conflict: his villain is an artist in his own right—a famous hairdresser, a master with international competitions to his credit. Lopakhin's artistic hands, which Petia had noticed in *The Cherry Orchard,* here take on a curiously ambiguous reality. King (Korolev) sees himself as an artist and a professional; the intelligentsia of the house sees him as a money-grabbing nouveau riche. His motives in buying the summer house are similar to Lopakhin's: to own a place whose previous owners look down on him and who dismiss his art as service. He is right: they look down on his occupation and are quick to see the situation as symbolic of lamentable changes in society: "It's some sort of plague! . . . They are taking over everything. Barbers move to center stage. . . ."[31]

The sixty-year-old Tabunov, the writer's brother, chastises his son-in-law, a scientist, for trying to supplement his meager salary with construction work: "It's no good, Leva, when a scientist dirties his hands with paint. His hands must be white . . . pampered . . . his nails pink. But you have whitewash under your nails."[32] The fact that the scientist and his friend, a poet, with all their education and refinement, have to put their work aside and engage in manual labor, while a hairdresser makes their monthly salary in one day, mixes up the social and moral sides of the conflict in much the same way as does Chekhov's play. The old owners once again cannot afford to hold on to their place, but their financial standing in no way diminishes their attitude of superiority, but perhaps even contributes to it. The irony of the situation is highlighted by the fact that Tabunov is not, in fact, the owner of the house but rather the owner's brother. His relation to the intelligentsia is suspect, based on nothing but his and his wife's haughty attitude. When he angrily remarks, "Would you look at this European celebrity . . . Unbelievable! Least of all were we interested in the achievements of barbers, sausage-makers, and beer-brewers. We had different European names in circulation,"[33] his wife tries and quite comically fails to produce a list of such names.

The intelligentsia's contempt for money, like Ranevskaya's, comes from pride in belonging to the elite. Again, the irony of the fact that Ranevskaya sneered at the dacha as a lower-class and vulgar phenomenon, while the children of Lopakhin's dacha project think of themselves as the elite with the right to sneer at everything they think of as lower class and vulgar, must have escaped the audience's attention. The satirical element of the play—that is, the Tabunovs' pretentiousness and the casting of a barber as villain, could have been perceived as such if the audience were less personally invested in the conflict. Instead, the play was seen as an elegiac look at the lifestyle and values of the intelligentsia, hence the critics' insistence that *Look Who's Here* echoes Chekhov's *The Cherry Orchard:* both plays are saying farewell to the vanishing aristocracy, real in one case, spiritual in the other. In both cases the approaching capitalist reality and mentality renders their existence and values unnecessary. Lopakhin's character once again feels too real for symbolic and complex rendering; he acquires the characteristics of a specific group, one that in the 1990s would be infamously called "the new Russians."

Sociologist Revekka Frumkina analyzes the play in terms of a crisis of the intelligentsia in the face of the impossibility of surviving in the new economic reality, *both* financially and spiritually:

> But the play is not only about how a victorious boor (*kham*) and nouveau riche asserts his right to buy the contemporary "cherry orchard." The play is about *the end of the era of junior researchers* (*mladshikh nauchnykh sotrudnikov*)[34] with connections (*s blatom*) or without them, but their status—and therefore their knowledge and culture—turned out to mean nothing when compared with the status delivered by money. It is no wonder that at the end of the play, the one who dies is precisely the overstrained "j.r." (*mns*), at the age of thirty four (supposedly Varia), instead of the old man who has been connected to the dacha the most throughout his life (supposedly Ranevskaya).[35]

The apocalyptic and angry sound of this broad sociological analysis is characteristic of 1990s discourse. In 1981, when the play appeared, the hindsight of the post-perestroika disappointment was not yet available; still, the play produced an uneasy sense of foreboding. Boris Minaev, who also takes for granted that Arro's play is "based on (*po motivam*) *The Cherry Orchard,*" stresses this apprehension:

> The details were not important, the important thing was the general feeling: something is happening, some kind of a change of values, a change of priorities. Soon it became clear: the play was premature. In about ten years there appeared *kooperatory* [private business entrepreneurs]. In another five—"new Russians." And then suddenly the new cherry orchard appeared as well. It took on shape. Its old branches started to rustle. On the scale of the whole country. [They] immediately started to cry over it. Defend it. Even fight for it.[36]

Arro's play has indeed come a little early: in the beginning of the 1980s the nascent crisis—economic, political, and spiritual—was not yet at the center of public attention. But had it appeared in the 1990s, it might have been lost in the multitude of heated debates on these issues that took place in both journalistic and literary discourse. Never before had the "cherry orchard" metaphor seemed this relevant to the pressing issues and ideologies of the time.

The 1980s and 1990s, a time of change and trouble in Russian history, elicited all kinds of responses, among which nostalgia takes a prominent place. It was driven in equal measure by the collapsing economy and the deterioration of living standards, by the diminishment of Russia's political clout, and by cultural shifts.[37] In a sadly ironic historical parallel, Russia experienced the advent of capitalism for the second time, and the reaction was similar to that at the end of the previous century. Chekhov's depiction of a clash between the old landowners' sensibility and Lopakhin's new capitalist one was suddenly relevant again. As an elegiac symbol, it is used in literary and everyday nonpolitical discourse. When a discussion turns to economic and political issues, Lopakhin, the agent of change and the garden's destroyer, is at the center of attention: he symbolizes the men of the new order and attracts a range of conflicting attitudes. Two forces propelled the "cherry orchard" image into the center of cultural discourse: its absolute metaphoric value and the historical parallels between the play's events and those of the last decades of the twentieth century.

In the journalistic discourse of the 1990s and the first years of the new century, "The Cherry Orchard" figures in the title of articles on poaching and bioterrorism in Russia, on the trials of the Russian population in independent Latvia,[38] on the decline of intellectualism in France, and even on the crash of the dot.com boom in Silicon Valley. There is a popular song, "The Cherry Orchard," by the group *Fristail*

(Freestyle), which mourns lost love: "We did not keep it warm and safe / did not shelter it from harm / we'll never be together again / in that old cherry orchard." There are restaurants, cafes, and beauty salons named "The Cherry Orchard," and "The Cherry Orchard" color of automobile paint. There is an ecological center called "The Cherry Orchard" and a "Cherry Orchard" project offered by a firm specializing in landscaping design. And, in the best case of all, it is the name of a gated cottage community near Moscow, in north Tushino, whose philosophy, as explained in their brochure, is the "renewal of the forgotten family tradition—to pass the ancestral estate from generation to generation. The children of the community residents will grow up together with the cherry orchard. Here a new generation will be born for whom the phrase 'to plant a tree' will not be empty of meaning."

The article on poaching and bioterrorism would have been better served by an allusion to *Uncle Vanya* and Astrov's ecologically minded speeches, perhaps; however, as a metaphor, the cherry orchard evokes an emotional response rather than providing substantive ground for discussion of the topic. The author is talking about ecological catastrophes, exacerbated in Russia by the new capitalists' disregard for ecological considerations: "On the verge of the twenty first century, having gotten the second wind amidst the fresh spaces of Russia, Lopakhin took his knife not only to orchards but even to woods. They are destroyed by dacha plots in order to serve the instantly materialized capitalist elite. Even national parks are threatened, those woodlands most preserved among protected natural areas."[39] The article appeared in a literary "thick journal" rather than at a scientific forum; accordingly, it uses metaphors of literary origins and allows free rein to the author's emotions. It is both angry and elegiac in tone and does not hesitate to assign the same anger to Chekhov: "the future does not belong to Lopakhins. Anton Chekhov had understood and showed it with conviction a century ago in his drama *The Cherry Orchard.*" One cannot help wondering how the editors of *Moskva,* a reputable literary journal, missed not only this improbable reading of Chekhov's play (where the future very much belongs to Lopakhin, although he might have been happier not to be its reluctant and constantly exhausted instrument), but even the wrong generic designation: *The Cherry Orchard* is a comedy, not a drama. It might be a sign of the general cultural impoverishment reaching even into the sacred offices of the thick journals, but more likely it is the ultimate result of a process of cultural familiarization. Unlike canonical familiarity, that which is cultural allows an image to become disconnected and function independently from it source. Usually such an image dominates cultural discourse for a limited time, repeatedly surfacing in popular fiction, films, and songs. The fact that Chekhov's play enjoys both canonical and cultural familiarity a hundred years after its appearance, and has outlived generations of other popular symbols, is a testament to its being a vital part of Russian cultural mythology. Like all myth constructions, it is not concerned with facts and molds itself to the user's purposes.

The review of a book about the Silicon Valley phenomenon by the American writer Christina Finn, which appeared on BBCRussian.com under the title "The Cherry Orchards of Silicon Valley," displays an obviously ironic pose.[40] The book's author refers to the end of the Silicon Valley computer boom as the disappearance of "the cherry orchards one by one." The author of the review is sufficiently amused by this migration of the Russian metaphor to use it in the title of his piece. The incongruous appearance of a cherry orchard in America's Silicon Valley is indeed funny. It seems that the farther the metaphor travels from its source, the less is the speaker's personal emotional involvement, and the more of its comic potential it retains. The function of the cherry orchard in this context is determined by neither literary nor factual parallels: it could be explained only by the proverbial use of the "the cherry orchard" image as standing for something good that is now lost. In the same vein, the article on the hardships of French intellectuals in these anti-intellectual times appears under the title "'The Cherry Orchard' in French,"[41] but it never gets around to developing the implied parallel: the author sees no need to explain or justify the obvious connotations of his title. Both texts rely on cultural familiarity with the image and use it as a point of departure or a shortcut to the motif of nostalgia.

The sales pitch for the gated community "The Cherry Orchard" disregards the origins of the image altogether. The part about renewing the tradition of land ownership through generations, and the symbolic planting of trees, produces an unintended comic effect: *The Cherry Orchard* is a play about the failure to do precisely that, to give the orchard intact to the children, to ensure that the tradition goes on. It is a play about forces of change, in the face of which people's desires and dreams do not matter. The showy advertisement with its claim to promote and symbolize continuity illustrates how cultural familiarization breaks literary connections and helps turn an image into a commodity. The advertisement exploits the cherry orchard image to sell those dreams and desires whose loss it connotes. The link between the cherry orchard metaphor and its original setting, Chekhov's play, is all but severed. The unintended comic effect of the advertisement fulfills, albeit unintentionally, Gromov's prediction that *The Cherry Orchard* will be a comedy in the future, once its elegiac connotations cease to reverberate for the audience. Russia's reintroduction to capitalism produces situations and narratives that range from the heartbreaking to the absurd, but advertisements are especially prone to ridiculousness in their incongruous mix of commercialism and cultural pretension. What the color of automobile paint, the beauty salons, and ecological projects have in common is that they build on and use as a commodity an image that in its original setting symbolized that which is incompatible with pragmatism and commercialism. The story of the cherry orchard metaphor traveling through contemporary cultural discourse is comic in the sense of Karl Marx's observation that recurring historical facts and personages appear as tragedy the first time and as farce the second.[42]

Literary uses of the cherry orchard metaphor too draw on the interconnection of the cherry orchard's canonical significance and its significance for pop culture. The writers who emphasize and develop the nostalgic implications of the image rely on readers' familiarity with the metaphor as much as the advertisements' authors do. While they do not commodify it, they rarely refer to its literary source. In Viktoria Tokareva's *Kheppi end*, the heroine muses: "as for us, today we look at the end of the nineteenth century and get nostalgic [. . .] longing for the cherry orchards and for the lost faith" (188). The plural "cherry orchards" in this melancholy reverie reflects the transformation of a concrete image into a cultural metaphor of loss. The critic Natalia Ivanova remarks, "There is the sound of an axe in the cherry orchard of Russian literature!"[43] and proceeds with her rather pessimistic analysis of contemporary prose. Galina Shcherbakova, in the short story "Avocado Pit," makes an explicitly sarcastic comment on the indiscriminate use of the cherry orchard in literary and journalistic discourse. Her narrator resigns herself to talking about the avocado even though she would have preferred the cherry as a subject. The cherry, however, she feels, is off-limits, an image too loaded and overused: "Although it would have been nice to write about the cherry, about how it blossoms, what a white smoke clouds above it. Such happiness grows inside that my ribs creak. But one can get it in the neck for the cherry orchard. We only have one—blossoming, axed down, burnt in a stove, sung by everyone to death, so don't go there. . . ."[44]

Using the cherry orchard as a metaphor for a better past does not, of course, take into account the fact that Chekhov never intended to portray the nineteenth century as a Golden Age. By its nature nostalgia idealizes the past, contrasting it to the present and assigning greatness to it. Lyudmila Petrushevskaya's 1999 story "Paradise, Paradise" employs and eventually deconstructs precisely this sort of nostalgic perception as it presents a sequence of losses, and the story explicitly addresses the way in which the motifs of the Garden of Eden and *Paradise Lost* became entangled in the consciousness of the intelligentsia in the twentieth century with the image of Chekhov's cherry orchard. The paradise of the story is equated with the cherry orchard, but the resulting image operates without additional references to Chekhov's play. The particular Chekhovian intertext is less important than the function of the concept of the cherry orchard in cultural memory.

The repetition in the title of the story reflects a repetition in the plot: paradise is lost twice. The story's plot is as simple as that of most Petrushevskaya stories: the younger generation builds a summer villa on a lot where the grandmother's old house used to stand. The money for the new project comes from renting out her apartment in the city. The old woman spends the summer at the luxurious villa accompanied by a hired housekeeper and a dog, and she is afraid of both of them. She thinks of the past as a better time and remembers warmly and sadly her little old house and garden. She remembers them as a cherry orchard. The neighbors pity her and reproach her children. The following summer the villa is empty, the old woman is not there, and the neighbors start thinking of the preceding summer as a happy time—indeed, paradise.

The dachas in Chekhov's play symbolize the spirit of the new time: commercial and ultimately vulgar. The landowners are unable to find a place in the new, capitalist society and thus literally lose their place, the house that holds their past and the memory of it. The old house in Petrushevskaya's story signifies the same thing. Unlike Arro's *Look Who's Here,* Petrushevskaya's story offers no ironic perspective on the concept of the dacha; it is purely an elegiac symbol. The sharp contrast between the little old house and the two-story new villa is of the same sort as that between Ranevskaya's house and Lopakhin's dachas: the conflict between the poeticized past and a harsh new commercialism. Petrushevskaya picks up Arro's equation of the intelligentsia with the old aristocracy, and of the dacha with the cherry orchard. But she changes the distribution of forces responsible for its destruction: this dacha is not sold but "improved," and not by an outsider but by the owner's children. The conflict is internalized, much as in Arro's *The Orchard*. The difference is that it is internalized within one family rather than within one consciousness.

The old woman, like Tabunov's family, belongs to a social group that is unable to cope with the new capitalist reality and whose time has gone—the intelligentsia: her neighbors call her an "un-adapted *intelligent*" (*neprisposoblennaia intelligentka*). Her house and little garden, together with the memory of them, are of no practical or sentimental value for the younger generation, who embrace the ethos of investment and profit. There is a peculiar nonmonetary twist, though, to their investment practice: "Sunsets, sunrises, and health—money should be invested in that."[45] Thus, a swimming pool and a tennis court, unheard of in the Russian countryside, replace the garden. The old dacha is replaced by a better dacha, one with a Western twist, a symbol more than a place to spend summers. "We've arrived at a better life," announce the owners who never actually find time to spend at the dacha. In the final paragraphs, the sad irony of this view of the good life comes through in the images of the overgrown tennis court and the empty, grassy swimming pool. The language of the new commercialized reality introduced in the description of the new dacha, as much a Western import as the villa itself, reveals its meaninglessness in the final picture of loss and emptiness.

The image of the cherry orchard enters the story slowly. Every time the discourse goes back to the little old house, the equation with the cherry orchard becomes more prominent. As it gains significance, the focus shifts from the basic connotations of the image of the cherry orchard to that of a lost paradise. In the middle of the story, the garden incorporates both images: paradise is a garden, a cherry orchard which has been lost. By the end of the story, however, it is paradise which becomes the governing image, and the idea of loss and memory comes to the foreground. The story, as it turns out, is about the nature of nostalgia: paradise is lost at least twice, and each time it is not recognized as such until it is too late.

The first mention of the orchard comes in the second sentence of the story, in parentheses: they "immediately began building and now (in the place of the decrepit little hut of a *dacha,* a hen-coop with a garden, twined-intertwined bushes and cherries)—they have built to the neighbors' amazement a two-story giant . . . ." At this point, "garden" and "cherries" are in close proximity, but not close enough to form a single verbal image. Moreover, the description makes it clear that the garden is a thicket of all kinds of trees and bushes. By the second mention, the notion of the cherry orchard is unequivocally introduced: "Elizaveta Fedorovna is quietly nodding, trying not to remember her little house, the intertwined curled paths, the pears—the cherries, the cherry orchard, in short" (*vishnevyi sad, koroche*).[46] It is clear that the cherry orchard comes to the narrator's mind not because the old woman's little garden reminds her of Chekhov's large and once-profitable orchard, but because it provides a metaphor, an image that captures the notion of loss, nostalgia, and memory. This is why it is a "cherry orchard, in short." At this point, the narrator gains access to the readers' cultural memory and evokes in them the emotional value of the image of the cherry orchard. The next two mentions of the cherry orchard take this further, engaging the reader's memory and building the nostalgic mood. The narrator directs her thoughts back to the old woman's past:

> Actually, the participants in the leisurely conversations live here *in paradise* four months of the year. And Elizaveta had lived like this until [they] *cut down her cherry orchard,* and appointed a sergeant to look after her (a dark force with a frying pan in one hand and ketchup in the other). As for her four friends, they still *live in paradise,* visiting one another in the evening [. . .]. They drink a little, eat a little and take Elizaveta's mind off the bitter memories of the cherry orchard and off the endless waiting for her son Serezha, who never comes and in whose place there regularly appears her daughter-in-law.[47]

Thus, the idea of paradise accompanies that of the cherry orchard and, near the end of the story—and the end of summer—replaces it. Elizaveta Fedorovna's daughter-in-law exclaims repeatedly that in the city it is "hell and hell. And here it is paradise, paradise, and paradise. Just step out of the car—quiet, fragrance, air, paradise" (2000, 121). The neighbors accuse the daughter-in-law of ruining the older woman's house, and consequently her life: "Had you let Elizaveta have her old house, you would not have any of her complaints. . . ."[48] The neighbors do not yet know that very soon, the very next summer, they will remember this summer as "paradise, paradise." They do not seem to take into account the nature of human nostalgia: everything appears to have been better, retrospectively, when seen from a temporal distance. The daughter-in-law, "fearless, experienced, capable," seems to be aware of this when she replies: "There were complaints! There would be complaints!"[49]

The story outlines the dynamic of loss. If human life is a succession of changes, Petrushevskaya chooses the final sequences of this succession when in old age each new state brings nothing but further decline. The repetition in the title, and the duplication of loss in the story, also forms a sequence, since the image of the cherry orchard opens up the perspective further into the past: the old dacha had itself replaced something, a real house maybe, perhaps Ranevskaya's estate. One would expect the chain to continue into the future, since presumably every new condition has the potential to be viewed as ideal later. However, Petrushevskaya characteristically puts an end to the succession with the impending death of her protagonist. She literally takes her out of the picture: the old woman is absent the next summer, and no one knows whether she is even alive. The internalization of the motif of change in Arro's *The Orchard* pointed to cyclical time and thus offered the hope of timeless repetition and rejuvenation. In "Paradise, Paradise," where change occurs within the three generations of a family, the breakdown of the cycle of succession is especially conspicuous. Even the obvious line of succession is skewed: the younger generation is represented by the daughter-in-law, not by the old woman's son, who never appears and whose absence undermines the notion of the future inherent in cyclical family time. Moreover, the story ends with an image of utter absence: the villa is empty and the neighbors come together and cannot stop talking about "that happy summer, when everything blossomed wildly and brought forth fruit, when everyone was alive [. . .] and when, as it turned out, everything was coming together into a quiet happiness, and indeed, paradise, paradise."[50]

The temporal perspective at the end is one of Petrushevskaya's major techniques. Whether her characters go on living after the last full stop of a story, or actually die in the course of it, her stories are overwhelmingly about the end—the end of hopes, illusions, love, childhood, friendship, family, or life itself. In any case, the world of Petrushevskaya's stories has no continuation. When she draws intertextually on works pivotal to the Russian cultural tradition, she takes on their moral and/or ideological argument and attempts to put closure to it. Significantly though, in order to have the last word on the subject, she has to activate the reader's memory of it and thus revitalize the older works.

The nostalgia that propels "Paradise, Paradise" into the past is one of the most representative themes in contemporary culture. Nostalgia, as Linda Hutcheon observes, depends on "the *irrecoverable* nature of the past for its emotional impact and appeal. [. . .] The aesthetics of nostalgia might, therefore, be less a matter of simple memory than of complex projection; the invocation of the partial, idealized history merges with a dissatisfaction with the present."[51] The nostalgia in Petrushevskaya's story is all about dissatisfaction with the present, but the fact that we see a rapid succession of nostalgic waves in a short period of time highlights Petrushevskaya's tendency toward the postmodern blending of nostalgia with irony: the nostalgia is "invoked but at the same time undercut, put into perspective, seen for exactly what it is—a comment on the present as much as on the past."[52] The ironic deconstruction of the nostalgic drive in Petrushevskaya's story questions our inclination to idealize the past and dismiss the present in its favor. Yet the story is by no means an attempt to reverse our perception and thus fix the error; rather, it makes a statement on the human inability to do so. We are frozen in the stance of looking back, not realizing our failure to live in the present until there is no more present left. In this picture of the world, the future has no place, since only what has already happened and what is now happening interact and matter.

The passage of time as an irrevocable and tragic process of loss is among the central Chekhovian themes. In the principal division of time into past, present, and future, the present is the least privileged time in the world of Chekhov's characters. A multitude of his protagonists cast nostalgic glances to the past or turn with hope toward a distant future and regard their present as a period that needs to be suffered through rather than lived through fully. Nostalgia is a persistent mood and a source of Chekhov's lyricism, but it also contributes to a disjunction between the presentation of the past and the present by the protagonists and the narrator, respectively. Chekhov's narrator is less invested in the nostalgic outlook than his characters. A character contrasts the idealized past to the unsatisfying present through memory, internal or externalized in the form of a narrated story. The sense of loss, "whether it be the loss of an estate, the loss of an opportunity for love, the loss of youth, the loss of identity, or death,"[53] is a moving force in a number of Chekhov stories and all major plays, a force strong enough to make the characters deplore their present. The perception of the present as not worthy of the past is quite common to all epochs and countries; however, present-day literary and social discourse in Russia is remarkable in the scant attention it gives to the future, directing most of its creative energy toward the past. Throughout the nineteenth century, including Chekhov's lifetime, expectations for the future were a given of social discourse and one of the main driving forces of the philosophy of art, whether it was the democrats' "bright future" or the modernists' leap toward the ideal. Strikingly absent from the recent discussion of the social, political, and literary situation in Russia are attempts to make projections into the future, however distant. The present period is certainly seen as a hardship to be endured, but it is the past and not the future that attracts the attention of the contemporary journalist and author. The postmodernist notion of nostalgia as the other side of postmodernist irony may help to explain this "looking back" of an entire culture. Postmodernism, in Linda Hutcheon's description, "confronts and contests any modernist discarding of the past in the name of the future. It suggests no search for transcendent timeless meaning, but rather a re-evaluation of and a dialogue with the past in the light of the present."[54] Of all the theoretical premises of postmodernism, this attention to the past at the expense of the future and even the present is among the few that actually have concrete representation in the majority of texts of contemporary Russian culture. The other is, of course, intertextuality, which "takes over" contemporary literature because it too depends on memory and is of an inherently nostalgic nature.

An intertextually constructed text arises from the tradition and contributes to its reevaluation. It relies on memory with a specifically nostalgic orientation, that is, memory of a reconstructed cultural past. The cultural myths that organize that memory bring forward those texts of a culture that allow the present to be constructed in relation to it. Whether the resulting image is that of unrealized hopes, or ironic distortion of the older texts themselves, culture is perceived as a horizontal space where past and present coexist and a dialogue is possible. The future, however, does not participate in it, since even though, theoretically, every new text is but a thread in the vast fabric of intertexts, in practice it is always an attempt to have the last word on the subject. It is not surprising that the literature of a society that moves forward with chronological time, while constantly looking back to an idealized past, should be created from the pieces of old texts. Nor is it surprising that it does not matter whether the writer upholds a nostalgic view of the past or attempts to deconstruct it. In any case, the process itself reveals the importance of the literature of the past for contemporary literature.

Igor Iarkevich's *Intellect, Sex, Literature* (*Um, Seks, Literatura*) (1998) is a typical postmodern attempt to deconstruct the literary past that, also typically, ends up asserting its importance. Iarkevich's deconstructive irony is not as subtle as Petrushevskaya's, and that makes his text even more characteristic of the contemporary cultural situation. Iarkevich poses his novel as the last word in the whole of Russian culture. It does indeed belong to the postliterary world inasmuch as it announces the death of literature. As a combustible blend of nostalgia and irony, Iarkevich's novel is a postmodern textual tour de force. He reconstructs the past as harmonious and uncontaminated, albeit naïve, but undercuts his own nostalgic reconstruction by blaming the cultural past for the deplorable present. Literature, in Iarkevich's novel, is the victim of the crisis of the 1990s, but it is also the reason for it. Thus, the first-person narrator delivers a long monologue on the hardships imposed by literature on the minds of Soviet men and women. From the vantage point of the cultural crisis of the 1990s he demands vengeance: "I take revenge [. . .], I cannot do anything about the cultural abyss of the '90s. It is uncontrollable. But I can go back and make trouble there, in the back."[55] And this he does: he goes back to the last decade of Soviet rule, and in its fascination with literature he finds the source of the present "cultural abyss." Hardly a single writer is spared a sarcastic mention, from Tolstoy to Pasternak, from Proust to Borges. However, Chekhov holds the central position in Iarkevich's exposé, and *The Cherry Orchard* is his ultimate Exhibit A. Iarkevich's novel demonstrates how a dialogue deteriorates into parody, thereby losing complexity and literary value, if the referent texts are posed explicitly and exclusively as targets.

The Cherry Orchard, the narrator rages, has made life impossible for him and his fellow Soviet citizens because it pretends to be full of intellect but is steeped in sex. One suspects that "intellect" and "sex," terms used both in these statements and in the title, are conceptual puzzles. The foreword, titled "The Choice," pits each against its ostensible counterpart: one must choose, we are told, between intellect and honor, between love and sex, and also between literature and real life. Most of the binary oppositions in the chapter (including mummy vs. daddy, day vs. night) are confused or break down into equations, but those that stand out and are part of the title—such as love and sex, intellect and honor, literature and the "real boring world"—allow for a tentative interpretation. Sex appears to stand for freedom and all that is forbidden in the tedium of Soviet cultural discourse. Literature appears to function as an escape from reality, and intellect as the will to survive the reality of Soviet life, at the expense of honor if necessary. According to Iarkevich, it was sex, in *The Cherry Orchard,* which seduced the Soviet people with the illusion of freedom. But what they really needed was intellect, the means to survive Soviet reality. The men and women of the 1990s are victims of *The Cherry Orchard* because like all classical literature, it offered illusions and temptations that were useless as means of survival and were therefore harmful. "The Cherry Orchard promised them intellect, but when they went to get it, *The Cherry Orchard* gave them only sex. *The Cherry Orchard* gave them sex but did not explicitly direct them. This sex was their undoing; there is too much sex in *The Cherry Orchard* but one has to know how to handle it."[56] Buried under the mass of expletives is a rather old sentiment. It was best expressed by Vasily Rozanov as early as 1918: Russian literature is responsible for the misfortunes of Russian history.

The novel offers a staggering amount of sex and gratuitous violence and no plot except in the first chapter, "Intellect and Sex," which presents something of a love story. This "love story"—or, rather, "sex story"—is an account of young actors developing different stage concepts for *The Cherry Orchard* at the end of the 1980s. The play is easily molded into various political statements. The hero and his girlfriend come up with many ways to stage *The Cherry Orchard* in order "to break the neck of Soviet rule." The first version is "The Cherry Hell" (the wordplay is on *sad-ad*); the next is "The Cherry Ass" (with a play on *sad-zad*). The young lovers consider setting the play in Stalin's prison camps, in Afghanistan's soldiers' barracks, in a women's prison, in a zoo, and more. They therefore consider an all-male, all-female, even an all-animal cast. One constant, regardless of the settings, is that amidst the hardship, Chekhovian spiritual values survive and triumph. The various productions' settings cover most of Soviet history. Characters get raped physically and symbolically, a common metaphor for the totalitarian regime, especially in recent feature films. Thus, Soviet history emerges as the rape of the Soviet people, a crime in which the government is aided by Russian literature. When the protagonists assert their control over staging the canonical *Cherry Orchard,* they create their own heroic narrative of resistance and in the process obtain an illusion of freedom. They use their intellect to recover honor, sex to reclaim their freedom from Soviet ideology, and literature to deal with an unacceptable reality. However, by the end of the 1990s the project's participants lose interest. The postliterary world of the 1990s knows that narratives can provide neither honor nor freedom. "The end of the century," the hero laments, "no longer believes *The Cherry Orchard* [. . .]. The twentieth century expected intellect and sex from culture. But did not get a fuck. Culture fed the century with promise of intellect and sex, promise of something kind of real and big. It promised and promised, but the century stayed hungry."[57]

That Iarkevich should choose Chekhov to play the part of the accused in this trial is characteristic: Chekhov's texts play a central role in Russian cultural memory and provide a link to the whole of the Russian classical tradition. A number of writers and cultural notables are allowed in as codefenders, but Chekhov is center stage: *The Cherry Orchard* is to blame for cultural, moral, and economic disintegration. It is responsible for young Ukrainian and Belarusian girls having to sell their bodies on Tverskaia Street: "You think the Ukrainian young body ended up on Tverskaia by no one's fault but its own. [. . .] [B]ut someone obviously gave it a push. An oblique push. And you know who? Tarkovsky? Would you stop with that Tarkovsky? Let him rest in peace. Vysotsky? Would you stop with that alcoholic? Let him too rest in peace. Brodsky? Not Brodsky either. Chekhov—he is the one who gave the push. Chekhov, Chekhov, Chekhov, Chekhov."[58]

Iarkevich's attack on literature is literary through and through. Like all intertextually based texts, his depends on the reader's familiarity with the writers and texts it exploits. It is possible that Iarkevich demolishes familiar literary hierarchies and attacks accepted literary authority in order to free the reader from intellectual oppression and start him and her on the road to overcoming all kinds of oppression. The novel indeed celebrates freedom from any kind of order or convention, yet, interestingly, the resulting chaos does not allow for a dialogue; it allows only for an angry tirade. The novel remains a witty attack on (cultural) authority, and as such it is not a truly independent work of art. Its polemical thrust and formal audacity is of interest only to other participants in the discussion of the cultural crisis of the nineties, the critics who dubbed Iarkevich "the last Russian writer." This kind of destruction from within, when a writer announces the death of literature, presents a purely postmodern paradox: "postmodernism finds itself constrained to resort to narrative even while it strives to disrupt it."[59] Thus, by its very existence, Iarkevich's novel perpetuates that which it asserts to be dead. In its postexistence, literature continues to produce narratives, among which none can really claim to be the last; only complete silence would accomplish the full stop. By "combating" texts (in Bourdieu's terms), Iarkevich participates in the process of canonical familiarization that ensures that the very texts he combats remain in the foreground of cultural memory. Writers, theater directors, authors of magazine articles, beauty salon owners, and advertisers, all operate within the same cultural discourse, the same system of references and cultural metaphors. They contribute to the system as much as they are governed by it. Commercial uses of cultural metaphors rely on and perpetuate cultural familiarization. Similarly, literary intertextual dialogue capitalizes on canonical familiarization, and it ensures that cultural metaphors remain embedded in a narrative and thus perpetuates the canon. Through this interdependence, cultural myths and metaphors bridge ruptures, ensure continuity, and endure through times of cultural crisis.

CHAPTER 6

The Lady with a Dog

No More Illusions

At the present time [love] is unsatisfying, it gives much less than one expects.

—Chekhov's Notebook

CHEKHOV ONCE CHARACTERIZED his *Seagull* as the play with (among other things) "five tons of love." None of the play's characters, however, can claim happiness in love. The narrator of "About Love" delivers one of the most passionate statements on the subject in Chekhov as he relates the story of his love's failure. Nikitin, in "The Teacher of Literature," recoils from his wife almost in disgust less than a year into the marriage. In Chekhov's stories, love proves again and again to be an illusion, a phantom, at best a dream. It is a memory of a lost opportunity or a dream of future happiness, but almost never a present reality. "The Lady with a Dog" (1899) is in this respect unique: its characters "fall properly, really in love," and if it does not make them indubitably happy, it makes them better. The story's unique, albeit cautiously positive, view of love as having absolute value can be explained by the fact that Chekhov had already met the love of his life when he wrote it. It is also possible that he never refuted the possibility of "real" love, and, as with all other prescriptive attitudes toward reality, he rejected the naïve, vulgar, and ultimately simplifying view of it. In any case, "The Lady with a Dog," one of Chekhov's best stories, is among the most powerful and influential in Russian and world literature since his time.[1] Like the cherry orchard, the lady with a dog has become a metaphor, one denoting love encumbered with obstacles that are as tragic as they are mundane. Unlike the large-scale intelligentsia myth that defines a whole class, the-lady-with-a-dog metaphor has narrower applications because it concerns one's private emotions and choices. It is nevertheless a very Chekhovian metaphor: melancholic yet hopeful; unique yet recognizable in a multitude of individual stories.

Two overlapping motifs structure "The Lady with a Dog." One is the motif of love's mystical, life-altering power, and the other is the story's distinctively Chekhovian juxtaposition of the romantic and the vulgar, the poetic and the everyday. Lyudmila Petrushevskaya's stories "The Lady with the Dogs" and "Downhill" develop these two groups of motifs and subject the artistic and philosophical issues of Chekhov's story to a trial by her poetics of closure. Petrushevskaya's treatment of love, as well as of all ostensibly absolute values exalted by Russian classic literature, opens up into the discussion of a specific time period—the end of the twentieth century—when the particular political, economic, and cultural situation affects even ostensibly fundamental and unchanging human emotions. Petrushevskaya seems to be testing these against her times and her poetics; she is rewriting Chekhov's famous story, and the result is not so much a dialogue as an angry statement.

"The Lady with the Dogs" (*Dama s sobakami,* 1990), a part of the *Requiems* cycle, presents in less than three pages the life and death of a woman who liked to take care of stray dogs and whose only companion was her own dog. Even though the text itself does not establish any obvious connections, the title suggests an intertextual link with Chekhov's story "The Lady with a Dog" (*Dama s sobachkoi*). What is more, Chekhov's story is itself engaged in an intertextual dialogue with Tolstoy's *Anna Karenina.* By 1899, when "The Lady with a Dog" was written, Chekhov had largely rejected Tolstoy's philosophical teachings; nevertheless, he continued the literary dialogue in several of his late stories. The choice of title for a text is the easiest way for an author to announce intertextual intent and direct the reader toward the source-text or texts. The reader may therefore not be surprised by the title of "The Lady with the Dogs," but he or she will be hard-pressed to find the connection between the story's intertextual title and its protagonist, who is utterly unlike the Chekhovian heroine. A close look at Petrushevskaya's "The Lady with the Dogs" instead reveals some surprising, but definite, parallels not so much with Chekhov's story as with *Anna Karenina.* Although Petrushevskaya is following the line of dialogue started by Chekhov, her objective is even more ambitious than adding another link to the great intertextual chain: by retracing the intertextual links embedded in Chekhov's story, she intrudes on the latter's dialogue with Tolstoy. She picks up the main issues addressed by the two classics, relocates their characters by placing them in the Russian reality of the end of the twentieth century, and makes a statement of her own. Petrushevskaya's nameless lady with the dogs shares many features with Anna Karenina but is presented under Chekhov's title and accompanied by his heroine's dog, while being subjected by Petrushevskaya to a contemporary version of sexual passion, social decline, divorce, and suicide.

Immediate critical reactions to Petrushevskaya's stories in literary journals invariably touch upon the author's attitude toward the human tragedies she describes. She is generally considered to present an "unfeeling" stance toward the events presented, but opinions vary about the reasons behind her stance. Critics are evenly split: either Petrushevskaya's "harshness is saturated with pain" and the reader is forced into cathartic recognition of responsibility for everyone's pain, or this harshness signals a "certain indifference on the part of the author," which eventually results in the reader's "getting used to indifference."[2] The debate may, in my view, be resolved thus: in most Petrushevskaya texts there is a narrator who is clearly an authorial construction. This narrator is not openly contradicted by an authorial voice offering "corrections," however, or any other voice setting "things right." The implied author does not interfere, but her presence is nevertheless felt. Thus, while Petrushevskaya's silent, implied author may be seen as remaining within the humanistic tradition of Russian literature, her constructed narrators lack human compassion, crossing over into a sphere of callous indifference to suffering and degradation. Numerous critical discussions of stories such as "Night Time" (*Vremia noch'*), "Our Crowd" (*Svoi krug*), and "Such a Girl" (*Takaia devochka*) address this kind of apparently single-voiced narrative where any compassionate authoritative voice seems absent; and they point to the vital importance of unmasking the narrator as crucial to a proper understanding of the stories.[3] However, this story's proper understanding relies on the readers' response to its intertextual nature rather than to its narrator. A dramatized or unreliable narrator presupposes distance between him or her and the implied author. In "The Lady with the Dogs," as in many *Requiem* stories, Petrushevskaya withdraws so far from any authorial position that her absence is, in fact, total—apart from the title of the story and the intertextual links it establishes. I am suggesting that the effect of this technique is to force the reader to become the missing counterpart to the narrator's voice, to do the job of the implied author, as it were. In the case of "The Lady with the Dogs," the only nonnarratorial perspective that the reader gets is the intertextual contextualization of this contemporary story in terms of classic pre-texts. He, or she, is drawn into the dialogue between Tolstoy and Chekhov with the expectation of finding a third voice there, the voice of Petrushevskaya's story. In that case, there would be three conflicting attitudes toward love, life, and death, each of which reflects a different historical epoch. Yet, Petrushevskaya's implied author refuses to provide a discernible position to this clash of attitudes, even though she clearly refers to Tolstoy-Chekhov dialogue and inserts herself into it. That absence forces the reader to formulate a position which the author refuses to indicate by any other means, or at least to select one from the alternatives thus suggested—provided the reader has the literary competence to do so.

The Tolstoy-Chekhov dialogue as conducted between *Anna Karenina* and "The Lady with the Dog," has, of course, been noted repeatedly and critically dealt with many times;[4] what critics of Petrushevskaya's oeuvre have so far failed to see is that she adds a radically new dimension to this dialogue by sharply negating both of their positions through the intrusion of a third voice, the voice of her indifferent narrator. In formulating a statement on life in the present through allusions to literature of the past, she creates a juxtaposition of epochs that clearly favors older times without her having to imply this in any "authorial" way. Most readers are likely to mourn the keen interest in moral issues that the nineteenth-century texts demonstrate—in however different ways—and that contemporary reality seems to have lost, substituting moral indifference for earnest engagement. Having withdrawn authorial direction, Petrushevskaya leaves her readers at a loss and challenges them to engage in a search for a counterpoint to indifference. Since her story is intertextually constructed and the implied author's voice is absent, the voices of two classic authors provide the missing counterpoint to the narrator's voice. As the reader follows Petrushevskaya down the intertextual lane, he or she faces the gap between the narrator's vision of the world and the time-honored humanism of classic Russian literature.

As has been pointed out, Chekhov's portrayal of ordinary people has the effect of "broadening the social side of a given conflict."[5] "The Lady with a Dog" certainly expresses this author's "avowal of independence from traditional treatments" in regard to the theme of adultery,[6] juxtaposing his portrayal of an extramarital affair to Tolstoy's and, in effect, challenging Tolstoy's conservative approach to the themes of love and morality.[7] Chekhov brings Tolstoy's grand tragedy down to earth: in contrast to a strikingly beautiful society lady and a dashing army officer who are led to a tragic end by their fateful passion, his characters are ordinary people (a bank employee and a middle-ranking civil servant's wife in the provinces) facing love as the unexpected outcome of a banal summer affair. One scene in particular is crucial in sustaining and making obvious the intertextual link between Chekhov's and Tolstoy's texts, as well as the two authors' different stance in regard to adultery. It is the seduction scene, in which both Annas experience excruciating guilt and grief for their lost moral integrity. In this scene Chekhov brings Tolstoy's theme to its culmination and also turns away from Tolstoy in order to concentrate on his own artistic and philosophical goals.

Chekhov's seduction (perhaps it should be called the *after-seduction*) scene opens the same way as Tolstoy's: resolutely after the fact. The focus is on the characters' reaction to what has happened between them, which determines the function of the scene in each text. While the two women behave in very similar ways—with remorse and self-condemnation—the men do not. Thomas Winner points out that "unlike Vronsky, Gurov appears cynical. When faced with Anna's shame, he takes her unhappiness lightly and eats watermelon while she weeps."[8] Nabokov singled out this moment as well: for him, the image of Gurov calmly taking a slice of watermelon is a "realistic detail—another typically Chekhovian technique."[9] I would argue that this detail is the culmination of the Tolstoyan line of the story and one of the story's most important symbols. Anna's monologue imploring Gurov not to despise her mirrors that of Anna Karenina who "felt herself so criminal and guilty that the only thing left for her was to humble herself and beg forgiveness";[10] Anna Sergeevna cries out, "I am a wicked, fallen woman. I despise myself."[11] Annoyed, Gurov even thinks that she might be playing a part, the part, obviously, of a fallen woman. Indeed, if Anna Sergeevna is, subconsciously, following a literary model, the most famous and readily available one would be that of Anna Karenina. If Gurov sees Anna as repeating someone else's lines, he is free to not really hear her, to dismiss her monologue as theatrical and therefore inauthentic.

The pathos of this scene, so alien to Chekhov's style, is justified solely by his objective of entering into a dialogue with Tolstoy's novel, and it is consequently undercut in a very Chekhovian manner by Gurov's prosaic gesture of slicing the watermelon. There is more to this detail than realistic effect though: with this gesture Chekhov's story symbolically parts ways with Tolstoy's novel and rejects its message. In *Anna Karenina*, Vronsky becomes "infected" (to use a Tolstoyan term) with Anna's guilt and fear as he is invariably influenced by her emotions throughout the first part of the novel. This time, while Anna is overcome by humiliation and guilt, he feels "what a murderer must feel when he looks at the body he has deprived of life." The equation of adulterous sex with murder refers first of all to Vronsky's feelings and actions:

> But despite all the murderer's horror before the murdered body, he had to *cut* this body into pieces and hide it, he had to make use of what the murderer had gained by his murder. And as the murderer falls upon this body with animosity, as if with passion, drags it off and *cuts* it up, so he covered her face and shoulders with kisses.[12]

The twice-repeated "cut" is the detail Chekhov picks up in his story, but his character's cutting is decidedly literal, mundane, and practical, without a trace of pathos. Bored with Anna's speech, and seeing a watermelon on the table, "Gurov *cut* a slice for himself and started eating it without hurry."[13] Thus the scene includes both conspicuous similarities with Tolstoy's scene and the no less striking deviation from it. When Tolstoy equates adultery with murder to make his point, he goes to an extreme; when Chekhov shows Gurov becoming bored by Anna's guilt, he goes to the opposite extreme: not only is Gurov completely immune to Anna's feelings, but he sees their adulterous encounter as a most ordinary event on a par with the consumption of food.

This dramatic difference in the men's reaction to adultery and to the women's expression of guilt highlights the differences between Chekhov's and Tolstoy's artistic and philosophical objectives. Unlike Tolstoy, Chekhov underplays the moral aspect of the characters' situation. Just as his setting emphasizes the characters' ordinariness, so his tone shifts from Tolstoy's high moral indignation to the subtle lyricism of the love story that develops after the seduction. Tolstoy posits the contrast between love and passion through two male characters: the "infected" passionate Vronsky is contrasted to the healthy and compassionate Levin. Gurov incorporates both attitudes; he, in fact, makes the transition in the course of the story from purely sexual infatuation to compassionate love, thus proving false Tolstoy's "either/or" formula.

The transition that is far from begun in this scene will be complete in the story's last. In both scenes the frame, in which Gurov sees Anna—and, later, himself—defines a stage in his development. In the seduction scene, before Chekhov's Anna even starts to speak, Gurov has been contemplating his past affairs, trying to categorize Anna among his many lovers: as careless, good-natured, hysterical, capricious, cold, and so on. He cannot find a category for her and finally settles on a cultural reference: "Her features lengthened and drooped, and her long hair hung mournfully on either side of her face. She assumed a pose of dismal meditation, like a repentant sinful woman in some old painting."[14] Gurov is following a habitual impulse not to become emotionally involved, and it is easier to do so if he assumes Anna's words to be false and invests her pose with staginess and theatricality. Seeing Anna as a woman in a picture, Gurov frames Anna, just as Tolstoy frames Anna Karenina, several times in the course of his novel. Tolstoy repeatedly employs the device of ekphrasis. As Amy Mandelker has pointed out, by "framing" the character, Tolstoy emphasizes the problematic nature of the Western tradition of portraying women as the object of the male gaze and, in general, of portraiture as a closed and final version of a person. Every description of Anna's portraits in Tolstoy's novel represents someone's vision of her, someone's version of her essence. Gurov's gaze too denies Anna individuality and voice. The trope of framing, however, puts the lady with a dog in the context not only of personal but also of cultural experience. The image of the sinful woman, while referring to the biblical figure, also invokes its literary representations. In Tolstoy's novel, biblical references (starting with the epigraph) are linked to Anna's transformation from a "good wife" into an unrepentant sinner.[15] When Chekhov's character describes a real woman in terms of a portrait, his perception is likewise mediated: his reference is to "the cultural pose of the 'sinful' woman." Coming together with other intertextual links to Tolstoy's novel, and in light of the importance of the pictorial in *Anna Karenina,* Chekhov's technique allows us to read the "classical painting" as a classic novel, that is, as a reference to *the* literary image of a sinning woman—Tolstoy's masterpiece.

Gurov's transition from infatuation to love is a shift from the Vronsky-like mindset of passion to the Levin-like one of compassion, and this transition involves a visual image. Levin's meeting with Anna, the only one in the novel, is central to his psychological maturity. When Levin, just before meeting Anna, contemplates Anna's portrait and then sees her "live," as she "really" is, it initializes a far-reaching inner change that is the beginning of his subsequent spiritual conversion. The scene, in which the portrait and the real person are juxtaposed, in Mandelker's analysis presents the beginning of his "tolerance for the imperfection of human lives and his resulting compassion."[16] Unlike the artists who have "finalized" Anna, Levin leaves her "free." He departs from Anna's house feeling pity for her, a feeling that his wife immediately mistakes for love. Kitty may be too hasty in her conclusion that Levin "ha[d] fallen in love with that nasty woman," but she is fundamentally right in linking compassion and love: in Tolstoy's arrangement of values, only compassion, as opposed to passion, signals true feeling.

Significantly, Levin sees Anna's portrait before she enters the room, and he performs an action contrary to Gurov's, an un-framing, so to speak. He sees Anna "stepping out of the [portrait's] frame in a brilliant light," sees "not a painting but a lovely living woman."[17] Gurov's moment of framing, in contrast, is far from including compassion; it is rather a result of his inability to see a living woman. He puts her in a pictorial and "framing" context to ease and bracket off his own discomfort. He remains the free wielder of the gaze that forces Anna Sergeevna into the position of an object of interpretation, the position in which she has no voice. At the end of the story, however, Gurov has learned the same lesson as Levin—by looking at himself. He sees himself in a mirror: his gaze is directed back at him and prompts self-examination.[18] He realizes at that moment that he is not the free agent he thought he was when gazing at his crying mistress, but that both he and Anna are "framed" by circumstances, their situation, encroaching old age, and the passage of time—that there is no such thing as classification and objectification, but only a shared human condition. The mirror, the most faithful of portraits, forces Gurov to look inside himself, and there he finds compassion and tenderness for another by transferring self-pity to empathy. Looking at and into himself, he accepts that he no longer can bracket off life's challenges. He finally accepts love with all its consequences, which would have been impossible for the Gurov of the beginning of the story.

Furthermore, Gurov's ultimate response is emblematic of Chekhov's response to Tolstoy's view of morality in general. Chekhov renders Tolstoy's moralistic and social message ineffective by assigning inherent value to love. Whereas Tolstoy subordinates love to moral and social obligations, Chekhov acknowledges the difficulty of his characters' situation without criminalizing their breaking the rules of conventional morality. He operates with a moral code wholly different from Tolstoy's: devoid of the traditional religious element, this is a moral code whereby marriages for money or convenience, like those of both Annas and Gurov, are truly immoral, more immoral perhaps than the adultery that results from such marriages. This view of morality as a private struggle full of compromises is very different from Tolstoy's maximalist demand for complete hold on the world and its truths. With the subtlety that earned him the title of a writer without principles, Chekhov cancels out Tolstoy's moralizing by sidestepping rather than disputing it. Tolstoy recognized this by judging the story "on the other side of good."[19] Chekhov, however, was no more inclined to be influenced by this kind of criticism than Gurov is affected by Anna's pathetic plea.

Thus Chekhov is interested in the development of his characters' relationship and in its effect on them. The relationship is not over at the end of the story, and its outcome is difficult to predict. The only definite conclusion is that "love has changed them both." While Anna Karenina's story is unequivocally tragic, the other Anna's often-proclaimed unhappiness is subject to doubt. Karenina's fate is sealed and predicted in the first scene in which she appears. Chekhov's story's ending is famously open, in line with the heuristic nature of his poetics. And this is where Petrushevskaya comes in. In contrast to Chekhov's poetics of openness, hers might be called the poetics of closure. The raw material of her texts are dysfunctional families, broken hopes, abandoned children, sick mothers, misery and destitution, all of which produce an effect of unrelieved gloom.[20] This vision of the world allows neither for lyricism nor for moralizing. Nor does it allow for an open ending that at least theoretically offers the possibility of a positive outcome. In her "lady-and-dog story," she picks up where Chekhov left his story open and provides the ending—one that does not replicate Tolstoy's either, however.

Chekhov's story ends with the word "beginning": "the most complicated and difficult part was only just beginning." Vladimir Kataev has commented on the tension between the motifs of "ending" and "beginning" which informs the end of the story in the same way as the tension between "it seemed" and "it turned out" (*kazalos'/okazalos'*) propels its development throughout.[21] Jan van der Eng elaborates on the function of the word *end,* in particular: "the whole point of the story is, in fact, centered in the ambiguity with which the word 'end' is echoed through it."[22] He maintains that there are two kinds of "ends," opposing each other: a positive one, or the end of the protagonists' predicament, signaling the beginning of a new life, and a negative one—the end of the affair itself. The complexity of the motifs of end and beginning puts them in play against each other, contributing to the story's open-endedness.

Petrushevskaya subverts the dynamics of beginnings and endings: she foregrounds and manipulates both conventional expectations and Chekhov's use of beginnings and endings. She opens her story about the "lady with the dogs" with a pointed accumulation of the past tense "ended" and the verb denoting the ultimate end—death: "She had already died, and he had already died, their heinous affair had ended, and, interestingly enough, it had ended long before their death."[23] The sentence starts with the twice-repeated verb *died,* goes on to the also repeated *ended,* and ends with the noun *death.* This semantic overflow of "end" words, and the finality of the past perfect verb tenses in the very first sentence, clearly manifest the author's intention to set a morbid mood in and rigid boundaries to her story. Unlike Chekhov's, which ends with a beginning, her story has ended before it begins. Petrushevskaya's poetics of closure are in full force here: the character is dead before we learn anything about her; the subsequent portrayal is as finalizing and objectifying as only a posthumous one can be.

The dominant feature in the description of the lady with the dogs is the use of the past tense. The events of the story are doubly removed:

she had already died, and what is described happened long before that: "Long before, about ten years before, they had already broken up, he lived somewhere, and she came and settled at the Retreat for Creative Professionals (*Dom tvorcheskikh rabotnikov*), as if for show, alone and with a dog."[24] In the following passage, the past tense *was* and the words *memory* and *to remember* indicate the erosion of her social status:

> . . . the old memory of her was still alive there, of her escapades and scandals, of their drinking-bouts for the world to see, of the fact that she was the wife of a distinguished artist—but the stress is on the 'was.' However, they recalled that she was also a daughter of a distinguished government official of the past: and, powerless to do anything, they provided her with an apartment and she moved in there with her dog.[25]

The narrator shows remarkable knowledge of the lady's past and present situation, although she admits to having heard most of the facts from others, emphasizing that the lady's privileged status and scandalous life have held her at the center of public attention. Like Karenina, who in Dolly's assessment is "the wife of one of the most important personalities in Petersburg and a Petersburg *grande dame*,"[26] she once belonged to the highest circles of Soviet society. The artistic circles form a new, twentieth-century version of the glamorous high society in which Karenina shone a hundred years earlier. And like Karenina after her break with society, she too is now a pariah, an unwelcome intruder.

Once the reader retraces the line to Tolstoy's novel via Chekhov's story, the similarities between the lady with the dogs and Anna Karenina emerge with great clarity: there is in both texts a woman of remarkable beauty, a passionate and public love affair, an estranged child, people's contempt, and finally a suicide attempt. The beauty of the lady with the dogs is described in the past tense, as is everything else concerning her, and is contrasted with the condition of "the lady" in her postglamorous state, which the narrator knows best. The details of that description correspond exactly, in negated form, to Tolstoy's description of Anna:

> Her looks had changed a lot since the time of the divorce: her at one

> time full bosom now sagged, her hands were withered like potato shoots, the hair that she used to wear proudly over her straight back, she now hid under a wrapper, and all she had left was her love for trinkets.[27]

Compare this description to Anna Karenina's "full shoulders and bosom . . . and her rounded arms with their very small, slender hands"; her "full arms with bracelets on them, firm neck with its string of pearls"; her "holding herself extremely erect, as always"; "her once proud, gay, but now shame-stricken head"; "her beautiful, ring-covered hands."[28] The details are central to both descriptions: the full body, the thick hair, a proud and very straight posture, and the jewelry. In Petrushevskaya's story, both the beauty and the pride are things of the past, and the jewelry has become symbolically cheap. The suicide attempt is also very public, perhaps even staged, because the lady called several women acquaintances informing them that she is going to hang herself. Not surprisingly, they called for an ambulance which arrived just in time to save the lady's life. The tragedy is trivialized, modeled to fit the reality of the immediate post-Soviet era: the love is gone, the suicide is unsuccessful and somewhat embarrassing; the lady's beauty and life are destroyed by time, gossip, and moral as well as physical decay.

Petrushevskaya's reader is denied access to "the lady's" inner world. She remains an object of external description and a hostile, totally finalizing gaze throughout the short narrative. In this manner Petrushevskaya subverts one of the basic realistic techniques—psychologism. Tolstoy's novel is the exemplary model of nineteenth-century psychologism that penetrates into a character's inner world in order to illuminate in detail every motive, however conflicting, behind any and every action. Chekhov does not, of course, follow Tolstoy's omniscient approach; he nevertheless combines carefully selected details with occasional glimpses into the characters' thoughts to recreate their psychological state. Tolstoy attempts to "tell" and Chekhov to "show" (to use Lubbock's terminology) the psychological state of their respective characters. In both cases, albeit to varying degrees, the reader is allowed into the characters' thoughts and moods. Petrushevskaya's narrator does not gain even a glimpse into her protagonist's soul, and the narrator's authority is further undermined by the fact that gossip is the sole source of her knowledge. Petrushevskaya's commonly unreliable narrators freely make assumptions about characters' states of mind, motives, and thoughts—here there is not even the slightest attempt to verify even the most unreliable information.

Since the narration consistently undermines and ridicules the lady's life story, she remains both an object and a victim of the narration. When she does speak, the few words she utters are projected through other people's accounts and are interpreted (or misinterpreted) according to the narrator. The narrator's voice is the collective voice of gossip, notoriously unreliable and always mean. It poses the lady's actions and behavior as hypocritical and even suggests that her suicide attempt was faked. The only scene presenting the lady's words as direct speech and without an overtly deforming interpretation is the passage in which she brings back to the Retreat a dirty and hungry dog, one of the many she has taken under her wing. We overhear her addressing her own "socially conscious" and "proper" dog, which looks embarrassed trotting along with such a lowly creature:

> [S]he lectured her poodle that he had no right to turn away this miserable creature, this carrion, if someone wanted to give her some food. Everybody has the right to live, yelled (spoke softly, she thought) this Brigitte Bardot, one mustn't turn away anyone. Do not turn away, lest you be turned away![29]

The lady seems to be advocating pity toward those less fortunate. It is characteristic, however, that the narrator represents the only character to do so in the story as crazy, ridiculous, and unable to elicit pity or respect from others. Loud, deranged, and arrogant, she is as unwelcome in the Retreat's respectable environment as the stray dog she smuggles in. Her gesture of compassion is further undermined—at least by the narrator—when in the next paragraph her love of dogs is juxtaposed to her hatred of children: "by the way, she hated children and was constantly involved in scandalous quarrels with her rather adult child." The dogs serve as a preferable substitute for people[30] because they "are the only creatures that never scolded her"[31] or, in other words, never talked back. The lady attempts to monologically rule her world in the same way the narrator rules the larger world of the story. But the narrator's voice, louder and more spiteful than hers, intrudes into the lady's story and silences her point of view, in retaliation perhaps for the latter's intrusion into the proper world of the Retreat. If the reader feels inclined to distrust the narrator, he or she gets no help from the implied author: no other information or perspective is offered. In the absence of authorial direction, the narrator's perspective, with its obvious dislike of her subject, dominates the story.

The Lady's little speech to her own snobbish dog also introduces the motif of passing judgment, one of the most important in Tolstoy's novel and emphatically absent in Chekhov's story. On a critical evening in Karenina's life, the evening of the ball where she falls in love with Vronsky, Tolstoy has her say: "No, I will not cast a stone."[32] The phrase alludes to the scene in the Gospel (John 8: 1–11) of the woman taken in sin: "[Jesus] said to them, 'He that is without sin among you, let him first cast a stone at her.'" The phrase used by the lady with the dogs is modeled on the biblical "judge not, that ye be not judged" and has similar connotations. Both phrases, about casting a stone and about judging, have acquired in the language of the twentieth-century a quasiproverbial function. They nevertheless retain their biblical associations even as elements of nonreligious discourse. Petrushevskaya's lady's words, with their religious overtones, thus introduce the motif of who is entitled to judge a fellow being. In *Anna Karenina,* this phrase is one of the details foreshadowing the time when Anna becomes the target of many a stone. Tolstoy draws a clear distinction between God's judgment and that of society, but he nevertheless subjects Anna to both. Chekhov's characters, in contrast, replace abstract moral judgment with concrete private fears. Gurov keeps looking around while kissing Anna on the street; and while Anna is not afraid of God's judgment, she is incessantly afraid of incurring Gurov's disrespect. In Petrushevskaya's story, the narration itself is the voice of universal condemnation. Potential relief comes from the fact that while the narrator condemns the lady with the dogs, the reader is free to condemn the narrator for her refusal or inability to empathize. Her meanness and cruelty make her suspect; her voice rings too ostentatiously loud. This reaction on the part of the reader would therefore be produced by the *absence* of the conventional way of affecting the reader through the unmasking of the narrator. She unmasks herself by being given absurdly unlimited freedom to judge, making the reader feel uneasy, pushing him or her to search for a different viewpoint.

Because narrative remains a weapon aimed at the lady, the story emerges as devoid of human compassion. The people surrounding the protagonist do not have any pity for her; she, in turn, feels compassion only for stray dogs. And after her death, the narrator concludes that "not a single dog took pity on her" (*ni odna sobaka ee ne pozhalela*). That is, of course, idiomatic speech, but the "dogs" spoken of here are clearly not only an allusion to humans but also a reference to "real dogs," specifically the stray ones that the "Lady" had taken care of. The play on the differences in sound and meaning of dogs in the two stories' titles is brought to a conclusion here: having one proper dog as a companion is socially acceptable, as it was for Chekhov's lady with her little dog (diminutive *s sobachkoi*) at another resort. But the very coarseness of the phrase "the lady with the dogs" (plural and not diminutive *s sobakami*) demotes her to the position of ridicule, the position in which she is too removed for emotional involvement. The idiomatic "not a single dog" finally strips the lady not only of human, but also of her dogs', compassion. The atmosphere of the story is that of a world in which nothing is valued and no one is pitied; thus, even a suicide attempt is interpreted as a farce and a scandalous trick, and the notion of faithful dogs mourning their good masters is plainly ridiculed. While in Chekhov's stories human interaction based on love and compassion is rare and precious, in Petrushevskaya's it does not exist. This significant absence accounts for the terrifying vision of the world that emerges in her stories. While Chekhov often makes the lack of human connection a leading motif of his stories, intimating that this is an important source of human unhappiness and implying that it can be overcome, at least by some people, for Petrushevskaya's narrators it is an issue that does not exist. They do not ask themselves whether miscommunication exists since they have no epistemological uncertainties.

In the last paragraph of the story, the void created by the absence of compassion is especially apparent as the narrator arrives at the point in her story that deals with the lady's death. She calmly states the facts, or lack of facts: "No one knows, however, how she really died, on what hospital bed she expired, probably from cancer and in pain"; and she explains: "somehow it really had to end, this hideous life, crippled by who knows what." She then wonders what happened to the dog and whether it was allowed to wail over its owner's grave, before dismissing the thought by referring to the times: "no one will allow something like that in our times."[33] What are these times, one may ask, when not even a dog is allowed to howl at the grave of its dead owner and a human being dies alone and in pain in a hospital bed? The answer must be that these are the times neither of Tolstoy's nor of Chekhov's Anna. The questions that preoccupied Tolstoy and Chekhov are now far less urgent than they once were, and their ideas on love and death as important events in human life are suspect. The Anna Karenina of our time, as the invisible author behind the narrator constructs it, is not even able to commit suicide to end her torments and must go on living, losing the last shreds of dignity; similarly, the lady with a dog has outlived her beauty and her love and is left with nothing but a dog—but even that creature is, significantly, "the last of its kind,"[34] the last descendant of Chekhov's lady's companion.

It is clear that the loud, arrogant, and slightly crazy lady with the dogs carries no resemblance to Anna Sergeevna. Still, her story bears the title of Anna Sergeevna's story and opens with words that unequivocally connect it to Chekhov's, even when stating the opposite. Petrushevskaya's title announces that her story of the end relates to the dominant ethical tradition of nineteenth-century literature, even when it is denied (by the narrator). Chekhov, the last classic of the nineteenth century, tones down Tolstoy's story of unfaithful passion by bringing it into his times and making compassion its center. He brackets off the social and moral side of the situation and concentrates on love as a force capable of changing one for the better.[35] Petrushevskaya's "absent author," in turn, denies love and beauty any inherent value by having her character outlive them both and turn into a lonely and unappealing creature. In her story, compassion is denied even to and by dogs, and as in Tolstoy's novel, the motif of passing judgment is central. However, in Tolstoy, that is *one* of the forces contributing to Karenina's transformation into an angry, unreasonable, vengeful, albeit still pitiable, figure, while in Petrushevskaya, it is the only "moral" force operating in a world devoid of feeling. Everything else is discarded as fleeting and useless. Petrushevskaya, in effect, attempts to show the end not only of the love and life story of her protagonist, but of a whole cultural tradition that exalted morality, love, family, compassion, and other axioms of meaningfulness in human existence, even when it revalued and reinterpreted these. In her vision of contemporary reality, these values are deemed to be illusions, wherefore they cannot be reinterpreted or revalued. No one among the present-day writers in Russia better fits the description given by Lev Shestov of Chekhov's poetics: "Stubbornly, sadly, monotonously, during all the years of his literary activity, nearly a quarter of century long, Chekhov was doing one thing only: by one means or another he was killing human hopes."[36]

Chekhov's dialogue with Tolstoy in "The Lady with a Dog," however, is one of many examples to the contrary: it is, of course, not human hopes that Chekhov is contesting but a prescriptive attitude toward the complexity of human life and emotions. The passion of Tolstoy's heroine leads her to ruin; the love of Chekhov's characters gives meaning to their existence. Petrushevskaya seems to be skeptical about both possibilities. In "The Lady with the Dogs," her narrator seems to side with Tolstoy in condemning stormy passions that lead to fateful consequences, only to go a step further and deprive the character she tells us about even of the compassion allowed Anna Karenina.

By withholding anything but the most indirect authorial presence that serves as a counterperspective to the narrator's interpretation of events, namely, the intertextual linkages demonstrated above, Petrushevskaya creates a world of voids that the reader is forced to fill somehow. One reason why, most probably, a reader would distrust the narrator and her vision of reality is his or her experience of the Russian literary tradition with its emphasis on humanistic values, the experience called forth by the story's intertextual thrusts and so conspicuously lacking in the narrator. The psychological depth of Tolstoy's novel, the compassionate lyricism of Chekhov's story—these are the elements Petrushevskaya evokes to create a counterpoint to her narrator's loud voice. They serve as a reminder of the lost world of the nineteenth-century and contribute to the melancholy inherent in a requiem. Petrushevskaya's cycle *Requiems* mourns a debate discontinued and a quest terminated—in short, a past irrevocably lost except as echoed in remembrance.

"The Lady with the Dogs" thrusts the title recalling Chekhov's famous story in the reader's face and challenges him or her to find the connection. The title—misleading as it is since Chekhov's story is not the final destination—nevertheless serves to direct the reader toward Russian classical literature. While the 1996 story "Downhill" (*S gory*) does not similarly announce its intertextual nature in the title, it nevertheless displays striking similarities to Chekhov's "The Lady with a Dog" in its plot, its descriptions of characters, and its mood. Unlike "The Lady with the Dogs," "Downhill" does not at first glance oppose the cultural tradition to which Chekhov's story belongs. On the contrary, it seems to contribute to it since its subject is love as an unexpected outcome of a summer fling. But while it begins with Chekhov, it too ends with departure and challenges Chekhov's view of the transformative power of love.[37]

Like Chekhov's story, "Downhill" starts at a sea resort and ends in two winter cities. The characters of both stories are ordinary, even commonplace, people who start a summer romance and unexpectedly walk into real love. When their stay in Crimea is over, both return to their families but are unable to forget each other. They are allowed a brief moment of reunion. The build-up of parallels in the text throws a dramatic highlight on Petrushevskaya's ending, significantly different from Chekhov's.

The plot parallels are supported by the parallel details of the characters' descriptions, which either exaggerate or are the direct opposite of Chekhov's. Here is Chekhov's heroine in the theater scene: "this *small* woman, lost in the provincial crowd, in no way remarkable, holding a *vulgar* lorgnette in her hand. . . ."[38] And here is the woman in Petrushevskaya's story: "this woman, who looked offensively *vulgar* so vulgar in fact that it caught the eye"; "*small,* even on high heels."[39] The adjective *vulgar,* which in Chekhov refers to Anna Sergeevna metonymically, through an object belonging to her, in Petrushevskaya's story applies directly to the character and becomes, at least for a time, her main feature. Anna's vulgar lorgnette and her ordinariness are important elements enabling Chekhov to counteract the pathos of Tolstoy's novel. Petrushevskaya exaggerates the trait and thus links, while at the same time contrasting, her heroine with Chekhov's. She actually stands out in the crowd because of the vulgarity of her looks; the vulgarity cancels out the ordinariness and becomes the reason why this heroine attracts attention.

The following description of the female protagonist is remarkably full of details of clothing and makeup but devoid of facial or body features:

> And here is a sight for you: a too-short haircut, with some sort of hairdresser springs and curlicues, a cheap perm, dead hair after the recently done cold wave; also, plucked eyebrows dyed blue-black, and a garishly painted mouth—likewise on the vulgar side. Beauty from the drugstore, one-twenty a jar, as the saying goes. A short skirt, a pair of sandals of the cheapest and tawdriest variety, but

with some pretension to fashion—the wording is of the nineteenth century but fairly precise: with an ambition to keep up with the Joneses and be anyone's equal.[40]

In Chekhov's story, Gurov performs the function of defining Anna Sergeevna's position when looking at her "expression, the way she walked, her dress." In other words, by the common signs of social and marital status he concludes that "she was upper class, married. . . ."[41] Chekhov's narrator throughout the story concentrates on Gurov's point of view; in Petrushevskaya's story both the heroine and her beau are denied their voices and are equally objects in the narrator's design. The narrator of this story, like that of "The Lady with the Dogs," is an observer, and the characters are the objects of her attention and analysis: objects without their own voices. One of the effects of this detached "objectifying" narration is that the characters do not have names: the narrator assigns names to them. The nameless character is a dehumanized object of desire in Chekhov's story as well. Gurov fantasizes about an affair with "a woman whose very name he did not know."[42] At first, he learns Anna's name and patronymic, although not her family name, and the reader is informed about this moment in a conspicuously marked way; after the detailed account of the couple's first conversation, the last sentence of the paragraph adds, "And also Gurov learned that her name was Anna Sergeevna."[43] Gurov will not learn her last name until a week later, when they become lovers. In this way, the nameless lady with a pet dog slowly gains importance in Gurov's life and in the narration: by the time they become lovers, she has a full name. Since in Petrushevskaya's story the narrator does not provide access to the characters' points of view, they remain nameless to the end. The names that the narrator assigns them carry symbolic connotations. The woman is called Carmen, and the man The First Fellow. He gets his name through a succession of metonymic transformations: from a tall man in a serious gray suit to a serious man in a gray suit who wins the number one spot in the small crowd surrounding Carmen—hence The First Fellow. The color gray, a carry-over from Chekhov's story, remains one of the main features of his description. Carmen's name is motivated neither by her looks—she is blond and homely—nor by her behavior. Yet it has a definite effect: it establishes the observers in their role as spectators as if at the famous opera and foreshadows the tragic tone of the ending.

The voice of the narrator in Petrushevskaya's story is uncharacteristically subtle. Unlike the unfeeling narrator of "The Lady with the Dogs," whose harshness, unbalanced by a definable authorial position, leads the reader to deplore and resist it, this narrator speaks with something close to compassion. She opens with an exposition, which is very rare for Petrushevskaya: a few thoughts on the nature of life at a resort and its influence on people. Life at the seashore is described as an unnatural existence "away from daily reality."[44] The unnatural freedom from the problems of real life results in illusions that trick a person into believing that this leisurely, problem-free life is the reality. The narration then moves on to provide an example of a woman and a man caught up in the illusion. The sequence of thesis and example gives the story the feel of a parable; one might expect a moral at the end.

The narrator belongs to the real world outside the summer resort. She is strictly an observer, philosophically detached, and, probably because of that, more compassionate than the narrator of "The Lady with the Dogs." The latter relied on gossip; this one is a first-hand witness: "We watched this woman—I mean us living opposite their big holiday home."[45] The plural "we watched" is akin to the plural of Chekhov's opening sentence: "[They] said . . ." (*Govorili . . .*). It emphasizes the similarity between the two stories' settings: the idle resort crowd, gossip, and the anticipation of a fleeting romance. The arrangement of the narration follows in slightly distorted form the order of events in Chekhov's story, but since "Downhill" is only about three pages long, the swiftness of the relationship's development is accelerated, compressing Chekhov's short story even further. The stages of development of the characters' feelings and relationship unfold during their short stay at the resort, with only the final paragraph left to describe their winter existence. Thus the notion of change—"this love changed them both"—to which Chekhov leads his reader toward the end of his story appears in the middle of Petrushevskaya's. The transformative event that in Chekhov finishes the story and simultaneously opens it into the future is in Petrushevskaya the story's center. Everything that follows is the downhill tumble toward the tragic consequences of falling in love.

The motifs of ordinariness and typicality are crucial to both Chekhov's and Petrushevskaya's narratives. In her presentation of the ordinary, Petrushevskaya plays with the signs established by Chekhov. The motifs of vulgarity and the color gray are symbolic signs common to both stories. In Chekhov's story, gray is a noncolor, used negatively in the description of the dusty and tasteless hotel room coupled with the gray fence across the street from Anna's house, and positively in Anna's gray dress, Gurov's favorite. In Petrushevskaya, gray represents typicality and stability: the "gray fellow" exchanges his gray suit for gray shorts and, thanks to the connotations of the word *gray,* remains the epitome of ordinariness. He stands as a foil to Carmen's extravagant vulgarity. Yet, both are typical people of their times, as typical as Gurov and Anna were of their time and class. He is an everyman, "a fellow (*na muzhike*) who always carries the burden on his back, the whole world";[46] she is an ordinary woman looking for a scrap of happiness. Because they are so typical, the narrator is able to dissect them both with ease. However, there comes a point when they surprise the spectators. Both couples cross the boundaries of the typical when they fall in love.

Chekhov lowered the tone of his story compared to Tolstoy's novel. Petrushevskaya lowers it even further by extensive use of animal imagery. Tolstoy reacted to what he perceived as immoral in Chekhov's story by claiming that its characters remain beyond good and evil and therefore "they are practically animals." Yet while Chekhov's use of natural imagery of "male and female" (*samets i samka*) is limited to a reference to birds in a metaphor that reverberates with poetic melancholy—"a pair of birds of passage, male and female (*samets i samka*), caught and forced to live in different cages," Petrushevskaya permeates her story with coarse animal similes. She designates her characters as dog and bitch ("*samets*" and "*samka*"): the First Fellow is "an earnest famished male in his best bib and tucker" (*ser'eznyi, golodnyi samets pri parade*) who is later seen "protecting his miniature female" (*malen'kuiu samku*).[47] The animal imagery grows out of the curious image of a dog pack surrounding a bitch in heat (the Russian metaphor is a "dog's wedding"). It is a striking touch, a playful pointer to the story's connection with "The Lady with a Dog": this not-much-of-a-lady is followed not by one little dog but by a whole pack of dogs. After one wins out, there is only one dog left at the woman's side. Taking the story down to the primal level of animal imagery allows Petrushevskaya to position it at the extreme lower end of the emotional scale.

The primal and therefore simple nature of the relationship at its beginning does not elicit negativity on the part of the narrator. According to her, such relationships are the norm in the unnatural setting of the resort. It is *after* the couple fall in love that people sense their otherness and condemn it: "it is increasingly obvious that the two of them are in love and are apart from the rest; and the crowd, too, seems to reject them, recoiling in disapproval—even in the general crush they have an oddly condemned look, as though they don't belong." The change is physical, apparent, and as visible as if they have been "stamped with the same suffering, imminent parting, and longing that go with love."[48] Most of all, the change affects the woman. As the dog pack disappears from her side, the patina of vulgarity falls off her image. Everything that was pathetically vulgar in her appearance—the tight curls and cheap make-up—gives way to soft waves of hair, a natural tan, and shining eyes. In other (Chekhov's) words, "love changed them both." The key sign of genuine love is the feeling of compassion. In Carmen's eyes, there is "love and pity," as in Chekhov's Gurov, who "felt deep compassion, wanted to be sincere, tender. . . ." The change has occurred, ostensibly for the better, but the story does not end at that. If it did, it would conform to a traditional view of the transformative power of love that does not need proving: Russian classic literature has made this point. The problems of adulterous love as well as numerous other complications that keep lovers apart have always been among the main motivations of the classics' plots. Petrushevskaya's story is untraditional in presenting love as "the most awful misfortune": "Yes, it has happened to them, the most awful misfortune. Sadness shines out of their all but tearful eyes."[49] Thus, she contests one of the main ideas of Chekhov's story: love changes both of her story's characters, but it also ruins them.

Chekhov's heroine repeatedly proclaims that she is unhappy: "I have never been happy, I am now unhappy, and never, never will I be happy, never!" In the last scene, the narrator concludes the account of her sad thoughts with the question, "Was not their life broken?"[50] The form of the question, however, implies that the answer is left to the reader. At least one possible answer is that Gurov and Anna Sergeevna are blessed with real love and escape the lot of those who know neither real pain nor real happiness. In other words, Chekhov equates real love with happiness. In one of the story's key moments, the theater scene, when looking at Anna Sergeevna, Gurov realizes that she "was his misery, his joy, the only happiness that he wished for himself."[51] Misery and joy become one in a peculiarly positive way.[52] The open ending of the story helps to sustain this ambiguity as well as its cautious optimism. Petrushevskaya, on the other hand, is explicit in outlining the hopeless conclusion of her characters' encounter. Unlike Chekhov, she does not assign inherent value to love. For her characters, love equals suffering, and the inevitable separation is worse than death:

> As though hurtling downhill, a man clenches his jaws and turns to stone, eyes narrowed, heart sinking, his entire willpower focused on the final crash at the foot—but it is not about survival he is thinking, what is looming ahead is far more terrible, and there the man is on his own. His love is hurtling downhill beside him, and it is to wane in a different direction, any moment now they will part their ways. It is not about personal death, this is beside the point, and the awful thing is eternal separation.[53]

The key technique that allows Petrushevskaya to substantiate the sorrowful mood is the emphasis on the unnaturalness of the story's setting, stressing the illusory nature of everything that takes place there. To a large extent, the contrast between the sea town and the faraway cold towns is similar to the contrasting pair Yalta/Moscow in Chekhov's story. In Chekhov, Yalta stands for warmth and ease, and Moscow for cold and strain. In "Downhill," however, the resort town symbolizes deception, the trickery and the deadly illusion of happiness. Toward the end of the story, the resort town loses its definite features and becomes a general, unspecified home of fantasy. The characters also become increasingly metaphorical, less real people than symbolic figures:

> But our lovely couple is not there; Carmen, the golden blonde, and First Fellow, her faithful husband, tall, sinewy, brown,—they have both passed into oblivion and are flying up there somewhere in the frozen blue, in different aircrafts, going home, to their parts, to join their children and spouses, toward winter, snow and toil.[54]

In the last paragraph, the narrator sheds the persona of a witness to events and, in the manner of an omniscient narrator, casts a glance at the characters' last encounter. She sees how Carmen will run to the post office, how the First Fellow will order a ten-minute long-distance phone call and the two will weep together for the last time:

> . . . and there, on the phone, they will again join hearts long distance, and will together bemoan their lot across thousands of miles, and will sob and shout for exactly ten minutes, as much as he has

> ordered and paid for—just as back then, in summer, it was exactly twenty-four days paid for. They will sob and shout, deceived by an illusion of holiday, by the eternal light of paradise, both seduced and abandoned.[55]

The picture is full of poignant melancholy. Chekhov too leaves his characters struggling with the unbearable difficulty of their situation. Significantly, though, they talk face-to-face, and the fact that they are together at this moment diminishes at least somewhat the overall gravity of their situation. In Petrushevskaya's story, the two heroes cry on the phone, separated by a vast distance and circumscribed by time. The illusory "eternal" love is contrasted to the rigid, temporal boundaries of their encounter: they had exactly twenty-four days together and exactly ten minutes on the phone. The stress on temporal limits and on the commercially defined settings of their love story contrasts with the open ending and the lyricism of Chekhov's story. Petrushevskaya makes a radical departure from Chekhov's portrayal of love. It is a force, she admits, but it is still an illusion for which one can pay, and sometimes dearly. Where Chekhov's story ends with "beginning," the word "abandoned" is the last in her story.

C. R. S. Cockrell finds the essence of Chekhov's art in the tension between two extremes: between "hope and hopelessness, between potentiality and actuality, between what could be and what is, between the idea and the reality." He goes on to assert that in "The Lady with a Dog" Chekhov reaches "a synthesis of these two streams: an awareness of life's futility and hopelessness and yet at the same time, however paradoxical it may sound, a sense of hope."[56] Petrushevskaya goes in the opposite direction when she not only foregrounds hopelessness but finds the illusion of hope almost criminal. The last sentence of "Downhill" brings up the notion of illusion and thus connects it to the story's beginning. The sequence of thesis and illustration ends with the affirmation of the thesis: unnatural settings breed illusion, and believing in illusion leads to personal tragedy. In the process, Petrushevskaya has equated love with harmful illusion and has refuted the very idea of happy love. Most important, since her story is openly intertextual, it is clear that the object of Petrushevskaya's deconstruction is not love per se but love as literary theme. Literature has held romantic love among its most cherished fantasies. It is one of the distinguishing features of Petrushevskaya's art, perhaps the main one, that she sorts through every human assumption and belief in order to expose their illusory nature. What many readers and critics perceive as ruthlessness toward her characters is ruthlessness toward their illusions. Remarkably, while most writers of the end of the twentieth century focus on the disappointment and loss of illusions in political and economic spheres, Petrushevskaya moves deeper into the private sphere, going to the heart of human emotional existence. She thus covers not only the changeable sociopolitical reality but that which has been considered unchangeable, valuable, and true—the importance of human connection. The tone of anger and disappointment not usually characteristic of a love story blends in with the generally angry and pessimistic tone of contemporary literature. Petrushevskaya's disagreement with Chekhov's tribute to the power of love in "The Lady with a Dog" is of the same nature as Iarkevich's attack on *The Cherry Orchard:* they both fault Chekhov, and by extension Russian classic literature, for the cultural, moral, and economic crises of the 1990s. The resort town of the story is more than Chekhov's Yalta; it is the home of Russian literature to which Chekhov provides an opening. Readers with cultural competency will recognize that Petrushevskaya poses disillusionment and the feeling of abandonment as the fault of the literature that turned out to be the illusory "eternal light of paradise," that aspired but failed to perpetuate basic humanistic values. This failure precipitated a backlash of all-embracing skepticism toward everything that was valued before. Russian literature is thus blamed both for the misfortunes of Russian political history, as Iarkevich repeats after Rozanov, and for the resulting moral deficit of the Russian people.

Petrushevskaya's worldview and artistic methods are similar to Chekhov's, with one crucial distinction: like most writers of the postmodernist period, Petrushevskaya does not hold a comforting albeit illusory belief in the existence of an ideal, no matter how unattainable. Chekhov's heuristic poetics presuppose a never-ending search for meaning; Petrushevskaya's poetics of closure attempts to put a stop to the search. In other words, while Chekhov admitted to not knowing the ideal, Petrushevskaya insists that it does not exist, and she warns against holding on to the illusion. Allan Wilde defines this principal difference between the modernist and postmodernist worldviews in a succinct statement: "paradise once lost is now abandoned."[57]

Significantly, whatever her intentions, Petrushevskaya's intertextual dialogue with Chekhov presupposes a memory-oriented reading and relies on the reader's cultural memory to activate the intertextual connections of her texts as well as those of the referent texts. The intertextual enters her stories effortlessly, often in the everyday speech of her narrators, as allusions and/or metaphors that form a semiotic system common to the Russian intelligentsia. The cherry orchard motif of "Paradise, Paradise" and the religious rhetoric in "The Lady with the Dogs" are elements of this system. On a deeper thematic and philosophical level, the reader's cultural memory is involved and trusted to bring forward the pivotal works and figures of Russian literature. This is the prerequisite of intertextual practice, without which the surface of the text remains impenetrable and its message hidden. To ensure the reader's participation, the author must ensure the availability of the referent texts. In other words, not only must the signs be conspicuous enough, but the text itself must be prominent enough to have a strong presence in cultural memory. Most writers of the Russian classic canon have this prominence; yet, Chekhov's role in cultural memory has become especially important at the end of the twentieth century and the beginning of the twenty-first.

In some critics' opinion, allusion to classic literature, Russian and otherwise, reestablishes Petrushevskaya's dark realism (*chernukha*) as high literature. As I have attempted to show, Petrushevskaya employs high literature not merely to gain status for her art. Her ambitions go beyond that: she intrudes into the dialogue between the classics of the tradition, and her loud narrators drown out other voices in the polemics. Yet, despite this aggressiveness, or perhaps because of it, ultimately she writes herself into the tradition. At the same time, the other effect of intertextuality comes to the fore: reviving the polemics means reviving the texts involved in them. While the overt hostility of her engagement with a classic at times denies a voice to the older text and brings the dialogue down to the level of parody, nevertheless, by challenging the tradition, Petrushevskaya ensures its continuation. While she mourns the past, blames it for the present, and exposes its values as harmful illusions, the past comes alive in her texts as it does in all intertextually based texts of contemporary culture.

During the last years of the twentieth century, critics began to announce the passing of postmodernism and the advent of new forms of realism, from new realism to neosentimentalism to trans-metarealism. Perhaps the rainy days of postmodernism are over. Once again Russian literature has preserved its integrity and continuity through its most reliable device—cultural memory. By keeping open the dialogue with its classics, by relying on intertextuality to remain a productive force and a defense mechanism of culture, Russian literature has once again survived revolutionary changes and once again may offer something to look forward to. In a 1994 cycle of poems, *Karamzin (Journal of Country Life)*, Petrushevskaya envisions a future that is still caught in cyclical regressions into the past, still reinvents traditions, replays the old plots, postpones solutions for a hundred years, and measures itself against Chekhov:

> O!
> what life will come
> what people will live here!
> Chekhov kept waiting for them!
> in another hundred years
> they will invent a wooden wheel . . .[58]

AFTERWORD

Chekhov without Borders

> [Pushkin] was discovering the America that Chekhov made into a beaten track.
>
> —Abram Tertz, *Strolls with Pushkin*

IT IS A CURIOUS FACT that no contemporary Russian writer has been dubbed a new Chekhov. One finds attributions of "Chekhovian motifs" and a "Chekhovian sensibility," often "Chekhovian themes and characters," and, more often still, a "Chekhovian influence"; but no one as yet has borne the full title despite Viktor Erofeev's insistence that "it is possible to become a Chekhov if one tries hard enough." Similarly, there is also no "new" Pushkin or Tolstoy, Gogol or Dostoevsky. The classics in the Russian cultural consciousness of the twentieth century, even though they have entered mythical space, have retained sufficient presence to stand on their own, to elicit awe and tribute as much as frustration and a need to challenge them. They are still active participants in the cultural process as key figures in literary debates and the main intertextual sources for contemporary writers; they are not removed enough to enter circulation with indefinite articles.

In the West, the situation is quite different. While most Russian classics are duly represented in school curricula, in bookstores, and on library shelves, they do not play a role in the literary process. But Chekhov has a genuine presence. "A good many Americans now, and especially American writers," writes George P. Elliott, "feel for Chekhov an affinity, a warmth of affection, a kinship, different from what we feel for other Russian writers, including the two who are commonly seen as towering above him. Tolstoy and Dostoevsky castigate us for our sins; he talks with us about what's gone wrong."[1] There clearly exists a different, Western version of the Chekhov myth—a foreign Chekhov that, when superimposed on common views of Russia and Russians, produces a stable image of a melancholy artist with the sharp eye of a physician. This Chekhov simultaneously exemplifies and deconstructs the Russian propensity to philosophize one's way through life. He is objective to the point of saintliness, for his objectivity never leads him to labels and judgments. All in all it is a very positive and consistent image. It poses Chekhov as both a founding father of the modern short story[2] and its absolute master. He is a quintessential classic; foreign, as most classics are, both worthy and safely removed as a model of emulation. Writers routinely cite Chekhov as an influence and welcome critical remarks on "the Chekhovian" in their texts. To be called, as Raymond Carver has been, "an American Chekhov of this century," is to achieve ultimate success as a writer. "I am, after all, one of perhaps ten American writers who are known as the American Chekhov," says John Cheever,[3] and then he hastens to defuse the presumption of his statement with a joke by adding, "but then I have been described as the Budd Schulberg of New England." One does not call oneself a Chekhov in earnest—one does not call oneself a genius. It is done by others, and mostly posthumously. But it is almost obligatory to talk about one's debt to Chekhov, one's admiration and deep personal connection: "I know him best through his letters. They were written to me."[4] This sense of personal affinity, impossible, for instance, with Dostoevsky or his characters, is based in almost equal measure on Chekhov's biography and personality, his innovation in method, and his typical protagonist. If, for contemporary educated Russians, multiple aspects of the Chekhov myth determine the range of readings and reactions that include and sometimes combine awe and mockery, the foreign Chekhov is a harmonious, if rigidly positive, concept. When a Western writer sees in Chekhov parallels with his or her time, these parallels are psychological and universal rather than historical. One reads Chekhov for that which is always true because, as Eudora Welty puts it, "emotions are the same. We are the same."[5]

For Raymond Carver, the personal connection with Chekhov reached a particularly poignant climax during the last months of his life when, dying of lung cancer, he found solace in a dialogue with the writer who died of tuberculoses at the age of forty-four. In the introduction to the poems in *A New Path to the Waterfall,* Carver's last collection, Tess Gallagher describes how much Chekhov was on Carver's mind during his last months and how this presence helped him write and live to the end. "It was to Chekhov," she writes, "we instinctively turned to restore our steadfastness. [. . .] [T]here was the sense that Chekhov had stepped toward us, and that while he remained in his own time, he seemed also to have become our contemporary."[6] Carver interacts with Chekhov as with a "companion soul"; when his poems "rewrite" Chekhov in verse, it is "as if Ray had somehow won permission through a lifetime of admiration to take up his work with the audacity of love."[7] Gallagher concludes that the titles of his obituaries—"The American Chekhov" and "America's Chekhov"—would have made Carver "humbly and deeply happy."[8]

The lifetime of learning from Chekhov and the tragically similar circumstances of their deaths allowed Carver to feel Chekhov's equal in art and life. Yet, of course, one need not be aware of Chekhov's biography, or to be a brilliant writer or die of lung disease, to feel affinity with Chekhov's characters. George P. Elliott observes that the dilemma of nineteenth-century Russian neurotic intellectuals was the same as that of American twentieth-century educated neurotics: "discontented and unreligious and liberal and they've read the right books but nothing seems to do right for them, love and so on."[9] Shame and guilt, two synonymous concepts according to Elliott, dominate the lives of Chekhov's characters and of present-day Americans. As "an extreme opinion," Elliott ventures that "[i]n Chekhov better than in any other writer of any age or nation, including our own, we can see what educated, cultivated, enlightened Americans now are essentially like."[10] There is nothing extreme in this view, of course, and it goes a long way to explain the appeal of a Chekhovian character and plot for the American or any other Western audience. As the Russian intelligentsia did throughout the twentieth century, educated Americans see themselves in Chekhov's weak, neurotic but redeemable characters, and they like what they see.

However, this feeling of affinity based on healthy admiration is drastically different from the personal engagement with Chekhov that Petrushevskaya and Iarkevich, P'etsukh and Tolstaya, Bitov and Erofeev establish in their texts. For them, the most important parallels are historical. Russian writers rarely emulate or pay tribute; rather, they engage in arguments with Chekhov, present him with lists of grievances, blame him, miss him, hold him responsible, and love him, all at the same time. Their stories rearrange, rethink, and re-accent Chekhov's characters, themes, and plots while they deal with the questions and problems that are pressing and real in their own times. When an American writer writes his or her "The Lady with a Dog," he or she does not, and in all fairness cannot be expected to, burden it with such concerns. Neither can the reader be expected to recognize all of the intertextual links that Chekhov's texts open into Russian nineteenth-century literature. American short stories intertextually based on Chekhov, or about him, range between paying tribute to the master, trying one's hand at a classic plot, or dealing with a universal "problem" insofar as it can be outlined using a Chekhovian plot. Outside Russia, Chekhov does not stand for a complicated relationship between history and literature, or literature and ideology; he does not provide an opening for a discussion on the traumas of the intelligentsia or a metaphor for the complexities of the nostalgic worldview. In short, in the West, Chekhov is just a classic, that is, a welcome influence and an uncontested model.

Raymond Carver states unequivocally that his story "Errand," about the last hours of Chekhov's life, is his tribute to the writer and his role in Carver's life: "I saw an opportunity to pay homage—if I could bring it off, do it rightly and honorably—to Chekhov, the writer who meant so much to me for such a long time."[11] The story gives the point of view of someone uninitiated, for whom the name Chekhov means nothing, the waiter who brings champagne to the room in a German hotel where Chekhov is dying. In the morning Olga Knipper, Chekhov's wife, sends the waiter on an errand to bring the mortician. As she outlines the importance of this errand and repeatedly asks, "Do you understand what I am saying?" the gap widens between the reader's understanding of the magnitude of the event—the death of a great man—and the waiter's confusion. The reader might see the nameless waiter as entering history, but from his point of view, that of someone who has never heard of Chekhov, he simply entered a room where a dead body lies and the widow is agitated; for him, it is merely an agonizingly awkward moment. While Knipper keeps repeating Chekhov's name, the waiter worries about the champagne cork that lies on the floor. This divergence of points of view might serve as a metaphor for the way Chekhov functions in the West: his authority and canonical status comprise a foreign cultural imperative that must be accepted without justification. Unless the waiter accepts that something of magnitude is happening, his story remains that of a missed opportunity to be part of history. Yet, the irony here is that this understanding belongs only to the reader and only in retrospect, confirmed by countless repetitions of Chekhov's name throughout the century. It has nothing to do with the waiter's personal experience or opinion; it is a given, a sign of cultural competency in the period that started on that very day. A Russian waiter in 1904 would have probably reacted no differently. A hundred years later, however, the Soviet school curriculum alone has ensured the broad canonical and cultural familiarity of Chekhov's name. And that highlights another issue in Carver's story—the relationship between a culture's literary circles and its nonreading public. Outside the self-consciously logocentric Russian culture, this relationship might be virtually nonexistent without causing anxiety to either group. In nineteenth-century Russia, however, the moral authority of the Word over the whole society was an assumption voluntarily shared by serious writers and their audience. The Soviet ideological machinery appropriated and built up on the myth, exploiting the nation's reliance on the Word's power to influence. Throughout the last two centuries, all literary and artistic developments in Russia have been inescapably entangled with political matters.

The heavy politicization of the cultural process has generated resistance of the kind we have seen in texts by Voinovich, Tertz, Petrushevskaya, and Iarkevich. The formation and the function of the Chekhov myth are exemplars of the ideological coercion of the classics into state-approved molds. While almost any Russian classic can serve to explicate the mechanisms of this process, the "apolitical" Chekhov, the model representative of the Russian intelligentsia, is especially relevant—indeed, the obvious choice for the writer who sets out to expose and deconstruct such mechanisms. Consider Vladimir Sorokin's deconstruction of the Chekhov myth in the short story "Jubilee." In it a factory kills and processes the bodies of Anton Pavlovich Chekhovs—people who bear the same name as the writer—to produce the material out of which they fashion stage props for Chekhov productions. Sorokin presents his narration as an official's speech at the factory's jubilee, delivered in the elevated and formulaic Soviet style whose familiar absurdity numbs the reader to the absurdity of the story's premise. Jubilee activities were an integral part of the Soviet ideological appropriation of the classics; and the Chekhov of the official canon is just a name, an empty form ready to be filled with whatever content is suited to the current ideology. In this case, the name is symbolically emptied of all content. It becomes a true simulacrum: a sound, a verbal image that, having no connection to reality, creates its own, in which people bearing the name Chekhov literally stand in for him. At the end of the story a group of visiting actors performs an incomprehensible mix of lines from Chekhov's plays using the factory's products as props and costumes. Like all Sorokin texts, this one is an extended metaphor: the State makes use of the dead name/body of the writer while his art remains lost. The intense violence of Sorokin's metaphor is all too characteristic of the post-Soviet rejection of the ideological restraints imposed by Soviet discourse on literature and their deadening effect on the Russian classics.

The title of Joyce Carol Oates's collection of short stories, *Marriages and Infidelities,* is a metaphor as well. She designates her stories "re-imaginings of famous stories," thus intimating "a kind of spiritual marriage"[12] between herself and the famous writers of the past, a union marred only by her infidelities to their visions when she diverges from them. Yet, compared to the dismemberment of the classic in Sorokin's story or with Petrushevskaya's radical disagreement with Chekhov's valuation of love in her rewritings of "The Lady with a Dog," Oates's infidelity is a mild transgression indeed. Her story "The Lady with the Pet Dog" is a story born out of love for Chekhov, born at a different time and bearing the signs of that difference. The plot of Oates's story is as similar to Chekhov's as the reality of the American 1970s will allow: there is a Nantucket beach in the place of Chekhov's Yalta, car rides, and telephone calls. The most significant difference, from which all others arise, is the point of view. In Oates it belongs to the woman. Yet, this change is as much a sign of contemporary America as the telephone. There are after all only two possibilities: one of the characters, either the man or the woman, must be the protagonist whose story we follow; neither author provided a balanced double point of view.[13] In Oates's story, the point of view includes the heroine's realization of the consequence of other people's views of her, especially those of her husband and her lover. The shift explains why the dog in Oates's story belongs to the male protagonist. The woman becomes a lady with a dog when the man makes a drawing of her holding the dog and calls her "lady with a pet dog." She becomes a lady with a dog in his drawing—his vision, with his dog—and Oates's heroine realizes it when she later looks at the drawing. The story is about seeing clearly, hence the striking detail of the man's blind son. Oates's heroine acquires clarity of vision at the end.[14] In place of Chekhov's open and only provisionally optimistic ending, Oates's Anna is unconditionally happy at the moment of the realization that she really is in love. Her triumph, her happy ending, is to finally determine her true feelings about herself and her lover. Chekhov's ending, like his beginning, rests on the same assumption: that clarity about one's feelings and circumstances is the only way to overcome the numbing tawdriness of the mundane. As much as Oates's story is a rewriting of Chekhov, it exists independently as a tale of a woman constructing her love and life story and struggling to acquire her own identity in the process. If Oates's story is a dialogue with Chekhov, it is certainly not an argument. As Oates plays with the signs and echoes of Chekhov, one has a feeling of both her profound understanding and love of Chekhov and her pleasure in rewriting his famous story. The feminist twist on the point of view is not enough to instill any sense of struggle. It is more a testament to the fact that the human condition depends on the same emotions that mattered to Chekhov's characters than a dialogue about these emotions.

This attention to similarities rather than differences is not exclusive to American culture; on the contrary, it is found in most "Chekhovian" stories outside Russia. Another rewriting of this Chekhov story is by the British writer William Boyd. In general, Boyd's works show the author's knowledge and admiration of Chekhov and abound with signs of this familiarity: there are quotes from Chekhov's letters; a character dying with a volume of Chekhov's plays in his hand; an unhappily married woman crying to her lover, "I married a lap-dog"; and a story about Chekhov's complicated relationship with the actress Lika Mizinova. Boyd's story "The Woman on the Beach with a Dog" is even closer than Oates's to Chekhov's story in spirit and in plot. There are the same plot elements; the mandatory list consisting of an American beach, a small white dog, hotel rooms, unloved spouses; and the characters' realization that their little holiday tryst has unexpectedly brought them love. Boyd leaves his characters, Garret and Anna, engaged in a conversation very similar to Gurov and Anna's: asking ourselves what to do. Both Boyd's and Oates's story agree with Chekhov that complicated love is better than emotional death; both posit Chekhov's plot as a master plot of the contemporary short story.

Of course, non-Russian writers' relationships with Chekhov are not entirely free of tension. A writer, especially a short story writer, might feel intimidated by the prospect of being measured against Chekhov. The novelist Walker Percy even explains that this is the reason he does not write short stories or plays: "because after reading a Chekhov play or short story one tends to be intimidated."[15] The recipient of the letter from Sherwood Anderson in which he chastises the young writer for trying to learn the craft from "flashy magazine writers" and recommends reading Chekhov instead might resist the reprimand just as Voinovich's and Tertz's hapless writers had for its "tactless" implication that "Chekhov wrote better than [they]." One aspiring writer finds his own stories wanting by comparison and writes a piece, "Why I Hate Chekhov?": "And then I read Chekhov. Chekhov violates all the rules set down by DeMarinis [in *The Art and Craft of the Short Story*]. For example, Chekhov's short stories have no beginning or end—they could be simply preludes to subsequent stories. Still, Chekhov ends up being the greatest short-story writer of all time." For this particular writer, a retired academic, Chekhov's "Lady with a Dog" is a reminder of the unscientifically mysterious nature of truly great literature. His "hatred," it is immediately apparent, is synonymous with admiration: "My little triptych of stories paled in comparison. [. . .] I hate Chekhov. Worse still, I can't stop reading him."[16] The sentiment is only superficially similar to that of Tertz's protagonist, the writer who feels that Chekhov and other classics "stole vacant places and I was faced with their competition without possessing one hundredth part of their inflated authority."[17] This graphomaniac's anger is genuine, albeit exaggerated, and neither implies nor masks admiration. When a Soviet writer resists the classics' authority, he resists a dogma endorsed by the government, and his fight is therefore political, whether he wants it to be or not. Iarkevich's claim that Chekhov's *Cherry Orchard* is responsible for young Ukrainian girls having to sell their bodies on Tverskaia Street is, of course, thoroughly political; it has little to do with Chekhov the writer. The nature of the relationship is different for American and Russian writers because for the latter the stakes are higher. Chekhov's texts and myth are part of the greater myth of Great Russian Literature, one of the myths that give Russian culture its cohesion even as they undergo reexamination. The Russian writers' dialogue with Chekhov is about much more than literary mastery: the writers are engaged in a heated discussion about Russian history and the fate of Russian culture, past and future.

During the last years of the twentieth century and the first years of the twenty-first, the cultural focus in Russia has shifted from the traditionally logocentric one to a more diverse one. This shift is the main reason why cultural critics describe the 1990s as a time of crisis. It has been hard for the intelligentsia to see the sacred Word demoted to merely one element of the free market, to accept the fact that mass literature, taboo during Soviet times, now dominates the market. Russians now have access to the best (and often the worst) that the world cultural and consumer market has to offer. Translated and native pulp fiction, romance novels, thrillers, feature films, and serials made according to Hollywood formulas have taken over bookstores and TV screens. It might be an expected reaction, a backlash against the decades when high literature reigned on the state-controlled market, "the market's revenge for the years of Soviet *cultural* imperialism—during most of which high literature occupied the place of honor in the pantheon of high culture—and Russia's *imperial* culture—during all of which high literature was the ever-present interlocutor in any high-minded 'discussion of ideas.'" [18] If high literature's status was indeed artificially maintained and state-imposed, then economic and political stabilization will put everything in its place. The optimistic prognosis would be that Russian culture will become healthily varied, providing material for consumer groups of different tastes and educational levels. High literature will have its audience, surely diminished in numbers but not in enthusiasm. Another possibility is that Russian culture is not as different as Russians would like to believe from the American culture that has chosen films and television over literature as the common source of cultural references. Time will tell whether Russian literature can survive the market mentality and the "banishment of high literature from the tables of commerce"[19] or, in other words, whether the importance of Russian literature in the life of the Russian people is a myth in the sense of a mode of explanation or in the sense of a false story. Meanwhile, Russian culture's best survival course has been the willingness to rethink and rewrite its myths and texts, allowing intertextuality to perform its regenerative function.

NOTES

Chapter 1

1. Yuri Lotman, *Besedy o russkoi kul'ture* (St. Petersburg: *Iskusstvo-SPB,* 1994), 9.

2. "Culture." *Britannica Concise Encyclopedia.* 2004. Encyclopædia Britannica Premium Service. Online. http://www.britannica.com/ebc/article?eu=387316.

3. See James Fentress and Chris Wickham, eds., *Social Memory* (Oxford: Blackwell, 1992); Paul Connertnon, *How Societies Remember* (Cambridge–New York: Cambridge University Press, 1989); Katherine Hodgkin and Susannah Radstone, eds., *Contested Pasts: The Politics of Memory* (London–New York: Routledge, 2003); Dan Ben-Amos and Lillian Weissberg, eds., *Cultural Memory and the Construction of Identity* (Detroit: Wayne State University Press, 1999).

4. Hodgkin and Radstone, 5.

5. Fentress and Wickham, 133.

6. The organizers of the Congress "Methods for the Study of Literature as Cultural Memory" see cultural memory in very broad terms as a means of preserving identities and traditions. It "enables an individual's acculturation, the construction of their identity in the discourse (knowledge, values, ideologemes, phantasms) of a certain community" (Marko Juvan). In this sense it is no different from memory as such. A more useful conceptualization of memory requires narrowing the focus to the process of memory formation, as it relates to the arrangement of artistic, or literary, form.

7. See Yuri Lotman, "*Pamiat' v kul'turologicheskom osveshchenii*," in his *Semiosphera* (St. Petersburg: *Isskustvo-SPB*, 2000), 673–76; and the volume *Genres as Repositories of Cultural Memory*, ed. Hendrik van Gorp and Ulla Musarra Schroeder (Amsterdam-Atlanta: Rodopi, 2000).

8. Maurice Halbwachs, *On Collective Memory*, ed. and trans. Lewis A. Coser (Chicago: University of Chicago Press, 1992), 40.

9. B. van den Bossche, "Myth as Literature, Literature as Myth: Some Remarks on Myth and Interpretation of Literary Texts," in *Methods for the Study of Literature as Cultural Memory*, ed. Raymond Viverliet and Annemarie Estor, Volume 6 of the Proceedings of the XVth Congress of the International Comparative Literary Association "Literature as Cultural Memory" (Amsterdam: Rodopi, 2000), 228.

10. John B. Vickery, ed., *Myth and Literature* (Lincoln: University of Nebraska Press, 1966), ix. The most representative examples of myth criticism are to be found in works by Northrop Frye, Richard Chase, and Francis Fergusson. See also Laurence Coupe, *Myth* (London–New York: Routledge, 1997).

11. Joseph P. Strelka, ed., *Literary Criticism and Myth* (University Park–London: The Pennsylvania State University Press, 1980), vii.

12. Yu. M. Lotman, and B. A. Uspensky, "Myth—Name—Culture," in *Soviet Semiotics*, ed. and trans. Daniel P. Lucid (Baltimore: The Johns Hopkins University Press, 1977), 234.

13. On primordial myths see Mircea Eliade, *Myth and Reality*, trans. Willard R. Trask (New York–Evanston: Harper & Row, 1963); E. M. Meletinsky, *Poetika mifa* (Moscow: *Iazyki russkoy kul'tury*, 1995); see also Geoffrey Hosking and George Schopflin, eds., *Myth & Nationhood* (New York: Routledge, 1997), for an analysis of connection between the national mythology and national consciousness.

14. Jurgen Habermas, *The Theory of Communicative Action*, trans. Thomas McCarthy (Boston: Beacon Press, 1983), 13.

15. Benedict Anderson, *Imagined Communities* (London: Verso, 1991).

16. Roland Barthes, "Myth Today," in his *Mythologies*, trans. Annette Lavers (New York: Hill and Wand, 1988), 110.

17. George Schopflin, "The Functions of Myth and a Taxonomy of Myths," in *Myth & Nationhood*, 20.

18. Homi K. Bhabha, ed., *Nation and Narration* (London: Routledge, 1990), 4.

19. Lotman and Uspensky, "Myth—Name—Culture," 242–43.

20. Mikhail Epstein, "The Origins and Meaning of Russian Postmodernism," in *After the Future: The Paradoxes of Postmodernism and Contemporary Russian Culture*, trans. Anesa Millr-Pogacar (Amherst: The University of Massachusetts Press, 1995), 191.

21. Lotman and Uspensky, "Myth—Name—Culture," 236.

22. Mikhail Bakhtin, *Problems of Dostoevsky Poetics*, ed. and trans. Carol Emerson (Minneapolis and London: University of Minnesota Press, 1997), 203.

23. Harold Bloom, *The Anxiety of Influence* (London: Oxford University Press, 1975), 32.

24. David Lowenthal, "Identity, Heritage, and History," in *Commemorations: The Politics of National Identity*, ed. John R. Gillis (Princeton: Princeton University Press, 1994), 53.

25. Vladimir Kataev, "Problems of Applied Literary Criticism," *Russian Studies in Literature* 35, no. 1 (Winter 1998–99): 60.

26. Halbwachs, *On Collective Memory,* 188.

27. Vladimir Slavetsky, "After Postmodernism," *Russian Studies in Literature* 30, no. 2 (Spring 1994): 41.

28. Alexander Ageev, "Conspectus of the Crisis: Sociocultural Conditions and the Literary Process," in *Re-Entering the Sign. Articulating New Russian Culture,* ed. Ellen E. Berry and Anesa Miller-Pogacar (Ann Arbor: University of Michigan Press, 1995), 176.

29. Mark Lipovetsky, *Russian Postmodernist Fiction. Dialogue with Chaos,* ed. Eliot Borenstein (Armonk: M. E. Sharpe, 1999), 4.

30. Epstein, "The Origins and Meaning of Russian Postmodernism," 191.

31. Lipovetsky, *Russian Postmodernist Fiction,* 11.

32. Ibid., 33, 35.

33. Andrew Wachtel, *Remaining Relevant after Communism. The Role of the Writer in Eastern Europe* (Chicago: The University of Chicago Press, 2006).

34. Julia Kristeva, "World, Dialogue, and Novel," in her *Desire in Language. A Semiotic Approach to Literature and Art,* ed. Leon S. Roudiez (New York: Columbia University Press, 1980), 66.

35. Ibid., 89.

36. Manfred Pfister, "How Postmodern Is Intertextuality?" in *Intertextuality,* ed. Heinrich F. Plett (Berlin: Walter de Gruyter, 1991), 210.

37. Kristeva, "World, Dialogue, and Novel," 97.

38. Roland Barthes, *Image—Music—Text,* trans. Stephen Heath (London: Fontana, 1977), 160.

39. Ibid., 146.

40. Ibid., 143.

41. Renate Lachmann, *Memory and Literature. Intertextuality and Russian Modernism* (Minneapolis: University of Minnesota Press, 1997), 30.

42. See, for instance, Margaret A. Rose, *Parody: Ancient, Modern, and Post-Modern* (Cambridge: Cambridge University Press, 1993).

43. Mikhail Bakhtin, *Problems of Dostoevsky's Poetics,* 193.

44. Linda Hutcheon, "Beginning to Theorize Postmodernism," in *A Postmodern Reader,* ed. Joseph Natoli and Linda Hutcheon (Albany: State University of New York Press, 1993), 251.

45. Linda Hutcheon, *A Poetics of Postmodernism. History, Theory, Fiction* (New York: Routledge, 1988), 26.

46. Bakhtin, 185. Emphasis in the original.

47. This large list includes Vladimir Tuchkov's "Terrible Vengeance" (*Strashnaia mest'*) and "Hunting Incident" (*Sluchai na okhote*), Konstantin Pleshakov's "Old-Fashioned Cheaters" (*Starosvetskie izmenshchiki*), and other titles mentioned below.

48. Wolfgang Karrer, "Titles and Mottoes as Intertextual Devices," in *Intertextuality,* 123.

49. See Wachtel, 166–81, for an analysis of Makanin's novel as a reaction to the cultural crisis of the 1990s.

50. Mark Lipovetsky, "*Rasstratnye strategii, ili metamorfozy 'chernukhi,'*" *Novy Mir* 11 (1999): 197.

51. Andrei Nemzer, "*Sovremennyi dialog s Gogolem*," *Novy Mir* 5 (1994).

52. See Judith Smith and Michael Worton, eds., *Intertextuality. Theories and Practices* (Manchester: Manchester University Press, 1990).

53. The Western literary tradition was not the only and certainly not the first instance of "borrowing" in Russian culture; the first was Christianity. The problematic standing of the Russian Church as a newcomer, and the way it was addressed in Metropolitan Hilarion's famous sermon, "Discourse on Law and Grace" (between 1037 and 1050), sets up the model for dealing with most of the later instances of Russia's "novice" position in relation to older and thus more developed traditions. Turning a presumably disadvantaged position into its opposite, into a source of pride—not late but last and therefore the only true church—enabled future generations of Russians to sidestep the problem of primacy altogether.

54. Charles Hamilton Newman, *The Post-Modern Aura. The Act of Fiction at an Age of Inflation* (Evanston: Northwestern University Press, 1985), 86.

55. D. S. Likhachev, *Razvitie Russkoi Literatury X–XVII vekov: Epokhi i stili* (Leningrad: *Nauka*, 1973), 22.

56. Lidiia Ginzburg, *O lirike* (Moscow: *Intrada*, 1997), 30.

57. V. E. Vatsuro provides a detailed analysis of the multitude of sources which "the elegiac school" adopted in the course of its development in his *Lirika Pushkinskoi pory* (St. Petersburg: *Nauka*, 1994).

58. Oleg Proskurin, *Poeziia Pushkina ili podvizhnyi palimpsest* (Moscow: *Novoe Literaturnoe Obozrenie*, 1999), 237.

59. Ibid., 172.

60. Ibid., 242.

61. Kristeva, "World, Dialogue, and Novel," 77.

62. David Bethea, "Where to Begin: Pushkin, Derzhavin, and the Poetic Use of Filiation," in *Rereading Russian Poetry*, ed. Stephanie Sandler (New Haven: Yale University Press, 1999), 66. Emphasis added.

Chapter 2

1. Anecdotes about Pushkin, like all anecdotes about historical personae, have an antimythical function and therefore can exist only in correlation to the myth. The same is true, for instance, for anecdotes about Chapaev, which provide the popular counterpart to the mythologization of the historical Civil War hero by Soviet literature and cinema.

2. Marcus C. Levitt, *Russian Literary Politics and the Pushkin Celebration of 1880* (Ithaca: Cornell University Press, 1989), 4.

3. Marcus C. Levitt, "Pushkin in 1899," in *Cultural Mythologies of Russian Modernism*, ed. Boris Gasparov, Robert P. Hughes, and Irina Paperno (Berkeley: University of California Press, 1992), 187.

4. Levitt, *Russian Literary Politics*, 160.

5. On different "images" of Dostoevsky in contemporary criticism, see, for instance, H. Mondry, "Nationalism in Literary Criticism in Russia Today," in *Twentieth-Century Russian Literature. Selected Papers from the Fifth World Congress*

of Central and East European Studies, ed. K. L. Ryan and B. P. Scherr (London: Macmillan, 2000), 307–18.

6. Boris Gasparov, "The Golden Age and Its Role in the Cultural Mythology of Russian Modernism," in *Cultural Mythologies of Russian Modernism*, 5–6.

7. Irina Paperno, "*Pushkin v zhizni cheloveka Serebriannogo veka*," in *Cultural Mythologies of Russian Modernism*, 19–51.

8. Boris Gasparov, "*Tridtsatye gody—zheleznyi vek (k analizu motivov stoletnego vozvrashcheniia u Mandelshtama)*," in *Cultural Mythologies of Russian Modernism*, 152.

9. Joan Delaney Grossman, "'Moi Pushkin': Briusov's search for the real Aleksandr Sergeevich," in *Cultural Mythologies of Russian Modernism*, 73–82.

10. Eric Hobsbawm, Introduction, in *The Invention of Traditions*, ed. Eric Hobsbawm and Terence Ranger (Cambridge: Cambridge University Press, 1983), 1.

11. John R. Gilles, "Memory and Identity. The History of a Relationship," Introduction, in his *Commemorations. The Politics of National Identity* (Princeton: Princeton University Press, 1994), 5.

12. See, for instance, Nikita Struve, "*Russkaia emigratsia i Pushkin (1987)*," *Russkii Mir* 4 (2001); V. Perelmuter, ed., *Pushkin v emigratsii. 1937*, (Moscow: *Progress-Traditsiia*, 1999); Angela Brintlinger, *Writing a Usable Past: Russian Literary Culture, 1917–1937* (Evanston: Northwestern University Press, 2000).

13. See Wendy Slater, "The Patriots' Pushkin," *Slavic Review* 58, no .2 (Summer 1999). See also Yurii Druzhnikov, "*Pushkin, Stalin i drugie*," in his *Russkie mify* (New York: Liberty Publishing, 1995), for an amusing account of the development of the official Pushkin myth.

14. Abram Tertz's *Strolls with Pushkin* (New Haven: Yale University Press, 1993) is one of the very few attempts to subvert the official Pushkin myth. It is important to remember that Tertz wrote this book in prison. See Catharine Theimer Nepomnyashchy, *Abram Tertz and the Poetics of Crime* (New Haven: Yale University Press, 1995); also see Slater, "The Patriot's Pushkin."

15. Vyacheslav P'etsukh, "*Dom na Moike*," in his *Gosudarstvennoe ditia* (Moscow: *Vagrius*), 1997), 82 (my translation).

16. Ibid.

17. On the relationship of anecdote and myth see, for instance, Leonid Stolovich, "*Anekdot i mif*," *Neva* 10 (2004).

18. Graham Roberts, "A Matter of (Dis)course: Metafiction in the works of Daniil Kharms," *New Directions in Soviet Literature*, ed. Sheelagh Duffin Grahamn (New York: St. Martin's Press, 1992), 142.

19. The English is in Avrahm Yarmolinsky, ed., *Treasury of Russian Verse* (New York: The Macmillan Company, 1949), 50.

20. For a detailed analysis of other aspects of Bitov's novel see Ellen Chances, *Andrei Bitov. The Ecology of Inspiration* (Cambridge: Cambridge University Press, 1993); Sven Spieker, *Figures of Memory and Forgetting in Andrej Bitov's Prose* (Frankfurt am Main: Peter Lang, 1996).

21. On Pushkin's museums and on Bitov's novel as part of the Pushkin myth, see Stephanie Sandler, *Commemorating Pushkin. Russia's Myth of a National Poet* (Stanford: Stanford University Press, 2004), chapters 2 and 7.

22. Lipovetsky, *Russian Postmodernist Fiction*, 42.

23. Ibid., 65.

24. Andrei Bitov, *Vychitanie zaitsa. 1825* (Moscow: *Nezavisimaia gazeta*, 2001), 110–11.

25. Abram Tertz, *Progulki s Pushkinym* (St. Petersburg: *Vsemirnoe slovo*, 1993), 6.

26. Bitov, *Vychitanie zaitsa*, 77.

27. Ibid., 72.

28. Tatiana Tolstaya, *Reka Okkervil'. Rasskazy* (Moscow: *Podkova*, 2002), 311. The English is based on Jamey Gambrell's translations. The story "*Syuzhet*" is my translation.

29. Ibid., 317.

30. Ibid., 314.

31. Ibid., 313.

32. Heinrich F. Plett, "Intertextualities," in *Intertextuality*, 25.

33. Tolstaya, *Reka Okkervil'*, 366.

34. Helena Goscilo, *The Explosive World of Tatyana N. Tolstaya's Fiction* (New York: M. E. Sharpe, 1996).

35. Simon Karlinsky in "The Gentle Subversive" makes explicit the connection between Chekhov's view of sex as "a morally neutral quantity, whose moral and ethical implications depend on the attitudes of the people involved" and Pushkin's "remarkably free treatment of sexual themes" (15). Pushkin, he writes, was "the last nineteenth-century Russian writer to have profound ties with eighteenth-century traditions [and] also the last to write openly and without guilt about the joys of sexual love" (15). Chekhov, in Karlinsky's view, approached the subject with the same open-mindedness he allowed any other in his work, that is, "without imposing moralizing sanctions" (16). As for Chekhov's stories on the theme of women and society, they should have been included "in the canon of the women's liberation movement" (18). Karlinsky bases this connection not on the actual similarities in Pushkin's and Chekhov's plots, but rather on their refusal to apply preformed moral standards to human relationships, including sexual ones. Simon Karlinsky, Introduction, "The Gentle Subversive," in *Letters of Anton Chekhov*, trans. Michael Henry Heim, selection and commentary Simon Karlinsky (New York: Harper & Row, Publishers, 1973).

36. Tolstaya, *Reka Okkervil'*, 240.

37. Ibid., 239.

38. Goscilo, *The Explosive World*, 90.

39. Tolstaya, *Reka Okkervil'*, 245.

40. Perhaps the inclusion of a Blok quotation implies an additional allusion to Blok's poem "To Pushkin House" (*Pushkinskomu domu*) quoted in an epigraph to Bitov's novel and celebrating Pushkin as a symbol of artistic freedom.

41. Tolstaya, *Reka Okkervil'*, 245.

42. Ibid., 247.

43. Ibid., 248.

44. Ibid., 247.

45. Ibid., 237.

46. In the fairy tale "Finist—Fair Falcon" (*Finist—Iasnyi Sokol*), the heroine

performs these very feats—"to wear out seven pairs of iron boots, break seven iron staffs in two, devour seven loaves of iron bread"—in order to find her beloved.

47. Tolstaya, *Reka Okkervil'*, 241.

48. Michael Riffaterre, "Compulsory Reader Response," in *Intertextuality. Theories and Practices,* ed. Michael Worton and Judith Still (Manchester–New York: Manchester University Press, 1990): "specific, specialized signs [that] can at once stand for the intertextual, point to its locus, and uncover its identity" (58–59).

49. Tolstaya, *Reka Okkervil'*, 241.

50. Ibid., 249.

51. Ibid.

52. Ibid., 250.

53. Anton Chekhov, *Polnoe sobranie sochinenii i pisem v tridtsati tomakh,* ed. N. F. Bel'chikov et al. (Moscow: *Nauka,* 1974–83), 8:9.

54. Carolina De Maegd-Soep, in her study devoted to women in Chekhov's life and works, analyzes the main types of women portrayed in Chekhov, concentrating on his attention to the social status of women and how it deprives them of any real choice in life except marriage. Carolina De Maegd-Soep, *Chekhov and Women. Women in the Life and Work of Chekhov* (Bloomington, IN: Slavica Publishers, 1987).

55. Chekhov, 9:131.

56. Ibid., 8:15.

57. Eliade, *Myth and Reality,* 187.

58. Peter Barta, "The Author, the Cultural Tradition and Glasnost. An Interview with Tatyana Tolstaya," *Russian Literature Journal* XLIV, nos. 147–49 (1990): 274.

59. Ibid., 275.

60. Louisa Saunders, "Heart and Soul," Interview with Tatyana Tolstaya, *Guardian* (Manchester, England), 24 May 1989: 21.

61. Ibid.

62. Tamara Alagova and Nina Efimov, "Interview with Tatyana Tolstaya," *World Literature Today* 67, no. 1 (1993): 52.

63. Barta, "The Author," 268.

64. Alagova and Efimov, "Interview with Tatyana Tolstaya," 52.

65. Lachmann, *Memory and Literature,* 184.

66. Ibid., 192.

67. S. Taroshchina, *"Ten' na zakate,"* Interview, *Literaturnaia Gazeta* 23 (July 1986): 7.

68. Osip Mandelshtam, *"Slovo I kul'tura."* In O. E. Mandelshtam, *Ob iskusstve* (Moscow: *Iskusstvo,* 1995), 204.

69. Translation is slightly modified from Peter Tempest's in *V. Mayakovsky. Selected Verse* (Moscow: *Raduga,* 1985), 107–8.

70. See Sandler, *Commemorating Pushkin,* 97–104.

71. Svetlana Boym sees this "dialogue" as a part of Maiakovsky's creation of his own myth. Svetlana Boym, *Death in Quotation Marks. Cultural Myths of the Modern Poet* (Cambridge: Harvard University Press, 1991), 134–36.

Chapter 3

1. Gasparov, "The Golden Age and Its Role in the Cultural Mythology of Russian Modernism," 4–5 (see chapter 2, n4).

2. See, for instance, the *Chekhov and Pushkin* volume in the *Chekhoviana* series. A. P. Chudakov, *"Pushkin i Chekhov. Zavershenie kruga,"* in *Chekhoviana. Chekhov i Pushkin,* ed. V. B. Kataev et al. Moscow: *Nauka,* 1998, 35–46.

3. A. P. Chudakov writes, "that which in Pushkin was found and declared, in Turgenev, Pisemsky, Goncharov, and Tolstoy not distinctly defined, and in literature of the 1870–80s was felt as a sign of the times, in Chekhov was completed, became the foundation of his manner, his artistic philosophy. The circle closed." A. P. Chudakov, *"Pushkin—Chekhov: Zavershenie kruga,"* in *Chekhoviana,* 45.

4. Boris Pasternak, *Doktor Zhivago* (Moscow: *Knizhnaya Palata,* 1989), 218. Trans. Max Hayward and Manya Harari (New York: Pantheon, 1958), 285.

5. Vladimir Nabokov, *Lectures on Russian Literature,* ed. Fredson Bowers (San Diego: A Harvest Book, Harcourt Brace & Company, Bruccoli Clark Layman, 1981), 250.

6. Alexander Ageev, "Conspectus of the Crisis: Sociocultural Conditions and the Literary Process," in *Re-Entering the Sign. Articulating New Russian Culture,* ed. Ellen E. Berry and Anesa Miller-Pogacar (Ann Arbor: University of Michigan Press, 1995), 179.

7. Alexander Blok, *Selected Poems,* trans. Alex Miller (Moscow: Progress, 1981), 247.

8. Mandelshtam, *"Shum Vremeni,"* in *Ob iskusstve,* 69.

9. Aleksandr Bogdanovich, *Gody pereloma: Sbornik kriticheskih statei* (SPB: *Mir Bozhii,* 1908), 118.

10. Karlinsky, "The Gentle Subversive," 3.

11. The cliché was exported to the West as well: Peter H. Srowell opens his book on Chekhov and James citing, "opposing impressions: a dying, consumptive, Russian peasant doctor distilling tightly compressed short stories and a few strangely elusive plays set against a well-fed and traveled American intellectual . . . ." H. Peter Stowell, *Literary Impressionism, James and Chekhov* (Athens: The University of Georgia Press, 1980), 3.

12. A notable exception is Chekhov's "Sakhalin trip" which, Michael Finke asserts, might have purported "to cast the traveling author as hero." Michael C. Finke, "The Hero's Descent to the Underworld in Chekhov," *Russian Review* 53, no. 1 (January 1994): 74.

13. On Pushkin's self-mythologizing writing see David M. Bethea, *Realizing Metaphors: Alexander Pushkin and the Life of a Poet* (Madison: University of Wisconsin Press, 1998); L. I. Volpert, *Pushkin v roli Pushkina* (Moscow: *Iazyki russkoi kul'tury,* 1998); Sandler, *Commemorating Pushkin.*

14. Dmitri Merezhkovsky, *Vechnye sputniki (Pushkin)* (Letchworth: Prideaux Press, 1971).

15. Dmitri Merezhkovsky, *Chekhov and Gorky* (Letchworth: Prideaux Press, 1975), 13.

16. Ibid., 15.

17. Zinaida Gippius, "*Nuzhny li stikhi?*" in her *Dnevniki* (Moscow: *Intelvak,* 1999), 242.

18. Zinaida Gippius, "*Slovo o teatre,*" in *Dnevniki,* 234.

19. Ibid., 234–35.

20. Chekhov, letter to Suvorin, Sept. 8, 1891. Karlinsky, 203.

21. Irina Paperno, "*Pushkin v zhizni cheloveka Serebriannogo veka,*" and Olga Matich, "Dialectics of Cultural Return: Zinaida Gippius' Personal Myth," in *Cultural Mythologies of Russian Modernism,* ed. Gasparov et al. (see chapter 2, n4).

22. Dmitri Merezhkovsky, "*Brat chelovechesky,*" in his *Akropol'. Izbrannye literaturno-kriticheskie stat'i.* (Moscow: *Knizhnaia palata,* 1991), 249.

23. Merezhkovsky, *Chekhov and Gorky,* 10.

24. Vladislav Khodasevich, "*O Chekhov,*" in his *Koleblemyi trenozhnik,* ed. V. G. Perelmuter (Moscow: *Sovetskii pisatel',* 1991), 251.

25. See Lia Bushkanets, "'*Obydennost' A. P. Chekhova,*" in *Almanach Melikhovo,* ed. Yu. A. Bychkov et al. (Moscow: *Druzhba narodov,* 2000), 47–62.

26. Vasilii Rozanov, "*Nash 'Antosha Chekhonte,'*" in his *Mysli o literature* (Moscow: *Sovremennik,* 1989), 303.

27. Ibid., 301.

28. Chekhov, letter to Shcheglov, March 22, 1890. Karlinsky, 163.

29. Ibid.

30. Chekhov, letter to Pleshcheev, Oct. 4, 1888. Karlinsky, 109.

31. H. Peter Stowell presents a case for Chekhov (alongside Henry James) as a literary impressionist. Insofar as Stowell defines impressionism as a borderline phenomenon, "caught between the ferocious revolt against subjectivity of romanticism and the headlong dash into the anarchy of modernism" and constituting the incipient moment of modernism, he is in agreement with Merezhkovsky. Stowell, *Literary Impressionism,* 13.

32. Vladimir Kataev, *Proza Chekhova. Problemy Interpretatsii* (Moscow: *Izdatel'stvo Moskovskogo Universiteta,* 1979), 118. The view shared by most critics is that Chekhov's worldview included the belief in the existence of a social ideal. It is the definition of it and the way to it that Chekhov refused to speculate on. Vladimir Kataev formulates this idea "not as found and known a priori, but rather as constantly searched for" (103). There is also a related and very complex question of Chekhov's religious views that is the subject of a growing field of studies.

33. Maria Semanova, *Chekhov i sovetskaya literatura* (Moscow: *Sovetsky pisatel',* 1966), 32–36.

34. Laurence Senelick, *The Chekhov Theater: A Century of Plays in Performance* (Cambridge: Cambridge University Press, 1997), 115.

35. Jeffrey Brooks, "Russian Nationalism and Russian Literature: The Canonization of the Classics," in *Nation and Ideology: Essays in Honor of Wayne S. Vucinich,* ed. Ivo Banac, John G. Ackerman, and Roman Szporluk (New York: East European Monographs, Columbia University Press, 1981), 315–16.

36. Alexander Lunacharsky, *Sobranie Sochinenii* (Moscow: *Khudozhestvennaia literatura,* 1963), 1:354.

37. Ibid., 365.

38. Ibid., 367.

39. Ibid., 371.

40. Several Chekhov landmarks in Taganrog now form the Chekhov Museum Complex which includes the family house, several houses of friends and relatives, the theater, and the school, also a Chekhov museum since 1935. The estate in Melikhovo had been designated a museum by 1940. By 1960 the main house had been renovated, or rather carefully replicated, and the museum officially opened on the centennial of Chekhov's birth. In 1954, on the fortieth anniversary of Chekhov's death, Malaya Dmitrovka Street in Moscow where Chekhovs had lived during the 1880s was renamed Chekhov Street. In the same year the town Lopasnya near Melikhovo was renamed Chekhov. There are Chekhov museums on Sakhalin Island; in the Ukrainian city of Sumy; in German Badenweiler, where he died; and even in Colombo, Sri Lanka, which Chekhov passed on his way from Sakhalin.

41. "When I finished the story last night, a feeling of outright terror took hold of me; I could not stay in my room and went out. I had a sensation that I too was locked in ward number 6" (*Vladimir Illich Lenin o Litrature i Isskusstve* [Moscow: *Goslitizdat,* 1960], 616). The comment became widely known after the publication in 1935 of A. I. Ul'ianova-Elizarova's memoirs.

42. See Druzhnikov, "*Pushkin, Stalin i drugie,*" in his *Russkie mify.*

43. Maurice Friedberg, *Russian Classics in Soviet Jackets* (New York: Columbia University Press, 1962), 187–89.

44. Ibid., 35.

45. Ibid., 87.

46. Ibid., 91.

47. On the canon see John Guillory, *Cultural Capital: The Problem of Literary Canon Formation* (Chicago: University of Chicago Press, 1993); Jan Gorak, *The Making of the Modern Canon. Genesis and Crisis of Literary Idea* (London: Athlone, 1991); E. Dean Kolbas, *Critical Theory and the Literary Canon* (Boulder: Westview, 2001).

48. Harold Bloom, *The Western Canon: The Books and School of the Ages* (New York: Riverhead Books, 1994), 35–39.

49. Mikhail Kuraev, "*Aktual'nyi Chekhov,*" *Druzhba narodov* 12 (1998), 174.

50. Vladimir Vysotsky, *Sochinenia v 4x tomakx* (St. Petersburg: *Tekxneks Possia,* 1992), 1:125.

51. Ia. A. Nazarenko, *Istoria russkoi literatuty XIX veka* (Moscow: *Gos. Izdatel'stvo,* 1926), 386.

52. Ibid., 388.

53. G. Abramovich, B. Braynina, A. Egolin, *Russkaya Literatura. Uchebnik dlia srednei shkoly, Chast' II* (Moscow: *Uchpedgiz,* 1935), 188–98.

54. Beatrice King, *Russia Goes to School: A Guide to Soviet Education* (London: The New Education Book Club, 1948), 66; Evgeny Dobrenko, *The Making of the State Reader* (Stanford: Stanford University Press, 1997), 146–62.

55. Here, for example, is an anecdotal but realistic account of teachers' dilemma after the end of Stalin's era, when they were ordered to expunge Stalin's name from the class materials: "It then turned out, however, that Stalin's name appeared in many other stories and poems, as well as in all the textbooks, with the

possible exception of mathematics books." Dora Shturman, *The Soviet Secondary School,* trans. Philippa Shimrat (London: Routledge, 1988), 62.

56. Similarly, the ideological value of the work, rather than its size, determined the time allotted to Nekrasov's lyrics—fourteen hours—while to Tolstoy's immense *War and Peace,* twenty-two hours.

57. N. N. Shneidman, *Literature and Ideology in Soviet Education* (Lexington: Lexington Books, 1973), 77–90.

58. Maxim Gorky, "*Rabochy class dolzhen vospitat' svoikh masterov kul'tury,*" in his *O Literature* (Moscow: *Sovetskii pisatel',* 1953), 343–49.

59. Vladimir Voinovich, *The Fur Hat,* trans. Susan Brownsberger (New York: Harcourt Brace Jovanovich, 1989), 22.

60. Tertz, *Fantastic Stories,* 200.

61. Ibid., 177.

62. Chekhov, letter to Alexei Peshkov (Maxim Gorky), January 3, 1899. Karlinsky, 338.

63. Nabokov, *Lectures on Russian Literature,* 252.

64. Ibid., 250.

65. Viktor Erofeev, "*La Sofi a dorme dezha (Chekhov—intelligentsiia—Frantsiia—Chekhov),*" in his *V Labirinte Prokliatykh Voprosov* (Moscow: *Soiuz fotokhudozhnikov Rossii,* 1996), 2:514.

66. Mikhail Kuraev, "*Chekhov poseredine Rossii,*" *Zvezda* 3 (1997): 125.

67. A. N. Sakharov, ed., *Istoria Rossii s nachala XVII do kontsa XIX veka* (Moscow: *ACT,* 1998), 407–73.

68. Petr Vail and Aleksandr Genis, "*Printsip matreshki,*" *Novy Mir* 10 (1989): 247.

69. Vladimir Potapov, "Coming Out of the Underground," *Soviet Literature* 5 (1990): 164.

70. Lev Shestov, "Chekhov. Creation from the Void," in his *Chekhov and Other Essays* (Ann Arbor: University of Michigan Press, 1966).

71. Nikolai Pereiaslov, "*Opravdanie postmodernizma,*" *Nash Sovremennik* 5 (1999): 279.

72. Slobodanka Vladiv-Glover, "The New Model of Discourse in Post-Soviet Russian Fiction," in Mikhail Epstein, Alexander Genis, and Slobodanka Vladiv-Glover, *Russian Postmodernism: New Perspectives on Post-Soviet Culture,* ed. and trans. Slobodanka Vladiv-Glover (New York: Berghahn Books, 1999), 229.

73. Alan Wilde, *Modernism and the Aesthetics of Crisis* (Baltimore: The Johns Hopkins University Press, 1987), 42.

74. Chekhov, letter to Suvorin, May 1888. Karlinsky, 104.

75. William Spanos, "The Detective and the Boundary: Some Notes on the Postmodern Literary Imagination," *A Journal of Postmodern Literature* 1 (1972): 147–68.

76. Ageev, "Conspectus of the Crisis," 179.

77. Jean-François Lyotard, *Answering the Question: What Is Postmodernism* (Manchester: Manchester University Press, 1986), 74.

78. Chekhov, letter to Pleshcheev, April 1889. In Anton Chekhov, *Polnoe sobranie sochinenii i pisem v tridtsati tomakh,* 3:184. Translation in Avraham Yarmolinsky, ed., *Letters of Anton Chekhov* (New York: Viking, 1973), 112.

Chapter 4

1. Lev Gudkov and Boris Dubin, "*Bez napriazheniia . . . Zametki o kul'ture perekhodnogo perioda,*" *Novy Mir* 2 (1993): 243.

2. The theme for the issue of *Russian Studies in Literature: A Journal of Translations* (Winter 1994–95) which was devoted entirely to the problem of the intelligentsia in post-Soviet Russia.

3. Natalia Ivanova, "*Nastol'iashchee. Retro na (post)sovetskom ekrane,*" *Znamia* 9 (1997): 204–11; Masha Gessen, *Dead Again. The Russian Intelligentsia After Communism* (London–New York: Verso, 1997).

4. Stanislav Rassadin, "The Intelligentsia As a Conciliar Concept Does Not Exist. It Has Played Out Its Role, Been Crowded Out, Destroyed, Leaving Us with Intellectualness," *Russian Studies in Literature* 31, no. 1 (Winter 1994–95): 32–41.

5. Evgenii Ermolin, "*Idealisty. Intelligentsiia bessmertna!*" *Novy Mir* 2 (2003): 156–61.

6. Some scholars see the Soviet intelligentsia as a "wholly new phenomenon, a stratum with characteristics never before seen in history." See Leopold Labedz, "The Structure of the Soviet Intelligentsia," in *The Russian Intelligentsia,* ed. Richard Pipes (New York: Columbia University Press, 1961), 66. Richard Pipes considers the majority of the Soviet intelligentsia "semi-intelligentsia." See Richard Pipes, "The Historical Evolution of the Russian Intelligentsia," in *The Russian Intelligentsia,* 55.

7. See Dobrenko, *The Making of the State Reader,* which describes the ideal Soviet reader as "the many millions of the intelligentsia from the people" whose consciousness was formed by images from Russian and, partially, Western classics (291).

8. Pipes also sees culture as the model on which the semi-intelligentsia fashions itself: "The hold this culture exercises on Russians is so strong that through it a class which is historically dead acquires, posthumously, ever new heirs and successors. In particular, a fraction of the technical and administrative semi-intelligentsia of the second and third generation, as it grows more secure and sophisticated, may be expected to model itself on it" (Pipes, *The Russian Intelligentsia,* 55). This observation made in the early 1960s applies to the rest of the Soviet period.

9. Nikolai Berdiaev, "*Filosofskaia istina i intelligentskaia pravda,*" in *Vekhi. Sbornik statei o russkoi intelligentsii* (Moscow, 1909): 1–22. Reprint Frankfurt: Posev, 1969.

10. Sergei Bulgakov, "*Geroizm i podvizhnichestvo,*" in *Vekhi,* 23–69.

11. Andrei Sinyavsky, *The Russian Intelligentsia,* trans. Lynn Visson (New York: Columbia University Press, 1997), 66–67.

12. Erofeev, "*La Sofi a dorme dezha,*" 2:514.

13. Rassadin, "The Intelligentsia As a Conciliar Concept . . . ," 32.

14. Ibid., 39.

15. Chekhov, letter to Orlov, 1899. Karlinsky, 341.

16. Vyacheslav P'etsukh, *Ia i prochee* (Moscow: *Khudozhestvennaia Literatura,* 1990), 219. All P'etsukh passages are my translations; the texts in Russian are in P'etsukh, *Ia i prochee;* P'etsukh, "*Palata 7,*" *Oktiabr'* 1 (1992): 117–22; P'etsukh,

Gosudarstvennoe ditia. Page numbers refer to these editions as 1990, 1992, and 1997, respectively.

17. P'etsukh 1990, 245.

18. Ibid., 333.

19. Critical literature addressing P'etsukh's work is rather scarce; a good short analysis of the novel can be found in George Gibian's article "The Quest for Russian National Identity in Soviet Culture Today," in *The Search for Self-Definition in Russian Literature,* ed. Ewa M. Thompson (Amsterdam: John Benjamins Publishing Company, 1991). Lipovetsky's *Russian Postmodernist Fiction. Dialogue with Chaos* includes a chapter with an analysis of P'etsukh's story "Central-Ermolaevo War." There are several articles in the Russian "thick" journals: L. Polikovskaia, *"Tragediia noveyshego obraztsa," Literaturnoe Obozrenie* 3 (1990); I. Mil'shtein, *"Moscow, Sankt-Peterburgskiy variant," Literaturnoe Obozrenie* 2 (1989); and Pavel Uliashov, "Authors and Positions," *Soviet Literature* 1 (1990).

20. P'etsukh 1990, 246.

21. Ibid., 333.

22. Ibid., 49.

23. Cultural critics Nancy Condee and Vladimir Padunov define this shift as a reaction, a backlash even, to the years of compulsory respect for culture: "In a sense, the symbolic banishment of high literature from the tables of commerce is the market's revenge for the years of Soviet *cultural* imperialism—during most of which high literature occupied the place of honor in the pantheon of high culture—and Russia's *imperial* culture—during all of which high literature was the ever-present interlocutor in any high-minded 'discussion of ideas.'" Nancy Condee and Vladimir Padunov, "The ABC of Russian Consumer Culture. Readings, Ratings, and Real Estate," in *Soviet Hieroglyphs. Visual Culture in Late Twentieth-Century Russia,* ed. Nancy Condee (Bloomington: Indiana University Press, 1995), 142.

24. This disappointment is usually expressed along these lines: "Being well-informed he [the alternative prose writer] does not find it easy to overlook the fact that neither the sermons of Dostoevsky and Tolstoy, nor the harmony of Pushkin, nor all of Russian literature could save our people and country from the tragic battering at the hands of history." Potapov, "Coming Out of the 'Underground,'" 162.

25. P'etsukh 1990, 218.

26. Michael Riffaterre, "Compulsory Reader Response," 58.

27. P'etsukh 1992, 117.

28. See Elena Zubareva, "'*Neponiatnaia dushevnaia trevoga*'" (*Motiv 'Palaty no. 6' v proze russkoi emigratsii 1970x–1980x gg.*)," in *Almanac Melikhovo,* ed. Yu. A. Bychkov et al. (Moscow: *Druzhba narodov,* 2000), 93–103. A number of contemporary texts develop the motif of the mad world in which only a madman is sane: Sasha Sokolov's "School for Fools" (1974), Iu. Aleshkovsky's "Little Blue Modest Kerchief" (*Sinen'kii skromnyi platochek*) (1981), and A. Zinov'ev's "Yellow House" (1980). Andrei Konchalovsky's critically acclaimed feature film "House of Fools" (2002) belongs to the same tradition.

29. Valerii Tarsis, *"Palata #7"* (Frankfurt: *Posev,* 1966), 8. For a translation see *Ward 7: An Autobiographical Novel,* trans. Katya Brown (New York: Dutton, 1965), 28.

30. Vyacheslav P'etsukh stated this in our phone conversation in March 2007.

31. P'etsukh 1992, 117.

32. Andrew Durkin, "Chekhov's Response to Dostoevsky: The Case of Ward 6," *Slavic Review* 80:1 (Spring 1981): 49–59.

33. Liza Knapp, "Fear and Pity in 'Ward Six': Chekhovian Catharsis," in *Reading Chekhov's Text,* ed. Robert Luis Jackson (Evanston: Northwestern University Press, 1993), 145–54.

34. Sally Wolff, "The Wisdom of Pain in Chekhov's 'Ward Number Six,'" in *Literature and Medicine. Fictive Ills: Literary Perspectives on Wounds and Diseases,* Vol. 9, ed. Peter W. Graham and Elizabeth Sewell (Baltimore: The Johns Hopkins University Press, 1990), 134–41.

35. N. N. Yudenich (1862–1933), Russian general and, in 1918, the Commander-in-Chief of the White Army in the North-West region.

36. P'etsukh 1992, 117.

37. Anton Chekhov, *Polnoe sobranie sochinenii i pisem v tridtsati tomakh,* 8:101.

38. P'etsukh 1992, 121–22.

39. Chekhov, 8:83.

40. Ibid., 8:97.

41. Chekhov, 8:75.

42. P'etsukh 1992, 118.

43. Chekhov, 8:100.

44. Ibid., 121.

45. Ibid., 119.

46. Ibid.

47. Ibid., 122.

48. Aleksandr Matrosov, the World War II hero who in 1943 covered a German machine gun with his body to shield his comrades during an attack.

49. Another look at Sergey Bulgakov's article "Heroism and Christian Selfless Devotion" ("*Geroizm i podvizhnichestvo*") is helpful in illustrating these conflicting notions of heroic impulse. Bulgakov distinguishes between heroic acts on the grounds of their motivations in much the same way as P'etsukh's character. Examining and comparing the intelligentsia's heroism and Christian selfless devotion, Bulgakov sees the principal difference in the intelligentsia's selfish pride in being heroic, in its dream of "saving mankind, or at least the Russian people [. . .] in its own name" (316), while the Christian devotee sees himself as a nameless "instrument of God's will" (331). Thus, to decide whether heroism is noble or reprehensible is to look into a hero's motives: is he a selfless devotee or a member of the intelligentsia driven by the selfish desire to become a hero? Doctor Krutov's motives do not seem to include the desire to promote himself to the status of a hero, because like Chekhov's madman Gromov he reacts to the surrounding evil almost automatically. By Bulgakov's definition, Krutov is a selfless devotee, an admirable figure because he does not expect rewards.

50. P'etsukh 1992, 122.

51. Nabokov, *Lectures on Russian Literature,* 251.

52. P'etsukh 1990, 36.

53. Ibid.

54. Ibid.

55. Ibid., 37.

56. See, for instance, Gary Soul Morson, "Prosaic Chekhov: Metadrama, the Intelligentsia, and Uncle Vanya," *Russian Literature TriQuarterly* 80 (1990–1991 Winter): 118–59.

57. Ibid., 38.

58. Chekhov, 8:332.

59. P'etsukh 1990, 40.

60. Ibid., 41.

61. Ibid., 38.

62. Ibid., 41.

63. Ibid.

64. Ibid., 42.

65. Vasily Rozanov, *The Apocalypses of Our Time and Other Writings,* trans. Robert Payne and Nikita Romanoff, ed. Robert Payne (New York: Praeger Publishers, 1977), 274.

66. See for instance Vyacheslav Kuritsyn's, "*Velikie mify i skromnye dekonstruktsii,*" in *Russky Literaturny Postmodernism* (Moscow: *OGI,* 2000), chap. 5.

67. P'etsukh 1990, 45.

68. On the event in Chekhov see Cathy Popkin, *The Pragmatics of Insignificance* (Stanford: Stanford University Press, 1993).

69. Raul Eshelman, *Early Soviet Postmodernism* (Frankfurt am Main: Peter Lang, 1997), 61.

70. For an in-depth analysis of the notion of the event in the short story see the collection *The New Short Story Theories,* ed. Charles E. May (Athens: Ohio University Press, 1994).

71. Newman, *The Post-Modern Aura,* 91.

72. As a recent critic comments: "In Soviet literature, much that was opposed to the aesthetics of Socialist Realism either consciously or unconsciously harkened back to Chekhov, starting with Zoshchenko and Dobychin, and ending with Trifonov and Makanin. Chekhov is the unrecognized forerunner of that cultural revolution that should have been completed in Russian in the first quarter of our century, the same revolution whose features can be seen in the chaos of the present crisis." Ageev, "Conspectus of the Crisis," 170–88.

73. Irving Howe, "Mass Society and Postmodern Fiction." *Partisan Review* 26 (1959): 426–36.

Chapter 5

1. The pince-nez easily metamorphoses into the more contemporary glasses, the persistent metonymical attribute of an intelligent—*ochkarik.*

2. Yu. N. Tynianov, "*O parodii,*" in his *Poetika. Istoriia Literatury. Kino* (Moscow: *Nauka,* 1977), 294.

3. Kolbas, *Critical Theory and Literary Canon,* 63.

4. Pierre Bourdieu, *The Rules of Art. Genesis and Structure of the Literary Field* (Stanford: Stanford University Press, 1995), 171.

5. E. H. Gombrich, *Ideal and Idols: Essays on Values in History and in Art* (Oxford: Phaidon, 1979), 12.

6. A source, but by no means the only source. There exists an extensive body of "sources," from real-life estates and orchards to Shakespeare and Turgenev; see, for instance, M. Gromov, *Chekhov* (Moscow: *Molodaia gvardiia,* 1993), 352–57. Donald Rayfield (*Understanding Chekhov: A Critical Study of Chekhov's Prose and Drama* [Madison: The University of Wisconsin Press, 1999], 265) posits Maupassant's short novel *The Poplars* as "one unquestionable European source for *The Cherry Orchard*." Undoubtedly, all of these played a part. It is also well-known that Chekhov admired *Anna Karenina,* and I consider the possibility of his picking up Tolstoy's use of the garden/orchard metaphor quite convincing.

7. Leo Tolstoy, *Anna Karenina,* trans. Richard Peaver and Larissa Volokhonsky (London: Allen Lane, 2000), bk. 6, chap. 29.

8. *Novoe Vremia,* April 1904, quoted in M. Gromov, *Chekhov,* 358.

9. Donald Rayfield, *The Cherry Orchard. Catastrophe and Comedy* (New York: Twayne Publishers, 1994), 13.

10. Richard Gilman, *Chekhov's Plays: An Opening into Eternity* (New Haven: Yale University Press, 1995), 200.

11. Gromov, *Chekhov,* 385.

12. Ibid., 374.

13. Anton Chekhov, *Five Plays,* trans. Roland Hingley (Oxford: Oxford University Press, 1998), 282.

14. See Stephen Lovell, *Summerfolk. A History of Dacha, 1710–2000* (Ithaca: Cornell University Press, 2003), 65–66, for a discussion of real-life instances of merchants buying gentlefolk's estates.

15. Galina Brodskaya, *Alekseev-Stanislavsky, Chekhov i drugie: Vishnevosadovskaia epopeia* (Moscow: *Agraf,* 2000), 338.

16. Quoted in Brodskaya, 341.

17. Konstantin Stanislavsky, *Moia zhizn' v iskusstve* (Moscow: *Iskusstvo,* 1972), 315.

18. Brodskaya, 363.

19. *"Besedy s Ol'goi Leonardovnoi Knipper": Sotsialisticheskii Donbas, Stalino,* May 26, 1939. Quoted in Brodskaya, 356.

20. Senelick, *The Chekhov Theatre,* 219–20.

21. Ibid., 221.

22. Ibid., 223.

23. Ibid., 208.

24. Vladimir Arro, *Koleia: P'esy* (Leningrad: *Sovetskii pisatel',* 1987), 65.

25. Ibid., 75.

26. Ibid., 97.

27. Ibid., 112.

28. Ibid., 116.

29. Ibid., 117.

30. Dacha is a frequent location in Russian and Soviet literature and film. An exhaustive history of *dacha* is found in Lovell's *Summerfolk.* A brief overview and analysis of the post-Soviet dacha is presented in Jane Zavisca, "Contesting Capitalism at the post-Soviet Dacha: The Meaning of Food Cultivation for Urban Russians," *Slavic Review* 62, no. 4 (Winter 2003): 786–810.

31. Arro, *Smotrite, kto prishel* (1980), 172.
32. Ibid., 168.
33. Ibid., 181.
34. The proverbial Junior Researcher—*mladshii nauchnyi sotrudnik*—might be considered the representative embodiment of mass intelligentsia, that is, the white-collar, college-educated middle class. For more on the intelligentsia as middle class, see Lyudmila Parts, "Degradation of the Word or the Adventures of the Intelligent in Viktor Pelevin's Generation P," *Canadian Slavonic Papers* 46, nos. 3–4 (September–December 2004): 435–49.
35. Revekka Frumkina, "*Predlagaemye obstoiatel'stva,*" *Neprikosnovennyi zapas* 4 (2002): 123. Emphasis in the original.
36. Boris Minaev, "*Sushenaia vishnia,*" *Ogonek* 4 (2004): 47.
37. There are a number of studies of post-Soviet nostalgia in relation to the political, economic, and cultural situation. For a few representative examples, see David S. Mason and Svetlana Sidorenko-Stephenson, "Public Opinion and the 1996 Elections in Russia: Nostalgic and Statist, Yet Pro-Market and Pro-Yeltsin," *Slavic Review* 56, no. 4 (1997): 698–717; Vida T. Johnson, "The Search for a New Russia in an 'Era of Few Films,'" *Russian Review* 56, no. 2 (1997): 281–85; and Svetlana Boym, "From the Russian Soul to Post-Communist Nostalgia," in *Representations,* Special Issue: *Identifying Histories: Eastern Europe Before and After 1989,* no. 49 (Winter 1995): 133–66.
38. Irina Tsygal'skaya, "*Moi zaroshie vishnevye sady. Neotpravlennoe pis'mo podruge,*" *Druzhba narodov* 1 (1988): 138–49.
39. Galina Ryzhova, "'*Vishnevyi sad.' Brakon'erstvo i bioterrorism v SNG,*" *Moskva* 9 (2003): 203.
40. "*Vishnevye sady Silikonovoi doliny,*" Online, BBCRussian.com, accessed 12/14/2001. http://news8.thdo.bbc.co.uk/hi/russian/life/newsid_1711000/1711437.stm/.
41. Sergei Romashko, "'*Vishnevyi sad' po-frantsuzski,*" *Russkii Zhurnal.* Online, accessed 03/11/2004. http://old.russ.ru/columns/nofocus/20040311_rom.htm.
42. Karl Marx, "The Eighteenth Brumaire of Luis Bonaparte," in *The Karl Marx Library,* ed. Saul K. Padover (New York: McGraw-Hill, 1972), 1:245–46.
43. Ivanova, "*Nastol'iashchee,*" 32.
44. Galina Shcherbakova, "Kostochka avocado," *Novy Mir* 9 (1995): 28.
45. Petrushevskaya 2000, 118.
46. Ibid., 119.
47. Ibid, 120. Emphasis added.
48. Ibid., 122.
49. Ibid.
50. Ibid., 123.
51. Linda Hutcheon, "Irony, Nostalgia, and the Postmodern," in *Methods for the Study of Literature as Cultural Memory,* ed. Raymond Viverliet and Annemarie Estor (Amsterdam: Rodopi, 2000), 195.
52. Ibid., 207.
53. Daria Kirjanov, *Chekhov and the Poetics of Memory* (New York: Peter Lang, 2000), 117.
54. Hutcheon, *A Poetics of Postmodernism,* 19.
55. Igor Iarkevich, *Um, Seks, Literatura* (Moscow: *Galereia Gel'mana,* 1998), 14.

56. Ibid., 17.
57. Ibid., 61.
58. Ibid., 15.
59. John McGowan, *Postmodernism and Its Critics* (Ithaca: Cornell University Press, 1991), 27.

Chapter 6

1. The 1960 feature film by Joseph Heifits, a winner of the Cannes Film Festival, helped to establish its status.

2. See Irina Murav'yova, "*Dva imeni,*" *Grani* 152 (1989): 121; Mark Lipovetsky, "*Tragediia i malo li chto eshche,*" *Novy Mir* 10 (1994): 231; Maria Vasil'eva, "*Tak slozhilos',*" *Druzhba narodov* 4 (1998): 208–17.

3. For analyses of "Night Time" see Helena Goscilo, "Speaking Bodies: Erotic Zones Rhetoricized," in *Fruits of Her Plume: Essays on Contemporary Russian Women's Culture,* ed. Helena Goscilo (Armonk, NY: M. E. Sharpe, 1993), 135–63; Helena Goscilo, "Mother as Mothra: Totalizing Narrative in Petrushevskaya," in *A Plot of Her Own: The Female Protagonist in Russian Literature,* ed. Sona Stephan Hoisington (Evanston: Northwestern University Press, 1995), 102–13; and Josephine Woll, "The Minotaur in the Maze: Remarks on Lyudmila Petrushevskaya," *World Literature Today: Russian Literature at a Crossroads* 67 (1993): 125–30. For analyses of "Our Crowd" see Patricia Carden, "The Art of War in Petrushevskaya's 'Our Crowd,'" *Studies in Short Fiction* 34:1 (1997): 39–54; and Woll, "The Minotaur in the Maze." For analyses of "Such a Girl" see Aleksandra Karriker, "Claustrophobic Interiors and Splintered Selves: Petrushevskaya's Prose in Context," *West Virginia University Philological Papers* 41 (1995): 124–31.

4. Not only in criticism: in Heifits's film, the connection is brilliantly introduced in the scene in which Gurov, already back in Moscow, sees a dog that looks just like Anna Sergeevna's white, nameless dog. He follows it and discovers that the dog's name is Frou-Frou, which is, of course, the name of Vronsky's horse in *Anna Karenina.*

5. B. Meilakh, "*Dva resheniia odnoi problemy,*" *Neva* 9 (1956): 187–88.

6. Thomas Winner, *Chekhov and His Prose* (New York: Holt, Rinehart and Winston, 1996), 223.

7. See Caryl Emerson, "Chekhov and the Annas," in *Life and Text: Essays in Honour of Geir Kjetsaa on the Occasion of His 60th Birthday,* ed. Eric Egeberg, Audin J. Morch, and Ole Michael Selberg (Oslo: Universitetet i Oslo, 1997), 121–32.

8. Winner, *Chekhov and His Prose,* 224.

9. Nabokov, *Lectures on Russian Literature,* 333.

10. Tolstoy, bk. 2, chap. 11 (see chap. 5, n5).

11. Chekhov, 10:132 (see chap. 4, n40).

12. Tolstoy, bk. 2, chap. 11.

13. Chekhov, 10:132. Emphasis added.

14. Ibid.

15. Julie de Sherbinin traces representations of the biblical sinner in Chekhov and throughout the Russian literary canon. The Christian paradigm of two

Marys, the virgin and the whore, which de Sherbinin designates the Marian paradigm, is fixed in popular imagination and in literary representation. Within this paradigm, Anna Karenina represents the sinner, "the woman who would transgress the boundaries of commonly shared religious/social beliefs to commit adultery (her body prostrate at Vronsky's feet after their first amorous encounter, announces literally a fallen woman)." Julie de Sherbinin, *Chekhov and the Russian Religious Culture: The Poetics of the Marian Paradigm* (Evanston: Northwestern University Press, 1997), 37.

16. Amy Mandeleker, *Framing Anna Karenina: Tolstoy, the Woman Question, and the Victorian Novel* (Columbus: The Ohio State University Press, 1993), 115.

17. Tolstoy, bk. 5, chap. 11.

18. Mirrors are also used in *Anna Karenina* as a potential pathway into self-consciousness, a path that Tolstoy's characters do not necessarily follow: Levin looks at himself in the mirror before entering Anna's house and refuses to acknowledge that he is drunk. On the other hand, when Anna looks in the mirror on the last day of her life, she does gain an insight into herself. She recognizes herself in the strange woman that is looking at her in the mirror (the "other woman" she referred to in her delirium some months before), and her acknowledgment "Ah, it's me" (bk. 7, chap. 27) is one of the last and decisive factors that drive her to suicide.

19. L. N. Tolstoy, diary entry, 16 January 1900, in *Tolstoy's Diaries,* ed. and trans. R. F. Christian (London: Flamingo, 1994), 347.

20. Virtually every work on Petrushevskaya makes a note of the unremitting bleakness of her world. See, for instance, Helena Goscilo's "Mother as Mothra" for a look at Petrushevskaya's subversive treatment of the traditional roles of mothers, wives, and daughters. For an analysis of the moral disintegration of Petrushevskaya's characters as representative of the disintegration of social norms, and of her stories as "testament of an arduous even horrible epoch," see Karriker, "Claustrophic Interiors," 127.

21. Kataev, *Proza Chekhova,* 257.

22. Jan Van Der Eng, "The Semantic Structure of *Lady with a Lapdog,*" in *On the Theory of Descriptive Poetics: Anton Chekhov as Story-Teller and Playwright. Essays by Jan Van Der Eng, Jan M. Meijer and Herta Schmid* (Amsterdam: Peter de Ridder Press, 1978), 75.

23. Lyudmila Petrushevskaya, "*Dama s sobakami,*" in her *Dom devushek* (Moscow: *Vagrius,* 1999), 199. (This story has not been translated into English; all translations are mine.)

24. Ibid.

25. Ibid.

26. Tolstoy, bk. 1, chap. 19.

27. Petrushevskaya, 200.

28. Tolstoy, bk. 1, chap. 22; bk. 1, chap. 23; bk. 2, chap. 7; bk. 2, chap. 11; bk. 2, chap. 24, respectively.

29. Petrushevskaya, 200. In 1976, Brigitte Bardot, the famous French actress who became one of the icons of female sexuality in the United States in the 1950s and 1960s, established the Brigitte Bardot Foundation for the Protection of Distressed Animals.

30. In "Niura the Beautiful" ("*Niura Prekrasnaia*"), another story of the *Requiems* cycle, a dog is again a substitute for a close family relationship, in this case an unfaithful husband and nonexistent child: "The husband has long lived on the sly with a girlfriend, and there has been a baby already, but Niura did not manage to have a child and walked everywhere with her dog" (242).

31. Ibid.

32. Tolstoy, bk. 1, chap. 22.

33. Petrushevskaya, 201.

34. Ibid.

35. First drafts of the story stated explicitly: "Made them both better." Chekhov cut the word "better" from this sentence during the last stages of working on the story, trusting the reader to reach the conclusion. See K. M. Vinogradova, "*Stranitsa iz chernovoi rukopisi rasskaza 'Dama s sobachkoi,'" Literaturnoe nasledstvo: Tom 68. Chekhov,* ed. I. I. Anisinom et al. (Moscow: *Izdatelstvo Akademii Nauk,* 1960), 133–40.

36. Lev Shestov, *Chekhov and Other Essays* (Ann Arbor: University of Michigan Press, 1996), 4.

37. In a personal (telephone) conversation with me in May of 2001, Lyudmila Petrushevskaya denied any Chekhovian influence in her work even though, she admitted, there was a time when she loved Chekhov and knew his stories by heart. She then mentioned her surprise that just the day prior to my call a Yalta newspaper called to ask for permission to reprint the story "Downhill." She did not see any reason for a Yalta newspaper to be interested in this particular story.

38. Chekhov, 10:139. Emphasis added.

39. Petrushevskaya, 9–11. Emphasis added.

40. Ibid. This translation is slightly modified from the one in the *Moscow News,* 06/22/2002.

41. Chekhov, 10:129.

42. Ibid.

43. Chekhov, 10:130.

44. Petrushevskaya, 9.

45. Ibid.

46. Ibid., 11.

47. Ibid., 10–11.

48. Ibid., 11.

49. Ibid.

50. Chekhov, 10:142.

51. Chekhov, 10:139.

52. In Tolstoy's *Anna Karenina,* Anna thinks of her love for Vronsky as her happiness and her unhappiness, yet clearly there is nothing positive about Anna's situation.

53. Petrushevskaya, 11.

54. Ibid, 12.

55. Ibid.

56. C. R. S. Cockrell, "Chekhov's The Lady with a Dog," in *The Voice of a Giant: Essays on Seven Russian Prose Classics,* ed. Roger Cockrell and David Richards (Exeter: University of Exeter Press, 1985), 86–87.

57. Wilde, *Modernism and the Aesthetics of Crisis,* 44.

58. Lyudmila Petrushevskaya, "*Karamzin Derevenskii dnevnik,*" *Novy Mir* 9 (1994): 6.

Afterword

1. George P. Elliott, "Warm Heart, Cold Eye," in *Chekhov and Our Age. Responses to Chekhov by American Writers and Scholars,* ed. James McConkey (Ithaca: Cornell University Press, 1984), 46.

2. I leave aside the large and independent field of Chekhov's role in world theater and dramaturgy and limit my analysis, as I have done throughout most of the book, to the short story.

3. John Cheever, "The Melancholy of Distance," in *Chekhov and Our Age,* 127.

4. Hollis Summers, "Beside the Point," in *Chekhov and Our Age,* 152.

5. Eudora Welty, "Reality in Chekhov's Stories," in *Chekhov and Our Age,* 122.

6. Raymond Carver, *A New Path to the Waterfall,* Introduction by Tess Gallagher (New York: The Atlantic Monthly Press, 1989), xx.

7. Ibid., xxii.

8. Ibid., xxix.

9. George P. Elliott, "Warm Heart, Cold Eye," 45.

10. Ibid., 47.

11. Raymond Carver, "On 'Errand,'" in *The Story and Its Writers. An Introduction to Short Story Fiction,* ed. Ann Charters (Boston: Bedford Books, 1999), 890.

12. Milazzo Lee, ed., *Conversations with Joyce Carol Oates* (Jackson: University Press of Mississippi, 1989), 19.

13. I therefore disagree with critics who overemphasize the significance of the shift in points of view (politicize it, really) to the extent that Oates is seen as challenging Chekhov on feminist grounds or even refuting him as a writer who sees women through the "lens of sexist imagination," as in Matthew C. Brennan, "Plotting against Chekhov: Joyce Carol Oates and 'The Lady with the Dog,'" *Notes on Modern American Literature* 3, no. 9 (Winter 1985): 13.

14. On the motif of seeing and being seen in Chekhov's story see Michael C. Finke, *Seeing Chekhov. Life and Art* (Ithaca–London: Cornell University Press, 2005), 145–46.

15. Walker Percy, "Novelist as Diagnostician of Modern Malaise," in *Chekhov and Our Age,* 71.

16. Maurice R. Berube, "Why I Hate Chekhov," *The Chronicle of Higher Education* 48, no. 25 (March 1, 2002): B5.

17. Tertz, *Fantastic Stories,* 200.

18. Condee and Padunov, "The ABC of Russian Consumer Culture. Readings, Ratings, and Real Estate," 142.

19. Ibid.

BIBLIOGRAPHY

Abramovich, G., B. Braynina, and A. Egolin. *Russkaya Literatura. Uchebnik dlia srednei shkoly, Chast' II.* Moscow: Uchpedgiz, 1935.

Ageev, Alexander. "Conspectus of the Crisis: Sociocultural Conditions and the Literary Process." In *Re-Entering the Sign. Articulating New Russian Culture,* ed. Ellen E. Berry and Anesa Miller-Pogacar. Ann Arbor: University of Michigan Press, 1995. 170–88.

Alagova, Tamara and Nina Efimov. "Interview with Tatyana Tolstaya." *World Literature Today* 67, no. 1 (1993): 49–53.

Anderson, Benedict. *Imagined Communities.* London: Verso, 1991.

Arro, Vladimir. *Koleia: P'esy.* Leningrad: Sovetskii pisatel', 1987.

Bakhtin, Mikhail. *Problems of Dostoevsky Poetics.* Ed. and trans. Carol Emerson. Minneapolis and London: University of Minnesota Press, 1997.

Barta, Peter. "The Author, the Cultural Tradition and Glasnost. An Interview with Tatyana Tolstaya." *Russian Literature Journal* XLIV, nos. 147–49 (1990): 265–83.

Barthes, Roland. *Mythologies.* Trans. Annette Lavers. New York: Hill and Wang, 1988.

———. *Image—Music—Text.* Trans. Stephen Heath. London: Fontana, 1977.

Ben-Amos, Dan and Lillian Weissberg, eds. *Cultural Memory and the Construction of Identity.* Detroit: Wayne State University Press, 1999.

Berdiaev, Nikolai. "*Filosofskaia istina i intelligentskaia pravda.* " In *Vekhi. Sbornik statei o russkoi intelligentsii.* Frankfurt: Posev, 1969. 1–22.

Berube, Maurice R. "Why I Hate Chekhov." *The Chronicle of Higher Education* 48, no. 25 (March 1, 2002): B5.

Bethea, David. "Where to Begin: Pushkin, Derzhavin, and the Poetic Use of Filiation." In *Rereading Russian Poetry,* ed. Stephanie Sandler. New Haven: Yale University Press, 1999. 58–70.

Bethea, David M. *Realizing Metaphors: Alexander Pushkin and the Life of a Poet.* Madison: University of Wisconsin Press, 1998.

Bhabha, Homi K., ed. *Nation and Narration.* London: Routledge, 1990.

Bitov, Andrei. "*Moi dedushka Chekhov and pradedushka Pushkin.*" In *Chetyrezhdy Chekhov,* ed. Andrei Bitov. Moscow: Izdatelstvo, 2004. 5–16.

———. *Pushkin House.* Trans. Susan Brownsberger. New York: Farrar, Strauss, Giroux, 1987.

———. *Vychitanie zaitsa. 1825.* Moscow: Nezavisimaia gazeta, 2001.

Blok, Alexander. *Selected Poems.* Trans. Alex Miller. Moscow: Progress Publishers, 1981.

Bloom, Harold. *The Western Canon: The Books and School of the Ages.* New York: Riverhead Books, 1994.

———. *The Anxiety of Influence.* London: Oxford University Press, 1975.

Bogdanovich, Aleksandr. *Gody pereloma. Sbornik kriticheskih statei.* SPB: Mir Bozhii, 1908.

Bourdieu, Pierre. *The Rules of Art. Genesis and Structure of the Literary Field.* Stanford: Stanford University Press, 1995.

Boym, Svetlana. "From the Russian Soul to Post-Communist Nostalgia." *Representation,* Special Issue: *Identifying Histories: Eastern Europe Before and After 1989,* no. 49 (Winter 1995): 133–66.

———. *Death in Quotation Marks. Cultural Myths of the Modern Poet.* Cambridge: Harvard University Press, 1991.

Brennan, Matthew C. "Plotting Against Chekhov: Joyce Carol Oates and 'The Lady with a Dog.'" *Notes on Modern American Literature* 9, no. 3 (1985): 13.

Brintlinger, Angela. *Writing a Usable Past: Russian Literary Culture, 1917–1937.* Evanston: Northwestern University Press, 2000.

Brodskaya, Galina. *Alekseev-Stanislavsky, Chekhov i drugie: Vishnevosadovskaia epopeia.* Moscow: Agraf, 2000.

Brooks, Jeffrey. "Russian Nationalism and Russian Literature: The Canonization of the Classics." In *Nation and Ideology. Essays in Honor of Wayne S. Vucinich,* ed. Ivo Banac, John G. Ackerman, and Roman Szporluk. New York: East European Monographs, Columbia University Press, 1981. 315–34.

Bulgakov, Sergei. "*Geroizm i podvizhnichestvo.*" In *Vekhi. Sbornik statei o russkoi intelligentsii.* Frankfurt: Posev, 1969. 23–69.

Bushkanets, Lia. "'*Obydennost' A. P. Chekhova.*" In *Almanach Melikhovo,* ed. Yu. A. Bychkov et al. Moscow: Druzhba narodov, 2000. 47–62.

Carden, Patricia. "The Art of War in Petrushevskaya's 'Our Crowd.'" *Studies in Short Fiction* 34:1 (1997): 39–54.

Carver, Raymond. "On 'Errand.'" *The Story and Its Writers. An Introduction to Short Story Fiction,* ed. Ann Charters. Boston: Bedford Books, 1999.

———. *A New Path to the Waterfall.* New York: Atlantic Monthly Press, 1989.

Chances, Ellen. *Andrei Bitov. The Ecology of Inspiration.* Cambridge: Cambridge University Press, 1993.

Cheever, John. "The Melancholy of Distance." In *Chekhov and Our Age. Responses to Chekhov by American Writers and Scholars,* ed. James McConkey. Ithaca: Cornell University Press, 1984.

Chekhov, Anton. *Five Plays.* Trans. Roland Hingley. Oxford: Oxford University Press, 1998.

———. *Polnoe sobranie sochinenii i pisem v tridtsati tomakh.* Ed. N. F. Belchikov et al. Moscow: Nauka, 1974–83.

———. *Plays.* Trans. Elizaveta Fen. London: Penguin Books, 1959.

Chekhov's Notebook. Online, accessed 09/12/2007. http://www.gutenberg.org/files/12494/12494.txt

Christian, R. F., ed. and trans. *Tolstoy's Diaries.* London: Flamingo, 1994.

Chudakov, A. P. "*Pushkin i Chekhov. Zavershenie kruga.*" In *Chekhoviana. Chekhov i Pushkin,* ed. V. B. Kataev et al. Moscow: Nauka, 1998. 35–47.

Cockrell, C. R. S. "Chekhov's 'The Lady with a Dog.'" In *The Voice of a Giant: Essays on Seven Russian Prose Classics,* ed. Roger Cockrell and David Richards. Exeter: University of Exeter Press, 1985. 81–92.

Condee, Nancy and Vladimir Padunov. "The ABC of Consumer Culture. Readings, Ratings, and Real Estate." In *Soviet Hieroglyphs: Visual Culture in Late Twentieth-Century Russia,* ed. Nancy Condee. Bloomington: Indiana University Press, 1995. 135–72.

Connertnon, Paul. *How Societies Remember.* Cambridge–New York: Cambridge University Press, 1989.

Coupe, Laurence. *Myth.* London–New York: Routledge, 1997.

De Wet, Karen. "Dialogues Generated by Pivotal Figures in Literary Systems: A Systematic Approach to the Study of Literature." In *Methods for the Study of Literature as Cultural Memory,* ed. Raymond Viverliet and Annemarie Estor. Amsterdam: Rodopi, 2000. 7–18.

Dobin E. S. "The Nature of Detail." In *Anton Chekhov as a Master of Story-Writing,* ed. and trans. Leo Hulanicki and David Savignac. Paris: Mouton, 1976. 39–59.

Dobrenko, Evgeny. *The Making of the State Reader.* Stanford: Stanford University Press, 1997.

Druzhnikov, Yurii. *Russkie mify.* New York: Liberty Publishing, 1995.

Durkin, Andrew. "Chekhov's Response to Dostoevsky: The Case of Ward 6." *Slavic Review* 80:1 (Spring 1981): 49–59.

Efimova, Nina. "*Motiv igry v proizvedeniiakh L. Petrushevskoi i T. Tolstoi.*" *Vestnik Moskovskogo Universiteta.* Ser. 9. *Filologiia* 3 (1998): 60–71.

Eliade, Mircea. *Myth and Reality.* Trans. Willard R. Trask. New York–Evanston: Harper & Row, 1963.

Elliott, George P. "Warm Heart, Cold Eye." In *Chekhov and Our Age. Responses to Chekhov by American Writers and Scholars,* ed. James McConkey. Ithaca: Cornell University Press, 1984. 46.

Emerson, Caryl. "Chekhov and the Annas." In *Life and Text: Essays in Honour of Geir Kjetsaa on the Occasion of His 60th Birthday,* ed. Eric Egeberg, Audin J. Morch, and Ole Michael Selberg. Oslo: Universitetet i Oslo, 1997. 121–32.

Epstein, Michael. "The Origins and Meaning of Russian Postmodernism." In *After the Future. The Paradoxes of Postmodernism and Contemporary Culture,* trans. Anesa Millr-Pogacar. Amherst: The University of Massachusetts Press, 1995. 188–210.

Ermilov, V. *Chekhov: ZHZL.* Moscow: Molodaya Gvardiya, 1949.

Ermolin, Evgenii. *"Idealisty. Intelligentsiia bessmertna!" Novy Mir* 2 (2003): 156–61.

Erofeev, Viktor. *"La Sofi a dorme dezha (Chekhov—intelligentsiia—Frantsiia—Chekhov)."* In his *V Labirinte Prokliatykh Voprosov,* t. 2. Moscow: Soiuz fotokhudozhnikov Rossii, 1996. 514–32.

Eshelman, Raul. *Early Soviet Postmodernism.* Frankfurt am Main: Peter Lang, 1997.

Fentress, James and Chris Wickham, eds. *Social Memory.* Oxford: Blackwell, 1992.

Finke, Michael C. *Seeing Chekhov. Life and Art.* Ithaca and London: Cornell University Press, 2005.

———. "The Hero's Descent to the Underworld in Chekhov." *Russian Review* 53, no. 1 (January 1994): 67–80.

Friedberg, Maurice. *Russian Classics in Soviet Jackets.* New York: Columbia University Press, 1962.

Frumkina, Revekka. *"Predlagaemye obstoiatel'stva." Neprikosnovennyi zapas* 4 (2002): 121–24.

Gasparov, Boris. "The Golden Age and Its Role in the Cultural Mythology of Russian Modernism." In *Cultural Mythologies of Russian Modernism,* ed. Boris Gasparov, Robert P. Hughes, and Irina Paperno. Berkeley: University of California Press, 1992. 5–6.

———. *"Tridtsatye gody—zheleznyi vek (k analizu motivov stoletnego vozvrashcheniia u Mandelshtama)."* In *Cultural Mythologies of Russian Modernism,* ed. Boris Gasparov, Robert P. Hughes, and Irina Paperno. Berkeley: University of California Press, 1992. 150–79.

Genette, Gerard. *Palimpsests: Literature in the Second Degree.* Trans. Channa Newman and Claude Doubinsky. Lincoln: University of Nebraska Press, 1997.

Gessen, Masha. *Dead Again. The Russian Intelligentsia After Communism.* London–New York: Verso, 1997.

Gibian, George. "The Quest for Russian National Identity in Soviet Culture Today." In *The Search for Self-Definition in Russian Literature,* ed. Ewa M. Thompson. Amsterdam: John Benjamins Publishing Company, 1991. 1–20.

Gilles, John R. Introduction. "Memory and Identity. The History of a Relationship." In *Commemorations. The Politics of National Identity,* ed. John R. Gillis. Princeton: Princeton University Press, 1994. 3–24.

Gilman, Richard. *Chekhov's Plays: An Opening Into Eternity.* New Haven: Yale University Press, 1995.

Ginzburg, Lidiia. *O lirike.* Moscow: Intrada, 1997.

Gippius, Zinaida. *"Nuzhny li stikhi?"* In her *Dnevniki.* Moscow: Intelvak, 1999.

———. *"Slovo o teatre."* In her *Dnevniki.* Moscow: Intelvak, 1999.

Glushkov, S. V. *"Chekhov v epokhu reform (Po materialam pressy 1985–1995 gg.)."* In *Chekhoivskie chteniia v Ialte: Chekhov i XX vek.* Vypusk 9. Moscow: *Nasledie,* 1997. 80–89.

Gombrich, E. H. *Ideal and Idols: Essays on Values in History and in Art*. Oxford: Phaidon, 1979.

Gorak, Jan. *The Making of the Modern Canon. Genesis and Crisis of Literary Idea*. London: Athlone, 1991.

Gorky, Maxim. "*Rabochy class dolzhen vospitat' svoikh masterov kul'tury*." In his *O Literature*. Moscow: Sovetskii pisatel', 1953. 343–49.

Goscilo, Helena. *The Explosive World of Tatyana N. Tolstaya's Fiction*. Armonk, NY: M. E. Sharpe, 1996.

———. "Mother as Mothra: Totalizing Nature and Nurture in Petrushevskaya." In *A Plot of Her Own: The Female Protagonist in Russian Literature*, ed. Sona Stephan Hoisington. Evanston: Northwestern University Press, 1995. 102–13.

———. "Speaking Bodies: Erotic Zones Rhetoricized." In *Fruits of Her Plume: Essays on Contemporary Russian Women's Culture*, ed. Helena Goscilo. Armonk, NY: M. E. Sharpe, 1993. 135–63.

Grahamn, Sheelagh Duffin, ed. *New Directions in Soviet Literature*. New York: St. Martin's Press, 1992.

Grekova, I. "*Rastochitel'nost' talanta*." *Novy Mir* 1 (1988): 252–56.

Gromov, M. *Chekhov*. Moscow: Molodaia gvardiia, 1993.

Gudkov, Lev and Boris Dubin. "*Bez napriazheniia . . . Zametki o kul'ture perekhodnogo perioda*." *Novy Mir* 2 (1993): 242–53.

Guillory, John. *Cultural Capital: The Problem of Literary Canon Formation*. Chicago: University of Chicago Press, 1993.

Habermas, Jurgen. *The Theory of Communicative Action*. Trans. Thomas McCarthy. Boston: Beacon Press, 1983.

Halbwachs, Maurice. *On Collective Memory*. Ed. and trans. Lewis A. Coser. Chicago: University of Chicago Press, 1992.

Hobsbawm, Eric. *The Invention of Traditions*. Ed. Eric Hobsbawm and Terence Ranger. Cambridge: Cambridge University Press, 1983.

Hodgkin, Katherine and Susannah Radstone, eds. *Contested Pasts: The Politics of Memory*. London–New York: Routledge, 2003.

Hosking, Geoffrey and George Schopflin, eds. *Myth & Nationhood*. New York: Routledge, 1997.

Howe, Irving. "Mass Society and Postmodern Fiction." *Partisan Review* 26 (1959): 426–36.

Hutcheon, Linda. "Irony, Nostalgia, and the Postmodern." In *Methods for the Study of Literature as Cultural Memory*, ed. Raymond Viverliet and Annemarie Estor. Amsterdam: Rodopi, 2000. 195.

———. *A Poetics of Postmodernism. History, Theory, Fiction*. New York: Routledge, 1988.

Iarkevich, Igor. *Um, Seks, Literatura*. Moscow: Galereia Gel'mana, 1998.

———. "Beginning to Theorize Postmodernism." In *A Postmodern Reader*, ed. Joseph Natoli and Linda Hutcheon. Albany: State University of New York Press, 1993.

———. *Kak ia i kak menia*. Moscow: Proza Press, 1996.

Ivanova, Natalia. "*Nastol'iashchee. Retro na (post)sovetskom ekrane*." *Znamia* 9 (1997): 204–11.

Johnson, Vida T. "The Search for a New Russia in an 'Era of Few Films.'" *Russian Review* 56, no. 2 (1997): 281–85.

Juvan, Marko. "Thematics and Intellectual Content: The XVth Triennial Congress of the International Comparative Literature Association in Leiden." Online, accessed summer 2004. http://clcwebjournal.lib.purdue.edu/clcweb99-1/juvan99.html.

Karlinsky, Simon. Introduction. "The Gentle Subversive." In *Letters of Anton Chekhov,* trans. Michael Henry Heim, selection and commentary Simon Karlinsky. New York: Harper & Row, 1973. 11–32.

Karrer, Wolfgang. "Titles and Mottoes as Intertextual Devices." In *Intertextuality,* ed. Heinrich F. Plett. Berlin: Walter de Gruyter, 1991. 122–34.

Karriker, Aleksandra. "Claustrophobic Interiors and Splintered Selves: Petrushevskaya's Prose in Context." *West Virginia University Philological Papers* 41 (1995): 124–31.

Kasymov, Aleksandr. "*Pomysel i promysel, ili pisateli o pisatel'stve.*" *Znamia* 4 (2000): 178–84.

Kataev, V. B. et al., eds. *Chekhoviana: Chekhov i Pushkin.* Moscow: Nauka, 1998.

Kataev, Vladimir. *Chekhov plius . . . Predshestvenniki, sovremenniki, preemniki.* Moscow: Iazyki slavianskoi kul'tury, 2004.

———. "Problems of Applied Literary Criticism." *Russian Studies in Literature* 35, no. 1 (Winter 1998–99): 57–68.

———. *Proza Chekhova. Problemy Interpretatsii.* Moscow: Izdatel'stvo Moskovskogo Universiteta, 1979.

Keunen, Bart. "Cultural Thematics and Cultural Memory. Toward a Socio-Cultural Approach to Literary Themes." In *Methods for the Study of Literature as Cultural Memory,* ed. Raymond Viverliet and Annemarie Estor. Amsterdam: Rodopi, 2000. 19–31.

Khodasevich, V. Introduction. In *A. P. Chekhov,* ed. Georgii Berdnikov. Rostov n/D: Feniks, 1997. 3–8.

Khodasevich, Vladislav. "*O Chekhov.*" In his *Koleblemyi trenozhnik,* ed. V. G. Perelmuter. Moscow: Sovetskii pisatel', 1991.

King, Beatrice. *Russia Goes to School. A Guide to Soviet Education.* London: The New Education Book Club, 1948.

Kirjanov, Daria. *Chekhov and the Poetics of Memory.* New York: Peter Lang, 2000.

Knapp, Lisa. "Fear and Pity in 'Ward Six': Chekhovian Catharsis." In *Reading Chekhov's Text,* ed. Robert Luis Jackson. Evanston: Northwestern University Press, 1993. 145–54.

Kolbas, E. Dean. *Critical Theory and the Literary Canon.* Boulder: Westview, 2001.

Kostiukov, L. "The Twentieth Century Renewal of a Great Destiny." *Russian Studies in Literature* 35, no. 1 (Winter 1998–99): 50–56.

Kristeva, Julia. "World, Dialogue, and Novel." In *Desire in Language. A Semiotic Approach to Literature and Art,* ed. Leon S. Roudiez. New York: Columbia University Press, 1980. 64–91.

Kuraev, Mikhail. "*Aktual'nyi Chekhov.*" *Druzhba narodov* 12 (1998): 168–79.

———. "*Chekhov poseredine Rossii.*" *Zvezda* 3 (1997): 116–36.

Kuritsin, Vyacheslav. *Russky Literaturny Postmodernism. 1992–1997.* Online, accessed 2000. http://www.guelman.ru/slava/postmod/html.

———. "Postmodernism: The New Primitive Culture." In *Re-Entering the Sign,* ed.

Ellen E. Berry and Anesa Miller-Pogacar. Ann Arbor: University of Michigan Press, 1995. 48–61.

Kuzicheva, A. P. "*O philosophii zhizni i smerti.*" In *Chekhov i Lev Tolstoy*, ed. L. D. Opul'skaia et al. Moscow: Nauka, 1980. 254–63.

Labedz, Leopold. "The Structure of the Soviet Intelligentsia." In *The Russian Intelligentsia*, ed. Richard Pipes. New York: Columbia University Press, 1961. 63–79.

Lachmann, Renate. *Memory and Literature. Intertextuality and Russian Modernism.* Minneapolis: University of Minnesota Press, 1997.

Lakshin, Vladimir. *Tolstoy i Chekhov.* izd. 2. Moscow: Sovetskii pisatel', 1975.

Lebedushkina, Olga. "*Kniga tsarstv i vozmozhnostei.*" *Druzhba Narodov* 4 (1998): 199–207.

Levitt, Marcus C. "Pushkin in 1899." In *Cultural Mythologies of Russian Modernism*, ed. Boris Gasparov, Robert P. Hughes, and Irina Paperno. Berkeley: University of California Press, 1992. 187.

———. *Russian Literary Politics and the Pushkin Celebration of 1880.* Ithaca: Cornell University Press, 1989.

Likhachev, D. S. "*O russkoi intelligentsii. Pis'mo v redaktsiiu.*" *Novy Mir* 2 (1993): 3–9.

———. *Razvitie Russkoy Literatury X–XVII vekov: Epokhi i stili.* Leningrad: Nauka, 1973.

Lipovetsky, Mark. "*Rasstratnye strategii, ili matamorfozy 'chernukhi.'*" *Novy Mir* 11 (1999): 193–210.

———. *Russian Postmodernist Fiction. Dialogue with Chaos.* Ed. Eliot Borenstein. Armonk, NY: M. E. Sharpe, 1999.

———. "*Tragediia i malo li chto eshche.*" *Novy Mir* 10 (1994): 229–32.

Lotman, Yu. M. and B. A. Uspensky. "Myth—Name—Culture." In *Soviet Semiotics*, ed. and trans. Daniel P. Lucid. Baltimore: The Johns Hopkins University Press, 1977. 233–52.

Lotman, Yuri. "*Pamiat' v kul'turologicheskom osveshchenii.*" In his *Semiosphera.* St. Petersburg: Isskustvo-SPB, 2000. 673–76.

———. *Besedy o russkoi kul'ture.* St. Petersburg: Iskusstvo-SPB, 1997. 8.

———. "*O semioticheskom mekhanizme kul'tury.*" In *Izbrannye stat'i v trekh tomakh.* Vol. 1, Tallinn: Aleksandra, 1993. 326–44.

Lovell, Stephen. *Summerfolk. A History of Dacha, 1710–2000.* Ithaca: Cornell University Press, 2003.

Lowenthal, David. "Identity, Heritage, and History." In *Commemorations. The Politics of National Identity*, ed. John R. Gillis. Princeton: Princeton University Press, 1994. 41–57.

Lunacharsky, Aexander. *Sobranie Sochineniy.* Vol. 1. Moscow: Khudozhestvennaia literatura, 1963.

Lyotard, Jean-François. *Answering the Question: What Is Postmodernism?* Manchester: Manchester University Press, 1986.

Maegd-Soep De, Carolina. *Chekhov and Women. Women in the Life and Work of Chekhov.* Bloomington, IN: Slavica Publishers, 1987.

Mandeleker, Amy. *Framing Anna Karenina: Tolstoy, the Woman Question, and the Victorian Novel.* Columbus: The Ohio State University Press, 1993.

Mandelshtam, Osip. "The Noise of Time." In O. E. Mandelshtam, *The Prose of*

Osip Mandelshtam. Trans. Clarence Brown. San Francisco: North Point Press, 1986.

———. *"Shum Vremeni."* In O. E. Mandelshtam, *Ob iskusstve* (Moscow: *Iskusstvo,* 1995). 24.

———.*"Slovo i kul'tura."* In O. E. Mandelshtam, *Ob iskusstve* (Moscow: *Iskusstvo,* 1995). 204.

Marx, Karl. "The Eighteenth Brumaire of Luis Bonaparte." In *The Karl Marx Library,* ed. Saul K. Padover. New York: McGraw-Hill, 1972.

Mason, David S. and Svetlana Sidorenko-Stephenson. "Public Opinion and the 1996 Elections in Russia: Nostalgic and Statist, Yet Pro-Market and Pro-Yeltsin." *Slavic Review* 56, no. 4 (1997): 698–717.

Matich, Olga. "Dialectics of Cultural Return: Zinaida Gippius' Personal Myth." In *Cultural Mythologies of Russian Modernism,* ed. Boris Gasparov, Robert P. Hughes, and Irina Paperno. Berkeley: University of California Press, 1992. Chapter 2, n4.

Matlaw, Ralphe E., ed. *Anton Chekhov's Short Stories. A Norton Critical Edition.* New York: W. W. Norton, 1979.

May, Charles E., ed. *The New Short Story Theories.* Athens: Ohio University Press, 1994.

Mayakovsky, V. *Polnoe sobranie sochinenii.* Compiled and with notes by V.A. Katanian. Moscow: Gosudarstvennoe izdatelstvo khudozhestvennoi literatury, vol. 1. 301.

———. *Selected Verse.* Moscow: Raduga, 1985.

McConkey, James, ed. *Chekhov and Our Age. Responses to Chekhov by American Writers and Scholars.* Ithaca: Cornell University Press, 1984.

McGowan, John. *Postmodernism and Its Critics.* Ithaca: Cornell University Press, 1991.

Meilakh, B. *"Dva resheniia odnoi problemy." Neva* 9 (1956): 187–88.

Meletinsky, E. M. *Poetika mifa. Vostochnaia Literatura RAN.* Moscow: Iazyki russkoy kul'tury, 1995.

Merezhkovsky, Dmitri. *"Brat chelovechesky."* In his *Akropol'. Izbrannye literaturno-kriticheskie stat'i.* Moscow: Knizhnaia palata, 1991.

———. *Chekhov and Gorky.* Letchworth: Prideaux Press, 1975.

———. *Vechnye sputniki (Pushkin).* Letchworth: Prideaux Press, 1971.

Meylakh, B. *"Dva resheniia odnoi problemy." Neva* 9 (1956): 184–88.

Milazzo, Lee, ed. *Conversations with Joyce Carol Oates.* Jackson: University Press of Mississippi, 1989.

Mil'shtein, I. *"Moscow, Sankt-Peterburgsky variant." Literaturnoe Obozrenie* 2 (1989): 69–70.

Minaev, Boris. *"Sushenaia vishnia." Ogonek* 4 (2004): 47.

Mondry, H. "Nationalism in Literary Criticism in Russia Today." In *Twentieth-Century Russian Literature. Selected Papers from the Fifth World Congress of Central and East European Studies,* ed. K. L. Ryan and B. P. Scherr. London: Macmillan, 2000. 307–18.

Morson, Gary Soul. "Prosaic Chekhov: Metadrama, the Intelligentsia, and Uncle Vanya." *Russian Literature TriQuarterly* 80 (Winter 1990–91): 118–59.

Murav'yova, Irina. "*Dva imeni.*" *Grani* 152 (1989): 99–133.
Nabokov, Vladimir. *Lectures on Russian Literature.* Ed. Fredson Bowers. San Diego: A Harvest Book, Harcourt Brace & Company, Bruccoli Clark Layman, 1981.
Nazarenko, Ia. A. *Istoriya russkoy literatury XIX veka.* Moscow: Gos. Izdatel'stvo, 1926.
Nemzer, Andrei. "*Sovremennyi dialog s Gogolem.*" *Novy Mir* 5 (1994): 208–25.
Nepomnyashchy, Catharine Theimer. *Abram Tertz and the Poetics of Crime.* New Haven: Yale University Press, 1995.
Newman, Charles Hamilton. *The Post-Modern Aura. The Act of Fiction at an Age of Inflation.* Evanston: Northwestern University Press, 1985.
Ognev, A. *Chekhov i sovremennaya russkaya proza.* Tver': Tverskoy Gosudarstvenny Universitet, 1994.
Paperno, Irina. "*Pushkin v zhizni cheloveka Serebriannogo veka.*" In *Cultural Mythologies of Russian Modernism,* ed. Boris Gasparov, Robert P. Hughes, and Irina Paperno. Berkeley: University of California Press, 1992. 19–51.
Parts, Lyudmila. "Degradation of the Word or the Adventures of the Intelligent in Viktor Pelevin's Generation P." *Canadian Slavonic Papers* 46, nos. 3–4 (September–December 2004): 435–49.
Pasternak, Boris. *Doctor Zhivago.* Trans. Max Hayward and Manya Harari. New York: Pantheon, 1958. 285.
———. *Doktor Zhivago.* Moscow: Knizhnaya Palata, 1989.
Percy, Walker. "Novelist as Diagnostician of Modern Malaise." In *Chekhov and Our Age. Responses to Chekhov by American Writers and Scholars,* ed. James McConkey. Ithaca: Cornell University Press, 1984. 71.
Pereiaslov, Nikolai. "*Opravdanie postmodernizma.*" *Nash Sovremennik* 5 (1999): 159–202.
Perelmuter, V. ed. *Pushkin v emigratsii. 1937.* Moscow: Progress-Traditsiia, 1999.
Petrushevskaya, Lyudmila. "*Rai, rai.*" *Znamia* 3 (2000): 118–123.
———. "*Dama s sobakami.*" In her *Dom devushek.* Moscow: Vagrius, 1999. 199.
———. *Dom Devushek.* Moscow: Vagrius, 1999.
———. "*Karamzin Derevenskii dnevnik.*" *Novy Mir* 9 (1994): 6.
P'etsukh, Vyacheslav. *Ia i prochee.* Moscow: Khudozhestvennaia Literatura, 1990.
———. *Gosudarstvennoe ditia.* Moscow: Vagrius, 1997.
———. "*Palata 7.*" *Oktiabr'* 1 (1992): 117–22.
Petukhova, E. N. "*Chekhov i drugaia proza.*" In *Chekhoivskie chteniia v Ialte: Chekhov i XX vek.* Vypusk 9. Moscow: Nasledie, 1997. 71–80.
Pfister, Manfred. "How Postmodern Is Intertextuality?" In *Intertextuality,* ed. Heinrich F. Plett. Berlin: Walter de Gruyter, 1991. 207–24.
Pipes, Richard, ed. *The Russian Intelligentsia.* New York: Columbia University Press, 1961.
Plett, Heinrich F., ed. *Intertextuality.* Berlin: Walter de Gruyter, 1991.
Plett, Heinrich F. "Intertextualities." In his *Intertextuality.* Berlin: Walter de Gruyter, 1991. 3–29.
Polikovskaia, L. "*Tragediia noveishego obraztsa.*" *Literaturnoe Obozrenie* 3 (1990): 51–53.
Popkin, Cathy. *The Pragmatics of Insignificance.* Stanford: Stanford University Press, 1993.

Potapov, Vladimir. "Coming Out of the Underground." *Soviet Literature* 5 (1990): 157–64.

Proskurin, Oleg. *Poezia Pushkina ili podvizhnyi palimpsest.* Moscow: Novoe Literaturnoe Obozrenie, 1999.

Rassadin, Stanislav. "The Intelligentsia as a Conciliar Concept Does Not Exist. It Has Played Out Its Role, Been Crowded Out, Destroyed, Leaving Us with Intellectualness." *Russian Studies in Literature* 31, no. 1 (Winter 1994–95): 32–41.

Rayfield, Donald. *Understanding Chekhov: A Critical Study of Chekhov's Prose and Drama.* Madison: The University of Wisconsin Press, 1999.

———. *The Cherry Orchard. Catastrophe and Comedy.* New York: Twayne Publishers, 1994.

Riffaterre, Michael. "Compulsory Reader Response." In *Intertextuality. Theories and Practices,* ed. Michael Worton and Judith Still. Manchester–New York: Manchester University Press, 1990. 56–78.

———. "The Interpretant in Literary Semiotics." *The American Journal of Semiotics* 3, no. 4 (1985): 41–55.

Roberts, Graham. "A Matter of (Dis)course: Metafiction in the works of Daniil Kharms." In *New Directions in Soviet Literature,* ed. Sheelagh Duffin Grahamn. New York: St. Martin's Press, 1992. 142.

Romashko, Sergei. "'*Vishnevyi sad' po-frantsuzski.*'" *Russkii Zhurnal.* Online, accessed 03/11/2004. http://old.russ.ru/columns/nofocus/20040311_rom.htm.

Rose, Margaret A. *Parody: Ancient, Modern, and Post-Modern.* Cambridge: Cambridge University Press, 1993.

Rozanov, Vasilii. "*Nash 'Antosha Chekhonte.'*" In his *Mysli o literature.* Moscow: Sovremennik, 1989.

———. *The Apocalypses of Our Time and Other Writings.* Trans. Robert Payne and Nikita Romanoff, ed. Robert Payne. New York: Praeger, 1977.

Ryzhova, Galina. "'*Vishnevyi sad.' Brakon'erstvo i bioterrorism v SNG.*" *Moskva* 9 (2003): 203–10.

Sakharov, A. N., ed. *Istoria Rossii s nachala XVII do kontsa XIX veka.* Moscow: ACT, 1998.

Sandler, Stephanie. *Commemorating Pushkin. Russia's Myth of a National Poet.* Stanford: Stanford University Press, 2004.

Saunders, Louisa. "Heart and Soul." Interview with Tatyana Tolstaya. *Guardian* 24 (May 1989): 21.

Schmidt, Siegfried J. "The Fiction Is That Reality Exists: A Constructivist Model of Reality, Fiction, and Literature." *Poetics Today* 5 (November 1984): 253–74.

Schopflin, George. "The Functions of Myth and a Taxonomy of Myths." In *Myth & Nationhood,* ed. Geoffrey Hosking and George Schopflin. New York: Routledge, 1997. 19–35.

Segal, D. M. "Problems in the Semiotic Study of Mythology." In *Soviet Semiotics,* ed. and trans. Daniel P Lucid. Baltimore: The Johns Hopkins University Press, 1977. 59–64.

Semanova, Maria. *Chekhov i sovetskaya literatura.* Moscow: Sovetskii pisatel', 1966.

———. *Chekhov v shkole.* Leningrad: Uchpedgiz, 1949.

Senelick, Laurence. *The Chekhov Theater: A Century of Plays in Performance.* Cambridge: Cambridge University Press, 1997.

Shcherbakova, Galina. "*Kostochka avocado.*" *Novy Mir* 9 (1995): 28–47.

Sherbinin de, Julie. *Chekhov and the Russian Religious Culture: The Poetics of the Marian Paradigm.* Evanston: Northwestern University Press, 1997.

Shestov, Lev. "Chekhov. Creation from the Void." In his *Chekhov and Other Essays.* Ann Arbor: University of Michigan Press, 1966.

———. *Chekhov and Other Essays.* Ann Arbor: University of Michigan Press, 1996.

Shishkova, Larisa. "*Nich'i babushki na zolotom kryl'tse.*" *Kontinent* 56 (1988): 398–402.

Shneidman, N. N. *Literature and Ideology in Soviet Education.* Lexington: Lexington Books, 1973.

Shturman, Dora. *The Soviet Secondary School.* Trans. Philippa Shimrat. London: Routledge, 1988.

Sinyavsky, Andrei. *The Russian Intelligentsia.* Trans. Lynn Visson. New York: Columbia University Press, 1997.

Slater, Wendy. "The Patriots' Pushkin." *Slavic Review* 58, no. 2 (Summer 1999): 407–27.

Slavetsky, Vladimir. "After Postmodernism." *Russian Studies in Literature* 30, no. 2 (Spring 1994): 40–51.

Smirnov, Igor. *Porozhdenie intertexta.* Wien: Wiener Slawistischer Almanach, 1985.

Smith, Judith and Michael Worton. Introduction. *Intertextuality. Theories and Practices,* ed. Michael Worton and Judith Smith. Manchester: Manchester University Press, 1990.

Sorokin, Vladimir. *Sobranie sochineniy.* Vol. 2. Moscow: Ad Marginem, 1998.

Spanos, William. "The Detective and the Boundary: Some Notes on the Postmodern Literary Imagination." *A Journal of Postmodern Literature* 1 (1972): 147–68.

Spieker, Sven. *Figures of Memory and Forgetting in Andrej Bitov's Prose.* Frankfurt am Main: Peter Lang, 1996.

Stanislavsky, Konstantin. *Moia zhizn' v iskusstve.* Moscow: Iskusstvo, 1972.

———. *My Life in Art.* Trans. J. J. Robbins. New York: Theatre Arts Books, 1952.

Startseva, Natal'ia. "Ladies with Dogs and Without." In *Skirted Issues. The Discretions and Indiscretions of Russian Woman's Prose.* Guest Editor Helena Goscilo. *Russian Studies of Literature. A Journal of Translations* (Spring 1992): 24–32.

Stepanian, Karen. "*Krizis slova na poroge svobody.*" *Znamia* 8 (1999): 204–14.

Stolovich, Leonid. "*Anekdot i mif.*" *Neva* 10 (2004): 193–98.

Stowell, H. Peter. *Literary Impressionism, James and Chekhov.* Athens: The University of Georgia Press, 1980.

Strelka, Joseph P., ed. *Literary Criticism and Myth.* University Park–London: Pennsylvania State University Press, 1980.

Struve, Nikita. "*Russkaia emigratsia i Pushkin (1987)*" *Russkii Mir* 4 (2001). Online, accessed summer 2004. http://ricolor.org/history/re/adaptation115/.

Summers, Hollis. "Beside the Point." In *Chekhov and Our Age. Responses to*

Chekhov by American Writers and Scholars, ed. James McConkey. Ithaca: Cornell University Press, 1984. 152.

Taroshchina, S. Interview. "*Ten' na zakate.*" *Literaturnaia Gazeta* 23 (July 1986): 7.

Tarsis, Valerii. *Palata # 7*. Frankfurt: Posev, 1966.

———. *Ward 7: An Autobiographical Novel*. Trans. Katya Brown. New York: Dutton, 1965.

Tertz, Abram. *Strolls with Pushkin*. New Haven: Yale University Press, 1993.

———. *Fantastic Stories*. Evanston: Northwestern University Press, 1987.

Thompson, Ewa M., ed. *The Search for Self-Definition in Russian Literature*. Amsterdam: John Benjamins Publishing Company, 1991.

Tokareva, Viktoria. *Kheppi end*. Moscow: Kvadrat, 1995.

Tolstaya, Tatiana. *Liubish'—ne liubish'*. Moscow: Olma-Press, 1997.

———. *Sleepwalker in the Fog*. Trans. Jamey Gambrell. New York: Alfred A. Knopf, 1992.

———. *On the Golden Porch*. Trans. Antonina W. Bouis. New York: Vintage International, 1990.

Tolstoy, Leo. *Anna Karenina*. Trans. Richard Peaver and Larissa Volokhonsky. London: Allen Lane, 2000.

Tsygal'skaya, Irina. "*Moi zarosshie vishnevye sady. Neotpravlennoe pis'mo podruge.*" *Druzhba narodov* 1 (1988): 138–49.

Tynianov Yu. N. "*O parodii.*" In *Poetika. Istoriia Literatury. Kino*, ed. Yu. N. Tynianov. Moscow: Nauka, 1977.

Uliashov, Pavel. "Authors and Positions." *Soviet Literature* 1 (1990): 107–11.

Vail, Petr and Aleksandr Genis. "*Printsip matreshki.*" *Novy Mir* 10 (1989): 245–52.

Van den Bossche, B. "Myth as Literature, Literature as Myth: Some Remarks on Myth and Interpretation of Literary Texts." In *Methods for the Study of Literature as Cultural Memory*, ed. Raymond Viverliet and Annemarie Estor. Vol. 6 of the *Proceedings of the XVth Congress of the International Comparative Literary Association*, "Literature as Cultural Memory." Amsterdam: Rodopi, 2000. 228.

Van der Eng, Jan. "The Semantic Structure of *Lady with a Lapdog*." In *On the Theory of Descriptive Poetics: Anton P. Chekhov as Story-Teller and Playwright. Essays by Jan van der Eng, Jan M. Meijer and Herta Schmid*. Amsterdam: The Peter de Ridder Press, 1978. 59–94.

Vasil'eva, Maria. "*Tak slozhilos'.*" *Druzhba Narodov* 4 (1998): 208–17.

Vatsuro, V. E. *Lirika Pushkinskoi pory*. St. Petersburg: Nauka, 1994.

Vekhi. Sbornik statei o russkoi intelligentsii. Frankfurt: Posev, 1969.

Vickery, John B., ed. *Myth and Literature*. Lincoln: University of Nebraska Press, 1966.

Vinogradova, K. M. "*Stranitsa iz chernovoi rukopisi rasskaza 'Dama s sobachkoi.'*" In *Literaturnoe nasledstvo: Tom 68. Chekhov*, ed. I. I. Anisinom et al. Moscow: Izdatelstvo Akademii Nauk, 1960. 133–40.

"*Vishnevye sady Silikonovoi doliny.*" BBCRussian.com. Online, accessed 12/14/2001. http://news8.thdo.bbc.co.uk/hi/russian/life/newsid_1711000/1711437.stm/.

Vladimir Illich Lenin o Litrature i Isskusstve. Ed. Leibovich et al. Moscow: Goslitizdat, 1960.

Vladiv-Glover, Slobodanka. "The New Model of Discourse in Post-Soviet Russian Fiction." In Mikhail Epstein, Alexander Genis, and Slobodanka Vladiv-Glover, *Russian Postmodernism. New Perspectives on Post-Soviet Culture,* ed. and trans. Slobodanka Vladiv-Glover. New York: Berghahn Books, 1999. 227–68.

Voinovich, Vladimir. *Maloe sobranie sochinenii.* Moscow: Fabula, 1993.

———. *The Fur Hat.* Trans. Susan Brownsberger. New York: Harcourt Brace Jovanovich, 1989.

Volpert, L. I. *Pushkin v roli Pushkina.* Moscow: Iazyki russkoi kul'tury, 1998.

Vysotsky, Vladimir. *Sochinenia v 4x tomakx.* St. Petersburg: Tekxneks Possia, 1992.

Wachtel, Andrew. *Remaining Relevant After Communism. The Role of the Writer in Eastern Europe.* Chicago: University of Chicago Press, 2006.

Welty, Eudora. "Reality in Chekhov's Stories." In *Chekhov and Our Age. Responses to Chekhov by American Writers and Scholars,* ed. James McConkey. Ithaca: Cornell University Press, 1984. 122.

Wilde, Allan. *Modernism and the Aesthetics of Crisis.* Johns Hopkins University Press, 1987.

Winner, Thomas. *Chekhov and His Prose.* New York: Holt, Rinehart and Winston, 1996.

Wolff, Sally. "The Wisdom of Pain in Chekhov's 'Ward number Six.'" *Literature and Medicine. Fictive Ills: Literary Perspectives on Wounds and Diseases,* Vol. 9, ed. Peter W. Graham and Elizabeth Sewell. Baltimore: The Johns Hopkins University Press. 134–41.

Woll, Josephine. "The Minotaur in the Maze: Remarks on Lyudmila Petrushevskaya." *World Literature Today (Russian Literature at a Crossroads)* 67 (Winter 1993): 125–30.

Yarmolinsky, Avrahm, ed. *Treasury of Russian Verse.* New York: Macmillan, 1949.

———, ed. *Letters of Anton Chekhov.* New York: Viking, 1973. 112

Zavisca, Jane. "Contesting Capitalism at the Post-Soviet Dacha: The Meaning of Food Cultivation for Urban Russians." *Slavic Review* 62, no. 4 (Winter 2003): 786–810.

Zolotonosov, Mikhail. "The Fountain at Rest: A Small Monograph on Postsocialist Realism." In *Re-Entering the Sign. Articulating the New Russian Culture,* ed. Ellen E. Berry and Anesa Miller-Pogacar. Ann Arbor: University of Michigan Press, 1995. 155–69.

———. *"Mechty i fantomy." Knizhnoe Obozrenie* 4 (1988): 58–61.

Zubareva, Elena. *"'Neponiatnaia dushevnaia trevoga'" (Motiv 'Palaty no. 6' v proze russkoi emigratsii 1970x–1980x gg.)."* In *Almanach Melikhovo,* ed. Yu. A. Bychkov et al. Moscow: Druzhba narodov, 2000. 93–103.

INDEX

www.ingramcontent.com/pod-product-compliance
Lightning Source LLC
LaVergne TN
LVHW091051080826
845145LV00002B/706